JUL 15 2014

D0166527

SPRINGDALE PUBLIC LIBRARY
405 S. Pleasant
Springdale, AR 72764

BOOKS BY MICHAEL FARQUHAR

*A Treasury of Royal Scandals: The Shocking True Stories
of History's Wickedest, Weirdest, Most Wanton Kings,
Queens, Tsars, Popes, and Emperors*

*A Treasury of Great American Scandals: Tantalizing True
Tales of Historic Misbehavior by the Founding Fathers
and Others Who Let Freedom Swing*

*A Treasury of Deception: Liars, Misleaders, Hoodwinkers,
and the Extraordinary True Stories of History's Greatest
Hoaxes, Fakes, and Frauds*

*A Treasury of Foolishly Forgotten Americans: Pirates,
Skinflints, Patriots, and Other Colorful Characters
Stuck in the Footnotes of History*

*Behind the Palace Doors: Five Centuries of Sex, Adventure,
Vice, Treachery, and Folly from Royal Britain*

*Secret Lives of the Tsars: Three Centuries of Autocracy,
Debauchery, Betrayal, Murder, and Madness
from Romanov Russia*

Secret Lives of
the Tsars

Secret Lives of the Tsars

THREE CENTURIES OF AUTOCRACY, DEBAUCHERY, BETRAYAL, MURDER, AND MADNESS FROM ROMANOV RUSSIA

Michael Farquhar

RANDOM HOUSE TRADE PAPERBACKS

NEW YORK

SPRINGDALE PUBLIC LIBRARY
405 S. Pleasant
Springdale, AR 72764

A Random House Trade Paperback Original

Copyright © 2014 by Michael Farquhar

All rights reserved.

Published in the United States by Random House Trade
Paperbacks, an imprint of Random House,
a division of Random House LLC, a Penguin
Random House Company, New York.

RANDOM HOUSE and the HOUSE colophon are registered
trademarks of Random House LLC.

ISBN 978-0-8129-7905-3
eBook ISBN 978-0-8129-8578-8

Printed in the United States of America on acid-free paper

www.atrandom.com

2 4 6 8 9 7 5 3 1

First Edition

Dedicated with love and appreciation

to the Foote/Rupp/Maloney clan—

Always in there pitching!

"In the house of the Romanovs, a mysterious curse descends from generation to generation. Murders and adultery, blood and mud . . . the block, the rope, and poison—these are the true emblems of Russian autocracy. God's unction on the brows of the Tsars has become the brand of Cain."

—DMITRI MEREZHKOVSKY (1865–1941)

The Romanovs — 1613 to 1796

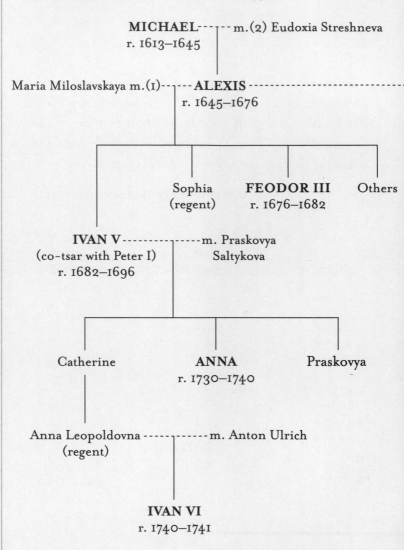

MICHAEL - - - - - m.(2) Eudoxia Streshneva
r. 1613–1645

Maria Miloslavskaya m.(1) - - - - - ALEXIS -
r. 1645–1676

Sophia   **FEODOR III**   Others
(regent)   r. 1676–1682

IVAN V - - - - - - - - - - - - m. Praskovya
(co-tsar with Peter I)   Saltykova
r. 1682–1696

Catherine   **ANNA**   Praskovya
                 r. 1730–1740

Anna Leopoldovna - - - - - - - m. Anton Ulrich
(regent)

IVAN VI
r. 1740–1741

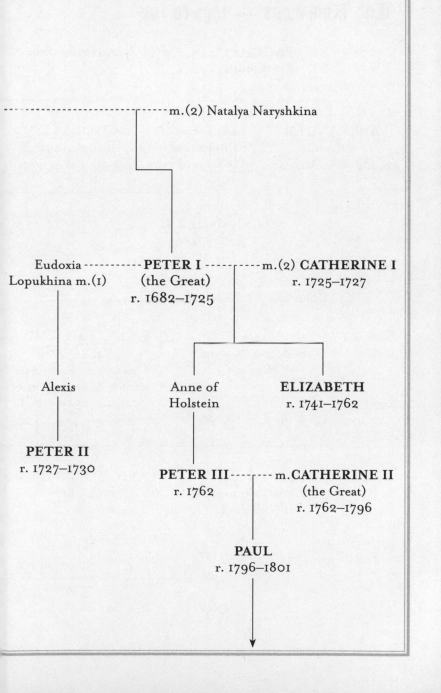

m.(2) Natalya Naryshkina

Eudoxia
Lopukhina m.(1)

PETER I
(the Great)
r. 1682–1725

m.(2) **CATHERINE I**
r. 1725–1727

Alexis

Anne of
Holstein

ELIZABETH
r. 1741–1762

PETER II
r. 1727–1730

PETER III
r. 1762

m. **CATHERINE II**
(the Great)
r. 1762–1796

PAUL
r. 1796–1801

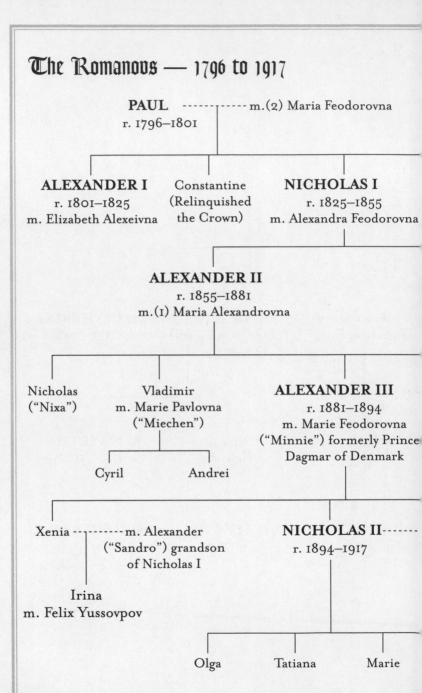

The Romanovs — 1796 to 1917

PAUL ----------- m.(2) Maria Feodorovna
r. 1796–1801

ALEXANDER I
r. 1801–1825
m. Elizabeth Alexeivna

Constantine
(Relinquished
the Crown)

NICHOLAS I
r. 1825–1855
m. Alexandra Feodorovna

ALEXANDER II
r. 1855–1881
m.(1) Maria Alexandrovna

Nicholas
("Nixa")

Vladimir
m. Marie Pavlovna
("Miechen")

ALEXANDER III
r. 1881–1894
m. Marie Feodorovna
("Minnie") formerly Prince
Dagmar of Denmark

Cyril   Andrei

Xenia ---------- m. Alexander
("Sandro") grandson
of Nicholas I

NICHOLAS II -------
r. 1894–1917

Irina
m. Felix Yussovpov

Olga   Tatiana   Marie

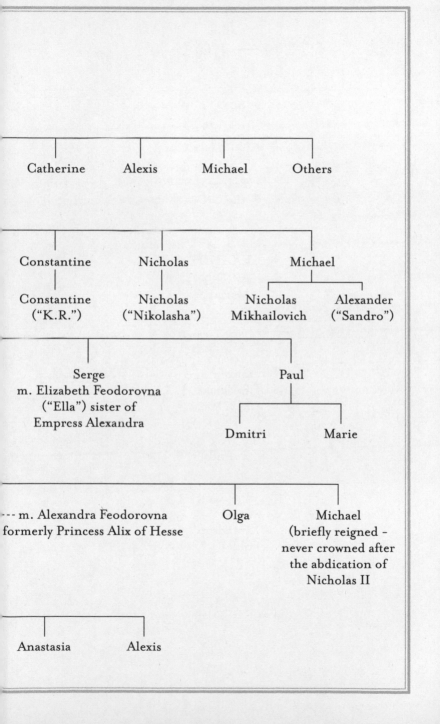

Catherine   Alexis   Michael   Others

Constantine   Nicholas   Michael

Constantine   Nicholas   Nicholas   Alexander
("K.R.")   ("Nikolasha")   Mikhailovich   ("Sandro")

Serge   Paul
m. Elizabeth Feodorovna
("Ella") sister of
Empress Alexandra

Dmitri   Marie

--- m. Alexandra Feodorovna   Olga   Michael
formerly Princess Alix of Hesse   (briefly reigned –
never crowned after
the abdication of
Nicholas II

Anastasia   Alexis

CONTENTS

Secret Lives of the Tsars

Introductory Chapter

The Time of Troubles and the
Rise of the Romanovs

The live animals came hurtling through the air, tossed off a Kremlin tower by the knee-high tyrant-in-training who would one day rule as Ivan the Terrible. There were no consequences for the demented lad's behavior then, nor would there be later when, as Russia's first crowned tsar, he slaughtered almost the entire city of Novgorod—accentuating the massacre by shoving a number of his victims under the ice of the frozen Volkhov River. Ivan barely blinked when he personally gutted one nobleman after mocking his royal pretensions by dressing him like a king and seating him on a throne, or when he ordered hundreds of his perceived enemies skinned, boiled, burned, or broken in an orgy of retribution on Red Square. Yet while this savage monarch murdered with impunity (which, not surprisingly, made him the favorite tsar of the twentieth-century monster, Joseph Stalin) there was one act of homicidal rage that Ivan IV would deeply regret; a fit of pique that changed the course of Russian history.

When, in 1581, the tsar's eldest son had the temerity to object to his father's kicking his pregnant wife in the stomach, Ivan became so incensed that he clobbered the younger man on the head with his iron staff. Rage instantly turned to regret, though, as the half-crazed sovereign cradled his dying heir in his arms. "May I be damned! I've killed my son! I've killed my son!" he cried. Indeed, he had. And with that bop on the head, Ivan had effectively destroyed the future of the ancient Rurik dynasty of sovereigns who had forged Russia into a nation.

Less than three years after killing his son, Ivan the Terrible was dead as well—felled by a stroke while playing chess. And though Russia began to recover from his ruinous policies, the relief was only temporary. In fact, Ivan IV's reign of terror turned out to be a mere prelude to a far more devastating era of famine, civil strife, and bloodshed known as the Time of Troubles. During this violently unsettled period, a succession of schemers, opportunists, and even an imposter occupied the Russian throne before young Michael Romanov was elected tsar in 1613 and began a storied royal dynasty that would endure for the next three centuries.

The transfer of power after the death of Ivan IV in 1584 had been peaceful enough; a deceptive lull, as it turned out. The bloody tsar was succeeded by his simple and uninspiring second son, Feodor I. "Of mind he has but little or . . . none at all," a Polish envoy wrote of the malformed monarch, who was guided by a group of regents. Among them was Tsar Feodor's brother-in-law, Boris Godunov, a shrewd politician and able administrator who emerged as the sole power behind the slow tsar's throne.

Early in Feodor's reign, Godunov crushed a revolt by the family of one of Ivan the Terrible's last wives,* Maria Nagaia, thwarting their effort to place on the throne the late tsar's

---

* Ivan the Terrible had between five and eight wives, but because of the frequency with which he wed, the church didn't recognize the legitimacy of some of the later spouses.

youngest son, Dmitri. The *tsarevitch* (tsar's son) and his mother, Maria, were exiled to the small principality of Uglich, and there, in 1591, the eight-year-old boy died under mysterious circumstances, his throat slashed. While Maria and her family loudly blamed their enemy Boris Godunov for Dmitri's death, inciting a deadly riot in the process, an investigative commission determined the child had been playing with a knife and fatally wounded himself with it during a seizure. Godunov was officially exonerated, but Dmitri would nevertheless loom large in his future.

In 1598, the enfeebled Tsar Feodor died without an heir, thus ending with a whimper the once-mighty Rurik dynasty. Boris Godunov, who had served as Russia's de facto ruler while Feodor merely reigned, was now selected to take his place. After a great show of reluctance, he was crowned amid general acclaim and seemed poised to bring Russia to greatness. Even with a severe economic crisis, crippling taxes, and an emerging policy that bound the majority of the population to the land against their will, Tsar Boris sat securely on his throne. But then the weather got really bad.

Climatic upheavals wrought by the Little Ice Age caused horrific famines during Boris Godunov's seven-year reign. "I swear to God that this is the truth," one witness to the disaster reported. "I saw with my own eyes people lying on the streets, eating grass like cattle in summer and hay in winter. Some were already dead, with hay and dung in their mouths and also (pardon my indelicacy) had swallowed human excrement. . . . Many dead bodies of people who had perished through hunger were found daily in the streets. . . . Daily . . . hundreds of corpses were gathered up at the tsar's command and carried away on so many carts, that to behold it (scarcely to be believed) was grisly and horrible."

In the midst of this unrelenting misery and deprivation, when nearly a third of Russia's population perished, a pretender appeared in 1604, claiming to be Ivan the Terrible's youngest son, Dmitri, miraculously rescued from Boris Godunov's attempt to assassinate him. Another boy had been killed, the False Dmitri asserted, and now he had come to claim his rightful place on the throne and to rescue the Russian people from the darkness and chaos caused by the sins of the usurper Godunov.

The true identity of the imposter remains a mystery. Some claimed he was a defrocked monk by the name of Gregory Otrepiev, who, backed by the Catholic king of Poland, had come to Russia to destroy Orthodoxy. Others have proposed that he may have been raised since childhood to actually believe he was in fact Dmitri. Whoever he really was, the pretender quickly gained a following among a disaffected populace desperate for relief and eager to believe that he was God's chosen.

In April 1605, while the rebellion that formed around the False Dmitri raged, Tsar Boris Godunov conveniently died, probably of heart disease. Two months later the pretender triumphantly entered Moscow, his path cleared by the strangulation of Godunov's son and successor, Feodor II. "Dmitri" created a stirring spectacle when he visited the tomb of Ivan the Terrible. "Oh, beloved father!" he cried. "You left me in this world an orphan, but your saintly prayers helped me through all the persecution and has led me to the throne." The next day he was crowned in the Kremlin's Cathedral of the Assumption. An imposter now sat on Russia's throne, but he would rule for less than a year.

No sooner had the False Dmitri been enthroned than a grasping boyar (noble) by the name of Vasili Shuisky began scheming against him. During the celebrations surrounding Dmitri's marriage to the Catholic Marina Mniszech, the pseudo-tsar met a ghastly end. He was hacked to death by his assassins. Then, with ropes tied around the feet and genitals, his naked corpse was dragged out to Red Square and left exposed to scorn and ridicule for three days. Finally, the body was incinerated; the ashes were mixed with gunpowder and shot from a cannon toward the southwestern frontier, where the imposter first appeared.

Having thus disposed of the False Dmitri, the unscrupulous Vasili Shuisky grabbed the crown for himself. His claim was shaky, however, and with discontent still roiling Russia, he occupied a very precarious throne. To bolster his regime, Vasili IV sought to discredit his predecessor by sowing incredible tales of the False Dmitri's evil deeds (many of which have lingered over the centuries). He even went as far as to produce the fresh corpse of a young boy and declared it to be the real Dmitri, uncorrupted by decay because of his saintly qualities and the source of many miracles. The body was ceremoniously transferred from Uglich to Moscow and placed in the Kremlin's Cathedral of the Archangel where it lay as a revered relic—until "St. Dmitri" started to stink and had to be hastily buried.

The cynical manufacture of the ersatz saint did little to placate the masses, or to discourage the appearance of a second False Dmitri in 1607. Like that of the first imposter, the identity of the second remains unknown. But such was the state of turmoil at the time that he gathered a significant following—his standing only enhanced when Marina Mniszech, widow of the first False Dmitri, "recognized" the new pretender as her miraculously saved husband and remarried him. (One Polish hetman wrote in his memoirs that about the only two things False Dmitris I and II had in common were that "they were both human and usurpers.")

Under threat from the second False Dmitri as he marched toward Moscow, Tsar Vasili ceded Russian territory to neighboring Sweden in exchange for a mercenary force. This, in turn, prompted Poland to seize the frontier town of Smolensk. "Russia's neighbours were beginning moving in like jackals on a dying beast to dismember the Empire," wrote historian Philip Longworth. "And still the chaotic civil war continued."

In July 1610, Tsar Vasili was forcibly removed from the throne by a mob and publicly shorn as a monk in Red Square. Then, the following December, the second False Dmitri was murdered by one of his own men. Now Russia was without a tsar—or even a fake tsar (although *yet another* False Dmitri would briefly gain a following before being killed)—and the descent into chaos rapidly accelerated.

Lawlessness, disease, and famine overtook the land; villages and fields were destroyed by marauding brigands. And when Polish troops came to occupy the Kremlin, the very citadel of power and authority, it seemed Russia had reached its very nadir. Thus, by 1613, people were clamoring for a powerful central authority to restore order and to lead ruined Russia back to greatness. They wanted an autocrat.

To elect a new tsar, a great assembly of the land, or *zemsky sobor*, was convened with representatives from all strata of society (except the enslaved serfs). There would be no more ambitious boyars, or duplicitous pretenders allowed to occupy the sacred throne; only a candidate who represented legitimacy, continuity, and true Orthodoxy would do. With these essential requirements, one name eventually emerged with near-total consensus: a teenager named Michael Romanov.

The frail, unassuming sixteen-year-old was an unlikely choice to lead a devastated realm into a new era of peace and prosperity—but he certainly had the right pedigree. His great-aunt was Ivan the Terrible's beloved first wife, Anastasia, who, with her gentle piety, had stood in such striking contrast to her homicidal husband. And Anastasia's brother, Nikita, Michael's grandfather, was one of Ivan's closest advisors, winning near-universal respect and adoration for his refusal to participate in his brother-in-law's most vicious assaults on his own subjects.

Michael's father, Feodor (who adopted the surname Romanov), had lost a power struggle with Boris Godunov after the death of his dim-witted first cousin Feodor I in 1598 and was exiled to the frozen outreaches of Siberia as a result. Although he and his wife Xenia managed to survive the brutal conditions there, both were forced to take religious vows and live apart—he as the unwilling monk renamed Philaret, she as the nun Martha. Feodor/Philaret's fortunes improved in 1605 when the False Dmitri made him metropolitan (or bishop) of Rostov, but soon after he became a prisoner of the king of Poland while visiting the kingdom as part of a Russian delegation. There he rotted in a Polish cell as his son Michael became Russia's new monarch.

The young man had not accepted the crown eagerly, having lived through all the tumult of "the troubles" since he was a five-year-old boy. It was then that his parents were dragged off to Siberia while he was sent to live in near poverty with an aunt. And later, during his father's imprisonment in Poland,

Michael and his mother were reduced to living as nomads, wandering from monastery to church and existing on whatever succor might be provided. So, when the representatives of the *zemsky sobor* arrived at the Ipatiev Monastery in Kostroma to beg Michael to rule over them, the shy teenager at first refused. The throne was too unsteady, he insisted. Indeed, it was akin to asking a toddler to tame a wounded bear. Only when the delegation assured him that all the people wanted him as their sovereign, and that he would sit securely on the throne, did Michael at last relent. He was about to inherit a seemingly insurmountable mess.

The young tsar saw the vast destruction all around him as he traveled from Kostroma to Moscow to accept the crown, and his dim prospects seemed all the more apparent at his coronation when the elaborate ceremonial robes all but consumed his slight frame. Nevertheless, Michael did enjoy near universal support from a strife-weary people desperate for his success. And with the help of the *zemsky sobor,* which met regularly during the early part of his reign, the tsar was able to achieve peace with his two most threatening neighbors, Sweden and Poland. The price was steep in terms of land concessions and indemnities, but at least it allowed Russia to focus on its slow recovery.

While Michael's early reign was accompanied by an unusual spirit of cooperation in the interests of the greater good, there were still elements of court intrigue and treachery that lingered after the Time of Troubles. This was particularly evident as the first Romanov tsar prepared to marry. His chosen bride, Maria Khlopova, was from an undistinguished aristocratic family, which left others of the boyar class seething with resentment over the bounty and privilege Maria's obscure clan would enjoy as a result of her exulted status. So they poisoned her. The powerful emetic placed in her food one evening caused violent convulsions, which were duly reported to the tsar as symptoms of an incurable disease, knowingly concealed by Maria and her family in their grasp for power. As a result of their "deception," the Khlopovas were banished to Siberia.

Six years into Michael's reign, his father was freed from his Polish imprisonment and returned home to become patriarch of Moscow and of all Russia. It was a joyful reunion, and the tsar was happy to cede the power Feodor/Philaret had long craved. Now the son was free to live as shadow sovereign, rarely seen except for the formal court ceremonials that required his presence. Compared to some of the weighty personalities of the later Romanov dynasty, like Peter the Great and Catherine the Great, he was about as bland as a Russian tsar could possibly be. His only real purpose was to sire an heir.

To that end, Michael did eventually marry—twice. His first wife died within a year while giving birth to a stillborn child. The second was chosen in an oddly traditional way. All the realm's eligible maidens—from the right families, of course, and with their virginity subject to verification—were assembled in Moscow for the tsar's inspection. Out of this mass, Michael chose Eudoxia Streshneva, a squire's daughter who, in 1629, bore the tsar an heir to carry on the fledgling dynasty.

Meanwhile, Feodor/Philaret continued to rule Russia until his death in 1633, after which the reign of Michael, the mildest of tsars, continued relatively uneventfully for another twelve years. He died in 1645—a colorless sovereign, certainly, but the founder of a royal line that was anything but.

Like his father, Alexis Romanov came to the throne at age sixteen. Unlike Michael, though, the second monarch of the dynasty presented the very image of power and majesty. A member of an English delegation later described the glory of Alexis seated on his throne:

"The Tsar like a sparkling sun darted forth most sumptuous rays, being most magnificently placed on his throne, with his scepter in his hand and having his crown on his head. His throne was of massy silver gilt, wrought curiously on top with several works and pyramids; and being seven or eight steps higher than the floor, it rendered the person of the Prince transcendentally majestic. His crown (which he wore upon a cap lined with black sables) was covered quite over with precious stones, terminating toward the top in the form of a pyramid with a golden cross at the spire. The scepter glittered also all over with jewels, his vest was set with the like from the top to the bottom and his collar was answerable to the same."

Alexis was known in his time as the mildest and most pious of tsars, which was at least partially true. Certainly he was devout, attending numerous masses and devotions throughout the day. The tsar's English physician reported, "On fast days he frequents midnight prayers, standing four, five, or six hours together, prostrating himself on the ground, sometimes a thousand times, and on great festivals, fifteen hundred." But when it came to rebellion in his realm, the God-fearing Alexis became something akin to Ivan the Terrible.

Witness the gentle tsar's grim retribution against Stenka Razin, who led a failed peasant revolt in 1670. The rebel's skin was shredded by a Russian whip known as the knout, after which he was branded with hot irons and subjected to a slow-drip water torture. Then Razin's limbs were torn out of their sockets and shoved back into place. Finally, he was cut into quarters while still alive; his torso and entrails were tossed to the dogs. (The tsar's heir, Peter the Great, would later embrace such cruel techniques and use the knout to lethal effect on his own son.)

Tsar Alexis married twice. His first wife, Maria Miloslavskaya, was picked from a parade of eligible brides, just as his own mother had been. (The tsar's first choice, like that of his father, was similarly sabotaged by jealous nobles.) The tsarina was a good spouse by the standards of the time, devoting her life to prayer, embroidery, and bearing children—thirteen in all, including two future tsars. She kept herself secluded, as all royal women did, in a palace chamber known as the *terem*, and remained thoroughly conservative in dress and outlook until she died in 1669 trying to deliver her fourteenth child.

Alexis was disconsolate, but not for long, for in less than a year he found a buxom new bride, nearly a quarter century his junior. Her name was Natalya Naryshkina, the young ward of the tsar's friend and chief advisor, Artamon Matveev. Having been raised in Matveev's unusually westernized household, with his Scottish wife as an example, the dark-eyed Natalya was rare among women of the day in that she didn't keep herself hidden from male guests, and even ventured to converse with them. The tsar was enchanted when he visited and sought her hand.

In an attempt to avoid the vicious scheming that had accompanied other royal marriages, Alexis decided to go through the motions of another presentation of eligible brides, with the prechosen Natalya among them. He hoped this charade would discourage the notion that Matveev, or Natalya's family, were maneuvering for power. It didn't work.

The relatives of the late tsarina Maria Miloslavskaya would stand to lose much of their privilege and prestige when the tsar remarried, and their resentment of Natalya and the Naryshkins would eventually turn to murderous hatred.

In the meantime, though, the vivacious new tsarina brought a refreshing element of modernity to the court. Some were scandalized by her boldness, such as one shocked observer who noted that she "opened the window of her carriage slightly." Previously, royal women traveled virtually hidden from view by veils and heavy dark curtains. Natalya also encouraged her middle-aged husband's natural curiosity, and spurred the introduction of some Western novelties, like the theater. Perhaps under the influence of his conservative first wife, Alexis had previously banned such entertainments— even going as far as to burn a pile of imported Western musical instruments in Red Square. Now he embraced them, although the resulting "music" was a little short of lilting. The tsar's English physician described the cacophony as being like "a flight of screech owls, a nest of jackdaws, a pack of hungry wolves, seven hogs on a windy day, and as many cats with their corrivals."

Yet despite the baby steps taken toward the West, Russia essentially remained in stagnant medieval mire, isolated and resistant to any variation of tradition. Perhaps this was most vividly apparent when Tsar Alexis, through the Orthodox patriarch, sought to implement some slight changes in church ritual to bring the Russian church more in harmony with its older Greek counterpart. It was decreed, for example, that three fingers rather than the traditional two should now be used by the faithful to cross themselves. But at a time when people sincerely believed that salvation absolutely depended upon the precise performance of ritual, many chose to burn themselves alive rather than be forced to switch fingers.[*]

This was the Russia Alexis left when he died in 1676, and it would be up to the son Natalya bore him to drag the realm out of its stupor. But before the future Peter the Great could do anything, he first had to contend with his big sister Sophia.

---

[*] These fanatic martyrs, known as "Old Believers," would be the bane of many a future Russian sovereign with their fierce resistance to change.

Chapter 1

Ivan V and Peter I (1682–1696):
One Autocrat Too Many

A princess endowed with all the accomplishments
of body and mind to perfection, had it not been
for her boundless ambition and insatiable desire
for governing.

—PETER I ("THE GREAT") ON HIS HALF-SISTER SOPHIA

*Tsar Alexis left three sons upon his death in 1676: two by his first
wife, Maria Miloslavskaya, Feodor and Ivan; and one by his second wife, Natalya Naryshkina, the future Peter the Great. (See
family tree.) The eldest son succeeded Alexis at age fourteen as Tsar
Feodor III. Though keen of mind, he was not a promising sovereign given the numerous physical ailments (including what is now
believed to have been scurvy) that left him weak and often immobilized. After a brief reign of six years, Feodor died without an
heir. The next in line was the even less impressive Ivan, who was
not only physically feeble but mentally disabled as well. Thus Ivan
was bypassed in favor of his vigorous half-brother Peter. But that's
when Ivan's big sister Sophia stepped in. A formidable woman at
a time when most were humble and passive, Sophia helped orchestrate a bloody revolt that left Russia with two co-monarchs and
Peter the Great with severe psychological scars that would remain
with him for the rest of his life.*

The petrified little tsar silently clutched his mother's hand as the mass of murderous pikesmen thronged beneath them, braying for blood. Then, amid a horrific roar, Prince Michael Dolgoruky was hoisted from a balcony above the frenzied crowd and violently cast down upon their sharpened weapons. He was instantly hacked to pieces. One by one, various boyars and other "traitors" were chopped to bits as well—their remains heaped onto a grisly pile that grew ever larger in Red Square. While young Tsar Peter watched the unfolding madness in stupefied terror (with the murder of his two uncles still yet to come), his older half-sister, Sophia, seemed to celebrate it. There was opportunity in the slaughter, and Sophia sensed it. Indeed, she emerged from the gore of the Kremlin massacre with autocratic powers no Russian woman had ever possessed before.

Sophia was never supposed to amount to anything—certainly not to become Russia's sovereign in all but name. She was the sixth child of Tsar Alexis by his first wife, Maria Miloslavskaya, born at a time when Russian women—even royal women—were considered weak and inferior possessions of their husbands and fathers. "To tell the truth, the female sex is not at all venerated amongst the Muscovites as it is amongst the majority of the nations of Europe," observed the Austrian envoy Augustin von Mayerberg. "In this country they are the slaves of men, who esteem them little. And the worst condition of all is that of the sisters and daughters of the Tsars."

These royal princesses (or *tsarevnas*) were virtual prisoners behind palace walls, consigned to live in secluded apartments known as the *terem*. Their lot was to pray, do needlework, and wallow in boredom. Marriage was denied the tsarevnas be-

cause their precious royal blood made every Russian man unworthy of their hand*—or even to look at them—while the
heretical religions of foreign princes made matches with them
impossible as well. Cut off from the world, without prospects,
these perpetual spinsters found their only companionship in
the dimly lit *terem* to be one another. "Not in one of the con-
vents of the day was there so much strictness and restraint, so
many fasts and prayers," observed one commentator. It was a
fate Sophia struggled against, and, remarkably, escaped.

"That strange alchemy which, for no apparent reason, lifts
one child out of a large family and endows it with a special
destiny had created Sophia," wrote biographer Robert K.
Massie. "She had the intelligence, the ambition, the decisive-
ness which her feeble brothers and anonymous sisters so
overwhelmingly lacked. It was almost as if her siblings had
been drained of normal health, vitality and purpose in order
to magnify these qualities in Sophia."

Alone among her sisters, Sophia was granted the unusual
privilege of being educated beside her brothers, and by all accounts she was a remarkably adept student. Her tutor, the
eminent monk and scholar Simeon Polotsky, described her as
"a maiden of great intelligence and the most delicate understanding, with an accomplished masculine mind." Given her
talents, there is some evidence to suggest that Sophia served
as a valued counselor during the reign of her brother Feodor
III. But when that frail, diseased tsar died childless in 1682,
Sophia was faced with the most unwelcome prospect of losing whatever freedom she had attained outside the *terem*.

By tradition, the crown should have passed to her younger

---

* As historian Grigorii Kotoshikhin wrote, "Princes and noblemen are
their [the tsarevnas'] slaves. And it would be considered an eternal disgrace if a lady were to be given away in marriage to a slave."

brother Ivan after Feodor's death, but the fifteen-year-old boy suffered a number of maladies that some believed disqualified him from inheriting. As the Dutch ambassador Johann van Keller noted at the time, "Tsarevitch Ivan is acknowledged to be incapable of ruling on account of his feeble-mindedness and other mental and corporal handicaps." That left the late Tsar Alexis's more vigorous son, Peter, by his second marriage to Natalya Naryshkina—even if he was only nine. Patriarch Joachim, head of the Russian Orthodox Church, gathered an assembly of various classes from the vicinity of the Kremlin and asked who they thought should rule: Ivan or Peter.

The decision, nearly unanimous for Peter, devastated Sophia. She saw the power of her family, the Miloslavskys, slipping away in favor of her stepmother's Naryshkin clan. And though the precise role she played in the bloody events that followed young Peter's election as tsar remains murky, one thing is certain: She emerged triumphant.

By some accounts, Sophia was the prime instigator of a revolt by the *streltsy*—the pikesmen and musketeers, fifty-five thousand strong, who guarded the Kremlin and who were sworn to defend the "true tsar." Through lies and innuendo, she appealed to the most reactionary instincts of this hereditary force of Old Believers[*] and other conservatives, described by Massie as "a kind of collective dumb animal, never quite sure who was its proper master, but ready to rush and bite anyone who challenged its own position."

It was said that Sophia's campaign against the new order began at the funeral of her brother Tsar Feodor, where, in defiance of all tradition, she made herself quite conspicuous,

---

[*] Old Believers were those who refused to adopt the new church rituals decreed by Tsar Alexis—see footnote, page 15.

weeping and wailing as she followed the body. Afterward, she suggested something sinister had not only taken her late brother away, but also deprived her surviving brother Ivan of the throne.

"Look, people, how unexpectedly our brother Tsar Feodor was dispatched from this world by enemies and ill-wishers," an anonymous Polish correspondent reported Sophia saying to a gathered crowd. "Be merciful to us orphans, who have neither mother nor father, nor our brother, the Tsar [Feodor]. Ivan our elder brother has not been chosen as tsar. If we have offended you or the boyars, release us alive to go to some foreign land and to Christian monarchs."

Sophia has gained an enduring historical reputation as a monster who stirred up murderous rebellion—a legacy reinforced by one contemporary Frenchman's unflattering (and unfounded) description of her as gigantic and hairy, with a bushel-sized head and a Machiavellian heart. Certainly the tsarevna was politically savvy, if not the ghastly ogress she was presented to be, but even without her coaxing, the *streltsy* were already ripe for revolt.

Discontent had been smoldering within a number of regiments due to various abuses by their colonels, some of whom embezzled their pay or made them work at the officers' private estates. The soldiers sought redress as Feodor III was dying, but it was Peter's mother, Natalya, serving as regent for the recently elected boy tsar, who inherited the problem. Unsure how to proceed, the new government capitulated to the demands of the inflamed regiments and the colonels were severely punished—some being whipped, others banished. Now, having sensed its own strength, the ill-educated and superstitious *streltsy* were poised to strike at any perceived threat.

There was already grumbling among the ranks about the elevation of Peter as tsar over Ivan. "The *streltsy* kept indicating that the election of the new Tsar had been improperly conducted," reported Heinrich Butenant, commercial agent to the king of Denmark and one of the more reliable witnesses of this restless period. "They could not believe that the elder Prince, Ivan Alekseevich,* was unfit to rule because of his poor eyesight and other accidents of fate." Furthermore, Butenant wrote, the *streltsy* "were most dissatisfied that the Naryshkins had become so powerful so quickly."

Indeed, the young tsar's relatives benefited tremendously from his accession and seemed to aggressively flaunt their status. Ivan Naryshkin, who, at the age of twenty-three, was elevated to the rank of boyar, gave particular offense with his arrogance. It was said, for example, that he had dared to try on the royal regalia, taken a seat on the throne, and grossly insulted Tsarevitch Ivan and the rest of the now-powerless Miloslavsky clan. Of what other evils were these upstart Naryshkins and their aristocratic allies capable?

"You yourselves can see what a heavy yoke the boyars have laid upon you and they have chosen God knows what kind of tsar," Prince Ivan Andrei Khovansky railed in a speech before the *streltsy*. "You'll see—not only won't they give you money and provisions, but you will have to do heavy labor as before and your children will be eternal slaves. What's worse, they will give you and us over to the bondage of a foreign foe, Moscow will be destroyed and the Orthodox faith eradicated."

---

* A Russian's first name was often followed by a patronymic—a variation of his or her father's given name. Thus, Ivan V, son of Tsar Alexis, was called Ivan Alekseevich. In the interest of simplicity, the author has avoided the use of patronyms, except in source quotations and in Chapter 5.

The atmosphere in Moscow was almost electric with tension that spring of 1682. "The discontent of the *streltsy* continues," reported the Dutch ambassador, Johann van Keller. "All public affairs are at a standstill. Great calamities are feared and not without cause, for the might of the *streltsy* is great and no resistance can be opposed to them."

Their fury was about to become lethally focused. "It was to take but a small spark to ignite the wrath of the already restive *streltsy* against the 'traitors' in the Kremlin," wrote biographer Lindsey Hughes, "and Sophia and her party were to reap the benefits, quite possibly without having put in much preparatory spadework."

The explosion came on the morning of May 15—a day the monk Sylvester Medvedev reported as dawning in a "disturbed" fashion, as "the air became still, then a great storm brewed up, and dark clouds came over." A rumor was spread among the *streltsy* that the Tsarevitch Ivan—Russia's rightful ruler in the view of many—had been murdered by the usurping Naryshkin clan. Hearing this, the soldiers erupted in fury and prepared to attack. "We are going to the Kremlin to kill the traitors and murderers of the Tsar's family!" they shouted. A monstrous bloodletting was about to begin.

The enraged regiments poured into the Kremlin before the gates of the great citadel could be closed, charged up the hill into Cathedral Square, and amassed before the Red Staircase, which led from the square into the government complex known as the Palace of Facets. There the rebellious *streltsy*—"milling in with loud voices and brazen uncouthness and insubordination," as one contemporary reported—demanded satisfaction. "Where is the Tsarevitch Ivan?" they shouted. "Give us the Naryshkins and the other traitors! Death to the traitors!"

Confronted with an armed mob screaming for blood, the Tsarina Natalya had no choice but to produce her stepson Ivan in order to prove he was still alive. It had to have been a terrifying ordeal, but the regent bravely appeared at the top of the Red Staircase with Peter and Ivan on either side of her, each holding her hand. Seeing this, the mutinous crowd was stunned into silence. Natalya then addressed them: "Here is the Lord Tsar Peter Alexeevich. And here is the Lord Tsarevitch Ivan Alexeevich. Thanks be to God, they are well and have not suffered at the hands of traitors. There are no traitors at the palace. You have been deceived."

Some of the *streltsy* were unconvinced and climbed the staircase to have a closer look. "Are you really Ivan?" they asked the half-blind and befuddled boy, who answered affirmatively. "No one is mistreating me," he said, "and I have no complaints against anyone." With that, the fury of the soldiers seemed to subside. Yet it was merely a lull.

Artamon Matveev, the friend and minister of the late Tsar Alexis (and caretaker of his wife, Natalya, before her marriage), was also a respected former commander of the *streltsy*. He managed to further placate the soldiers by gently admonishing them for their misguided rebellion, urging their dispersal, and reminding them of their duty to the tsar. But almost as soon as Matveev finished speaking and retreated back inside the palace, Prince Michael Dolgoruky, a commander of the *streltsy*, appeared before the simmering regiments and fiercely upbraided them for their outrageous behavior. It was a spectacularly ill-timed rebuke, for which Dolgoruky paid dearly at the business end of the *streltsy*'s pikes. Having now tasted blood, the beast was unstoppable in its search for more.

With their fury reignited, the *streltsy* stormed into the palace and spotted Matveev talking with the regent Natalya, who was still holding the hands of Ivan and Peter. The old man who had just managed to calm the agitated mob now fell victim to it. As the royal family looked on with horror, their confidant was ripped away from them, taken out front, and tossed over the stairway to be butchered the same way Dolgoruky had been. And the hunt continued. Rampaging through the palace, thrusting their pikes into any potential hiding place, the maddened *streltsy* searched for what appeared to be a preselected list of enemies.

Natalya and her son Peter were spared the *streltsy's* violent retribution, though certainly not the terror that accompanied it. Other members of their family weren't so fortunate. One of the regent's brothers, Afanasy Naryshkin, was slaughtered after a court dwarf led a pack of soldiers to his hiding place behind the altar of the Church of the Resurrection. Another, the despised Ivan, was tortured for hours before he, too, was torn to pieces.

With the death of these hated Naryshkins, the bloodlust of the *streltsy* had at last been satiated. But not their preening sense of self-importance and instinct to survive. In addition to their demands for enormous pay arrears, as well as amnesty for the revolt, they insisted a triumphal column be erected in Red Square celebrating their recent deeds—with the names of their victims attached to it on bronze plates. The *streltsy* also sought to correct what they perceived to be a gross mishandling of the royal succession, when Tsarevitch Ivan was bypassed in favor of his younger half-brother Peter. Threatening further violence, they demanded that the throne be shared by both boys, with Ivan serving as the senior tsar.

Sophia, who had emerged as the royal family's representative during the three days of unrest, heard the *streltsy's* demands—and acquiesced to them. Summoning the victorious regiments before her, she praised them for their loyalty and feted them with food and vodka. Then, after a show of reluctance, Sophia accepted their petition that she rule as regent while her younger siblings remained incapable due to the tender age of one and the multiple disabilities of the other. Thus, on June 25, 1682, Ivan V and Peter I were crowned together as co-tsars.

It was a strange tableau, unprecedented in European royal history: two sibling monarchs, in full ceremonial regalia, sharing the same throne. Seated listlessly on one side was the drooling half-wit Ivan V; on the other was his infinitely more robust half-brother Peter. "Nature develops herself with advantage and good fortune in his whole personality," the Dutch ambassador wrote of the younger tsar in 1685. "His stature is great and his mien is fine; he grows visibly and advances with as much in intelligence and understanding as he gains the affection and love of all. He has such a strong preference for military pursuits that when he comes of age we may surely expect from him brave actions and heroic deeds."

Missing from the scene, but controlling it nonetheless, was Sophia, sister of the tsars and the power behind them— literally—for at the back of Ivan and Peter's two-seated throne, hidden from view, was a chair upon which big sister Sophia or one of her representatives sat, whispering instructions to the young co-monarchs through an opening cut out for the purpose. Sophia was now Russia's de facto ruler; the young tsars merely props. "It is clear as day to many people that she is gifted with a high degree of talent for governing," one foreign correspondent reported. It was also clear that Sophia possessed a degree of ruthlessness that helped sustain her lofty position for seven years.

Within just three months of assuming power, at the age of twenty-five, Sophia demonstrated her might by taming the same force that had helped elevate her. The *streltsy* swaggered with increased confidence in the wake of their murderous revolt, as did the newly appointed director of their department, Prince Ivan Khovansky. So Sophia chopped off his head. The once-rabid *streltsy* was now left a writhing, leaderless mass that now sought only conciliation. "We have no evil intentions, nor shall we have," they assured the tsars in a statement. Thus a delegation of *streltsy* was permitted to go to Trinity Monastery, where, amid much weeping, the members humbled themselves before the royal family and swore to obey a stringent set of regulations set out before them. It was a triumph for Sophia, punctuated not long after when the column recently erected in Red Square at the *streltsy*'s insistence was torn down.

Though Sophia was now Russia's undisputed ruler, her strength and position depended entirely on her brothers—the co-tsars Ivan and Peter—remaining ineffectual puppets. Peter could one day rise to challenge her, as indeed he did, but for now his youth kept him at bay. Sophia was content to have him away from court while she attempted to build a power base around her ever pliable brother Ivan. "She guards Ivan so well that he never goes anywhere and no one visits him without her leave," one observer reported.

Like Sophia, Ivan was a Miloslavsky. And she needed her brother to sire more Miloslavskys to ensure that the succession would be perpetuated by their side of the family before Peter grew old enough to have his own sons. Accordingly, Sophia arranged a marriage for her decidedly less than sprightly sibling. The Austrian envoy, for one, was doubtful the marriage would be fruitful, writing, "In my humble opinion this seems a lost cause insofar as Tsar Ivan is very infirm and congenitally blind, with a growth of skin right over his eyes." Yet despite his numerous handicaps, Ivan V did manage to father three girls—including the future Empress Anna—but this was not enough to permanently secure Sophia's position. She needed to *reign* as well as rule.

The regent gradually began behaving as if she was in fact the third sovereign, adopting many of the monarchical trappings of the tsars themselves. Her face was stamped on coins. Portraits featured her in full royal regalia, which she often adorned herself with when meeting foreign visitors. In 1684, for example, after a Swedish delegation was received by the two enthroned tsars, Ivan and Peter, they were taken to another chamber to see Sophia, "who was seated on her royal throne which was studded with diamonds, wearing a crown adorned with pearls, a cloak of gold-threaded samite [a luxurious, heavy silk fabric] lined with sables, and next to the sables an edging of lace. And the sovereign lady was attended by ladies-in-waiting, two on each side of the throne . . . and by female dwarves wearing embroidered sashes and gold sable-lined cloaks."

Sophia's name was always included with her brothers' on all official documents, but in 1686 she began sharing the title of *autocrat* with them. The following year, she actually tried to get herself formally crowned—an effort that never gathered much momentum as no one was prepared to elevate a woman quite that high. Big sister would have to content herself looking and behaving like the sovereign, and for seven years she did. But then, in a most unwelcome development, half-brother Peter began to assert himself.

While Sophia was busy ruling Russia, Peter was often away from court at his late father's country estate, Preobrazhen-skoe, happily pursuing his own interests—particularly war games, which became increasingly sophisticated, and, later, shipbuilding. The young tsar only came to Moscow, most re-luctantly, when his presence was required at various ceremo-nials. Otherwise, he lived almost entirely free, indulged in his interests by an ambitious half-sister who was pleased to have him out of her way. It was an ideal state of affairs, but, inevi-tably, change was coming.

"Tsar Peter has already grown taller than all the gentlemen of the court," the Dutch ambassador recorded in July 1688. "We are convinced that this young prince will soon undertake the duties of a sovereign. If those changes do take place, then we shall see affairs taking a new direction."

Urged on by his adherents, including his mother, Natalya, Peter did gradually begin to take more of an active part in governing. Early in 1688, for example, it was reported that he joined Sophia and Ivan at a council meeting for the first time, and soon after he appointed some of his Naryshkin relatives to powerful posts. But it wasn't until the following year that Peter finally took on his sister, at a time when her regime was particularly vulnerable.

Sophia's chief minister (and reputed lover), Vasili Golit-syn, had led two disastrous military campaigns against the Crimean Tatars. But rather than acknowledge defeat, Sophia instead treated Golitsyn—"my lord and light and hope"—as a conquering hero. In the name of both tsars, Golitsyn was to be richly rewarded "for the glorious and splendid victory over the infidel." Peter, however, was having none of it. For a week he refused to sanction the gifts to Golitsyn and his officers, and only later reluctantly agreed under pressure.

"Everyone saw plainly and knew that the consent of the younger Tsar had not been extorted without the greatest difficulty," wrote General Patrick Gordon, a Scottish soldier in the Russian service, "and that this merely made him more excited against the generalissimo [Golitsyn] and the most prominent members of the other party at court; for it was now seen that an open breach was imminent."

On the night of August 7, 1689, Peter was roused from his sleep at his country retreat at Preobrazhenskoe and told that the *streltsy* were marching out from Moscow to kill him and his family. Wearing just his nightshirt, the terrified tsar leapt onto his horse, raced to a hidden copse, and waited for his clothes to be brought to him. Then he rode all night to the Trinity Monastery, where, it was reported, "he immediately threw himself upon a bed and fell a weeping bitterly relating the case to the abbot and desiring the protection and assistance of them." The wounds left seven years earlier, when the ten-year-old boy watched in terror as those closest to him were torn to pieces, were still raw.

Several accounts from the period insist there really was a plot hatched in the Kremlin to kill the young tsar, although some historians have asserted that it was Peter's own party—eager to force a confrontation with Sophia—that raised a false alarm. If so, it was an effective, though utterly heartless, ploy. The uncrowned regent now faced a formidable threat from an anointed tsar whose ire had been (perhaps artificially) aroused.

A week after arriving at the monastery, Peter sent a written summons to the colonels of all the *streltsy* regiments, ordering them to attend him there. Sophia tried to stop such a disastrous exodus with what Patrick Gordon described as an "eloquent oration," urging the *streltsy* to disobey and not "meddle themselves in the differences betwixt her and her brother." When several voted to go anyway, she "took them up very sharply, telling them that if any went thither, she would cause [to] interrupt them, and strike off their heads."

It was imperative to Sophia's survival that she quickly resolve the conflict that had so suddenly erupted. She set off with several of her sisters to see Peter, but before they could reach the monastery, the party was intercepted by a messenger from the tsar with orders to proceed no farther. When Sophia defiantly announced that she would continue the journey, another messenger arrived to inform her that she would be dealt with "dishonorably" if she continued to disobey.

The next day Peter stepped up his offensive by ordering that Feodor Shaklovity, director of the *streltsy* department and one of Sophia's most fervent supporters, be sent to him to face charges that he and his troops "intended to march to the village of Preobrazhenskoe and murder us, our mother, our sister and our courtiers." The order clearly implicated Sophia in Shaklovity's plot and so incensed her that she ordered the messenger bearing it to be immediately beheaded. Fortunately for him, an executioner could not be found on such short notice.

As Sophia's power ebbed away, she gathered the *streltsy* before her and delivered a series of rousing speeches, but to little effect. Shaklovity was arrested and, under torture, admitted to having considered killing the younger tsar and his family. Now, as the exodus to Peter's camp became a stampede, Sophia was left alone at the Kremlin, stubbornly resistant to whatever fate awaited her. Peter addressed the Sophia problem in a letter to his co-ruler, Ivan, with whom he had no quarrel, and indeed declared, "I shall be ready to honor you as I would my father." Ivan would continue to serve as the senior tsar, but Sophia had to go.

Realistically, Ivan V had little choice in the matter, and soon enough Sophia was hauled away to a convent—never to emerge again. It was perhaps worse than death for the woman who had dared assert herself outside the *terem* and for a brief period wielded unprecedented, intoxicating power. She was "a princess endowed with all the accomplishments of body and mind to perfection," Peter the Great later said of his half-sister, "had it not been for her boundless ambition and insatiable desire for governing."

Chapter 2

Peter I (1696–1725):

The Eccentricities of an Emperor

> . . . debauchery and drunkenness so great that it
> is impossible to describe it.
>
> —PRINCE BORIS KURAKIN

After the fall of the regent Sophia in 1689, Peter I continued to rule jointly with his half-brother Ivan V until the latter's death in 1696. Then, as sole autocrat, Peter proceeded to utterly transform Russia. He had grown to be a giant of a man, standing nearly seven feet tall, with grand ambitions to match his stature. With relentless will, he opened his insulated realm to the rest of Europe, eagerly adopting new ideas and customs while forcing his often recalcitrant subjects to do the same. Having transformed the army and building a navy from nothing, the tsar was able to crush the power of the Swedish Empire, seizing its Baltic possessions and, in so doing, achieving for his kingdom open access to the sea for the first time. In the process, he built his magnificent new capital of St. Petersburg—known as Russia's "window to the West"—undeterred by the marshy, inhospitable condition of the land he had chosen. It was these stunning accomplishments, among many, that earned Peter his sobriquet, "the Great." But there was another side to this most dynamic monarch, when he behaved more like a depraved maniac than the enlightened ruler he so wanted to be.

Mary Hamilton had a date with the executioner, and her escort to the fatal rendezvous was none other than her ex-lover, Peter the Great himself. She had hoped her past relationship with the tsar, as well as her status as one of his wife's favorite ladies, might save her from her fate. But not even the beguiling white silk dress she wore for the occasion, adorned with black ribbons, was enough to move the implacable monarch—even as he stood by her side—for Mary's crimes were unpardonable. Not only had she stolen the tsarina's jewels and mocked her ruddy complexion, but, far worse, she had done away with a succession of unwanted children immediately after delivering them.

"I cannot save you without breaking laws both human and divine," Peter whispered in his former mistress's ear. "Accept your punishment in the hope that God will pardon you if you repent." Although the tsar's final words to her were delivered with a kiss, it was certainly not the reprieve Mary hoped to hear.

Having bid her farewell, Peter turned away while the headsman completed his grisly task. But the tsar wasn't quite finished with the woman who had once shared his bed. There was a lesson to be learned and, ever the eager instructor, Peter didn't waste the opportunity. Approaching the bloody heap that had been Mary Hamilton, he reached down and grabbed her head, lifted it up, and addressing the gathered spectators, began pointing out some of the anatomical features that had been exposed by the decapitation—the neatly sliced vertebrae, the gaping windpipe, and the draining carotid arteries. Having finished this impromptu lecture, Peter brought Mary's cold lips to his, kissed them, then tossed her head back to the ground and strode away.

Perhaps it was the lingering horror of a ten-year-old boy, his own fate uncertain, being forced to watch as his uncles and other close family associates were torn to bits by a crazed mob of *streltsy*. Or maybe it was some kind of neurological disorder, manifested in those disconcerting episodes when the tsar's eyes would roll back in their sockets while his body convulsed in severe tremors. Whatever the cause, Peter the Great showed himself to be decidedly unbalanced at times—his most impressive attributes often mingled with bizarre, sometimes vicious behavior.

Here was a sovereign whose insatiable curiosity drove him admirably to learn and master innumerable crafts—from shipbuilding to carpentry—but woe to that poor subject with a toothache, say, for he might find the wild-eyed tsar coming at him with a pair of pliers, ready to rip out the offending tooth as he honed his dentistry skills. There was no option but to submit. And while most monarchs left the death penalty to their professional executioners, Peter was known to hack off a few heads himself—yet another art mastered.

Absorbing and implementing the knowledge of the West was one of Peter the Great's most ardent passions, and to that end he embarked on a tour of Europe in 1697. Hoping to avoid all the ceremony that would normally be due his rank as a visiting sovereign, the tsar traveled incognito. And though his identity was hardly a secret, he did manage to utilize his time learning rather than enduring endless cycles of hospitality. Peter was entranced by all the scientific, mechanical, and artistic wonders at his disposal. But at one point, during an anatomical lecture in Holland, he became infuriated at the squeamishness of his companions when a human corpse was dissected. In retaliation, he made each man march up to the dead body and take a bite out of it.

After long days of learning, the tsar liked to unwind a little—much like a Viking. While Peter was visiting England during his extended European tour, the diarist John Evelyn's elegantly appointed home was made available to him and his traveling companions for three months. It ended up in shambles, laid waste by a horde of drunken Russians led by their monarch. Windows were smashed, floors so stained with ink and grease that they had to be replaced, portraits used as target practice, feather mattresses and pillows shredded, furniture reduced to firewood. And that was just inside. Evelyn had spent years cultivating beautiful lawns and gardens, only to find them trampled into mud and dust, "as if a regiment of soldiers in iron shoes had drilled on [them]." Neighbors even reported seeing the drunken tsar pushed along in a wheelbarrow—a then-unknown contraption in Russia—right into the estate's carefully cultivated hedges.

Despite much evidence to the contrary, Peter wasn't a complete animal while visiting Europe. When the occasion called for it, he did manage to behave himself: "The Tsar surpassed himself during all this time," wrote a member of the Prussian court. "He neither belched, nor farted, nor picked his teeth—at least I neither saw nor heard him do so." And he absolutely enchanted Sophia, Electress of Hanover (mother of Britain's future king George I), who recorded her impressions of the tsar after spending an evening with him:

"He has a great vivacity of mind, and a ready and just repartee. But, with all the advantages with which nature has endowed him, it could be wished that his manners were a little less rustic. . . . We stayed in truth a very long time at table, but we would gladly have remained there longer still without feeling a moment of boredom, for the Tsar was in very good humor, and never ceased talking to us. . . . He told us that he worked himself in building ships, showed us his hands, and made us touch the callous places that had been caused by work. . . . He is a very extraordinary man. It is impossible to describe him, or even to give an idea of him, unless you have seen him. He has a very good heart, and remarkably noble sentiments. I must tell you also, that he did not get drunk in our presence, but we had hardly left when the people of his suite began to make ample amends."

The tsar returned from his nearly yearlong European sojourn filled with dreams of breaking Russia free from its backward isolation and transforming it into an evolved, enlightened kingdom worthy of the civilized world's respect. He started with the beards, which Russian men had worn with pride for generations as symbols of their faith and ancient values. To Peter, these bushy totems were nothing short of barbaric—the most outward reflection of crippling superstition and complacency. He ordered them off, but, of course, he couldn't just leave that to the barbers. No, the tsar attacked with a razor the hairy faces of his courtiers, many of whom lost a fair amount of skin in the process. For those who could not bear to part with their beards, a special tax was instituted. Those who opted to pay were issued a bronze medallion to be worn around the neck, which (sometimes) protected them from the government's roving enforcers.

The forced shearing led some to believe that Peter was actually the Antichrist, come to destroy the venerable Orthodox faith. "Look often at the icons of the Second Coming of Christ," one treatise warned, "and observe the righteous standing at the right side of Christ, all with beards. At the left stand the Muselmen and heretics. Lutherans and Poles and other shavers of their ilk, with just whiskers, such as cats and dogs have. Take heed whom to imitate and which side you will be on."

Driven as he was to win wars and reform Russia, Peter never neglected the booze—prodigious amounts of it, enough to poison most men, which was in fact a distinct possibility many of the tsar's drinking companions confronted as he demanded their full participation in his alcoholic excesses. As one commentator later wrote, "above all the apparent jollity and revelry of life there reigned the iron will of the head pedagogue, which knew no bounds—everyone made merry by decree and even to the sound of drumbeats, they got drunk and made merry under compulsion."

Alcohol was one of Peter the Great's ultimate pleasures—his fondness for it established as a young man during his frequent visits to Moscow's German Suburb (the neighborhood set aside for non-Russians), where he would spend the day learning about the West from the foreigners who resided there and the night indulging in what Prince Boris Kurakin called "debauchery and drunkenness so great that it is impossible to describe it." Peter gradually organized these bacchanals into a formal club, "the Most Drunken Synod of Fools and Jesters," whose members, the tsar and his drinking buddies, seemed to take special delight in mocking organized religion—particularly Roman Catholicism, with a dash of contempt toward traditional Russian Orthodoxy tossed in as well.

The hierarchy of the Drunken Synod mimicked that of the church, with a "Prince-Pope" at the top, gradually descending from bishops down to lowly deacons. As he was wont to do in other arenas, like the military, the tsar took a lesser ecclesiastical title—but there was no question who *really* headed the motley bunch.

"Peter seems to have expended as much energy and imagination on [the Synod] as he did on many of his more serious projects," wrote historian Russell Zguta. "He was constantly adding to or changing its statutes, drawing up elaborate procedures for the induction of new members, or . . . singlehandedly working out the details for the election and installation of a new Prince-Pope."

The primary rule of membership was that "Bacchus be worshiped with strong and honorable drinking and receive his just dues." To help facilitate this, the tsar had built a massive palace of "worship," where drinking and orgies were treated as sacraments. Often, though, the Synod would spill out to the streets in gaudy pseudoreligious processions, like on one Palm Sunday when the Prince-Pope and a retinue of twelve cardinals—"each carefully chosen from among the most physically deformed stutterers," as one described the red-capped drunks—rode on oxen and asses, or in sleighs pulled by pigs, bears, and goats.

One of the Synod's early Prince-Popes was the tsar's former tutor, Nikita Zotov, who was an eighty-four-year-old widower when Peter decided to marry him off to a widow a mere half century his junior. The wedding was a spectacle, showcasing the tsar's warped sense of fun. Perhaps in honor of the octogenarian groom, ancient and decrepit was the wedding theme. Old men were appointed as attendants, waiters, and stewards, with four fat runners selected because of their obesity and disabling gout. At the cathedral, the couple was "joined in Matrimony by a priest a hundred years old," one witness recounted, "who had lost his eyesight and memory, to supply which defect a pair of spectacles were put on his nose, two candles held before his eyes, and the words sounded in his ears, which he was to pronounce."

When old Zotov died several years later, it was time to elect a new Prince-Pope in a ritual proscribed by Peter that seemed to parody papal elections in Rome. Nearly two hundred members of the Synod were sealed into their pleasure palace to ensure secrecy in the balloting. Next, the candidates for office were seated in specially designed stools to have their sex verified—a pseudo-precaution apparently inspired by the widespread belief that a female pontiff, "Pope Joan," had once been elected by the College of Cardinals. With the candidates' appropriate genitalia confirmed, it was time for the election. The eligible voters approached the "Arch-Abbess" present at the proceedings, kissed her breasts, and then dropped an egg (colored to indicate "yes" or "no") into a chalice before each candidate. When Peter Buturlin emerged the victor, Peter decided it was only appropriate that the new Prince-Pope marry his predecessor's widow. Their wedding bed was then placed on public display at Senate Square.

Though it was clearly his favorite pastime, drinking wasn't the tsar's only diversion. There were dwarfs as well. While many royal courts of the era had their complement of little people to amuse them, Peter found them especially hilarious and kept scores of them near him. He loved to surprise his guests by having a naked dwarf pop out of a gigantic pie, or have them participate in the mock ceremonials he so frequently staged. On one memorable occasion, as part of the wedding celebration of his niece Anna (future empress and daughter of Peter's late co-tsar, Ivan V), a contingent of dwarfs was brought in to replicate the royal nuptials. Friedrich Christian Weber, the Hanoverian envoy, recorded the scene:

"A very little dwarf marched to the head of the procession, as being the marshal . . . conductor and master of the ceremony. He was followed by the bride and bridegroom neatly dressed. Then came the Tsar attended by his ministers, princes, boyars, officers and others; next marched all the dwarfs of both sexes in couples. They were in all seventy-two. . . . The Tsar, in token of his favor, was pleased to hold the garland over the bride's head according to the Russian custom. The ceremony being over, the company went . . . to the Prince Menshikov's palace. . . . Several small tables were placed in the middle of the hall for the new-married couple and the rest of the dwarfs, who were all splendidly dressed after the German fashion. . . . After dinner the dwarfs began to dance after the Russian way, which lasted till eleven at night. It is very easy to imagine how much the Tsar and the rest of the company were delighted at the comical capers, strange grimaces, and odd postures of that medley of pygmies, most of whom were of a size the mere sight of which was enough to produce laughter. One had a high hunch on his back, and very short legs, another was remarkable by a monstrous big belly; a third came waddling along on a little pair of crooked legs like a badger; a fourth had a head of prodigious size; some had wry mouths and long ears, little pig eyes, and chubby cheeks and many such comical figures more. When these diversions were ended, the newly married couple were carried to the Tsar's house and bedded in his own bedchamber."

It should perhaps be noted that Peter's interest in dwarfs extended beyond mere amusement. He was fascinated by "oddities" of all kinds, human and animal, and among the numerous objects he collected for his cabinet of curiosities— displayed beside such items as the neat rows of teeth he had extracted from his subjects and the severed head of Mary Hamilton pickled in alcohol—were the remains of deformed infants he encouraged his subjects to send him, dead dwarfs, and the skeleton of a giant who stood nearly eight feet tall.

Entertainment for Peter sometimes took on a menacing quality. "In the winter he has large holes cut in the ice and makes the fattest lords pass over them in sleds," reported Foy de la Neuville (a possible pseudonym for an unknown diarist). "The weakness of the new ice often causes them to fall in and drown." Prince Boris Kurakin reported that on some occasions people's clothes were torn off them and they were made to sit on ice, their bare behinds exposed, then violated with candles, with air blown up them with bellows. There was at least one fatality from this unique form of fun, but Peter at play was still far less dangerous than when his wrath was stirred.

This was especially evident in 1698, after an abortive uprising by four regiments of the *streltsy*—those "begetters of evil," as Peter called them, whose vicious rampage sixteen years earlier had left the young tsar in mute terror as they slaughtered his family in front of him. Now the nightmares that had haunted him ever since became real again. Only this time, he was no longer a helpless little boy. And though otherwise progressive in his thinking, Peter the Great delivered a retribution that was utterly medieval in its barbarity.

The tsar had already done much to humble the unruly and arrogant *streltsy* in the years following their first revolt, essentially reducing them to common foot soldiers deprived of all the privileges and prestige they had once enjoyed. Thus sparked the second revolt, which erupted while Peter was away on his extended tour of Europe. The uprising had been quickly crushed and a number of participants already tortured and executed, but not nearly enough to satisfy Peter. He canceled the rest of his planned itinerary in the West and immediately sped home to deal with the treasonous *streltsy* himself.

After hacking off the beards of his subjects, the tsar started hacking off heads. But first he was determined to discover if there had been a larger conspiracy behind the *streltsy* revolt, and, if so, how high among his boyars it went. Two thousand or so rebels still languished in prison, and Peter wanted answers from them. To that end, what author Robert K. Massie termed as "an assembly line of torture" was set up outside the tsar's country estate of Preobrazhenskoe. Bones were broken, flesh seared, and backs lashed and shredded—with Peter presiding over the interrogations, which lasted for weeks—but many of the *streltsy* remained stubbornly mum about any greater plot.

The Austrian envoy Johannes Korb left a vivid account of the revolt and its aftermath, including the tsar's frustration when it became apparent that being racked and roasted was not enough to elicit the answers he was seeking from one poor soul. "The Tsar, tired at last of this exceedingly wicked stubbornness, furiously raised the stick which he happened to have in his hand, and thrust it so violently into his jaws—clenched in obstinate silence—to break them open, and make him give tongue to speak. And these words too that fell from the raging man, 'Confess, beast, confess!' loudly proclaimed how great was his wrath."

As numerous historians have pointed out, cruel torture was hardly unusual in the seventeenth century, but rare was the monarch who personally conducted such bloody business like the Russian tsar did, week after week, without a trace of mercy. "Peter never hesitated to be a participant in the enterprises he commanded, whether on the battlefield, on shipboard or in the torture chamber," Massie noted. "He had decreed the interrogation and destruction of the *Streltsy;* he would not sit back and wait for someone to bring him news that his command had been obeyed."

Gradually the tsar gleaned that the *streltsy* had planned to march on Moscow, kill the foreigners there, and restore the old order under the potential leadership of their old ally Sophia. But Peter found no conspiracy among the ranks of the boyars, and even after personally interrogating his once fearsome half-sister in her convent, he could find no hard evidence against Sophia, either. Still, the woman who had loomed so large in his youth did not entirely escape his vengeance. After nine years of relatively luxurious confinement in the convent, where she never actually became a nun, Sophia's head was shaved and she was forced to take the veil as Sister Susanna. And just to remind her of the *streltsy's* treachery, three of their rotting corpses were hung outside the window of her cell—close enough to touch, and smell.

After endless rounds of torture, the executions began in batches, and would continue over the next year. The first group was hauled to the gibbet outside Preobrazhenskoe in carts, two doomed men in each, holding lighted tapers as their weeping relatives ran beside them. Many were too broken by their interrogations to make it up the scaffold without help, but all died stoically. During another round of retribution, the tsar ordered some of his associates to lop off *streltsy* heads themselves. Some went about the task eagerly, like Peter's friend Alexander Menshikov, who bragged of completing twenty decapitations without getting a single drop of blood on himself. Others, however, were more reticent. Indeed, one wielded the axe so limply that he succeeded only in striking a blow to his victim's back. Peter himself set an example by rolling up his sleeves and beheading at least five men, perhaps more, as accounts vary.

The heads and bodies of the hated *streltsy* were put on gruesome display throughout Moscow; some corpses were even left hanging from the Kremlin walls. "What strange sentries!" Korb exclaimed in his diary. Those who survived the massacre spent the rest of their lives without ears and noses, which had been lopped off, while the remaining *streltsy* regiments were forever disbanded.

Peter the Great had demonstrated in the most vivid way possible the fate of those who would dare threaten the realm or interfere with his reforms. But the lesson seems to have been lost on one of those closest to the tsar: his very own son, Alexis.

Peter had never been much of a father to the young tsarevitch, possibly due to his distaste for the boy's mother, Eudoxia Lopukhina, a colorless, ultra-Orthodox woman he had married in 1689 only because his mother willed it.* He was seventeen at the time, bursting with vigor, and far from ready to settle down with the dull, clingy spouse imposed upon him. Peter soon abandoned Eudoxia, and, with her, the son she had delivered a year after the couple wed.

But as Alexis grew up, the tsar began to take more notice, and he was bitterly disappointed by what he saw. While Peter was relentlessly energetic in the pursuit of his grand designs, his heir was a lazy intellectual, content to let the world pass him by as he dallied with his mistress and drank himself stupid. Certainly the sovereign shared his son's fondness for drink, but he was appalled by Alexis's indolence, as well as his

---

* Prince Boris Kurakin wrote of Eudoxia: She was "fair of face, but mediocre of mind, and no match for her husband."

apparent affinity with those conservative factions resistant to the tsar's efforts to westernize Russia. Peter was determined to reconstitute the tsarevitch into a man more like himself—an effort that would have devastating consequences in the end.

It began with constant cajoling, which served to frighten the young man rather than improve him. After Alexis returned from a year of study in Germany, for example, he completely panicked when his father asked him what he had learned about geometry and fortifications; Alexis was terrified that the tsar might require him to execute drawings on the subject about which he was entirely incompetent. It was too horrible to contemplate, and rather than face such an ordeal, he returned to his home, picked up a pistol, and tried to shoot himself in the hand. The shot missed, but his hands were badly burned by the powder flash.

In the face of what he viewed as his son's complete dereliction of duty as heir to the Russian throne—particularly in learning the martial arts the tsar deemed essential in a future monarch—Peter sent Alexis a letter in 1715 expressing his deep dissatisfaction and frustration:

"Remember your obstinacy and ill-nature, how often I reproached you for it and for how many years I almost have not spoken to you. But all this has availed nothing, has affected nothing. It was but losing my time, it was striking the air. You do not make the least endeavors, and all your pleasure seems to consist in staying idle and lazy at home. Things of which you ought to be ashamed (forasmuch as they make you miserable) seem to make up your dearest delight, nor do you foresee the dangerous consequences for yourself and for the whole state."

The tsar concluded his missive with a threat. If Alexis persisted in his waywardness, "I will have you know that I will deprive you of the succession, as one may cut off a gangrenous limb." Rather than heed the warning and improve himself, though, the tsarevitch simply waived his rights as heir. Such easy capitulation unsettled Peter, as did Alexis's apparent willingness to become a monk when confronted with that dire fate. Then the tsarevitch did the unthinkable. He ran away from home and sought asylum with the Austrian emperor.

Peter was livid when he learned of Alexis's ignominious flight. Not only had his heir shamed him in front of the world, but his escape would undoubtedly give those dissident elements in Russia encouragement to revolt in support of Alexis. The tsar sent his agents in pursuit of his son, but the Austrian emperor was reluctant to hand him over to an uncertain fate. Ultimately, though, Peter managed to lure the young man back to Russia with false promises of indemnity and even permission to marry Alexis's peasant mistress, Afrosinia. In responding to his father's siren song, Alexis sealed his doom.

"Have you heard that that fool of a Tsarevitch is coming here because his father has allowed him to marry Afrosinia?" wrote Prince Vasili Dolgoruky to Prince Gagarin. "He will have a coffin instead of a wedding!"

The tsar appeared conciliatory, at first, but as his suspicions of a conspiracy became inflamed, scores of people associated with the tsarevitch and his infamous escape were tortured to get to the truth. Soon enough, it was Alexis's turn. With Peter's permission, the young man was subjected to the uniquely Russian form of "interrogation" known as the knout—a thick leather strap that would slice into a man's back with every blow. Fifteen to twenty-five lashes were considered standard; anything over that could easily prove lethal. On the first day of questioning, Alexis received twenty-five blows but made no additional confessions. Five days later, with his back already in shreds, he was subjected to fifteen more lashes. In this state of extreme agony, the tsarevitch admitted to telling his confessor that he wished for his father's death and that he would have willingly paid the emperor for a supply of foreign troops to seize Peter's throne. It was enough.

A secular convocation of 127 senators, ministers, governors, generals, and officers of the Imperial Guard unanimously condemned Alexis to death, but it was up to the tsar to sign the warrant. Even for a monarch as ruthless in the face of treason as Peter the Great, signing his son's life away would be a staggering act of retribution. Fortunately, Alexis spared him this burden by conveniently expiring two days after last being knouted. The cause of death was surrounded by much speculation and remains a mystery to this day. Some said the tsarevitch had been secretly done away with, although some historians believe the torture Alexis endured was sufficient to kill him.

Whatever the cause of death, Peter made no false demonstrations of grief. In fact, the next day he attended a banquet and ball in celebration of Russia's victory over Sweden at the Battle of Poltava nine years earlier. As far as the tsar was concerned, the death of his son, though tragic, was also necessary. Alexis had proven himself an enemy of progress and, had he lived, would have destroyed everything his father had built. To commemorate Russia's deliverance from such a calamity, Peter had a medal struck. It featured a crown lit by the sun with its rays piercing the clouds and included an inscription that read: "The horizon has cleared."

Chapter 3

Catherine I (1725–1727):

The Peasant Empress

One cannot help wondering at God's Providence whereby the empress has been elevated from the lowly position into which she was born and in which she lived to the pinnacle of human honors.

—FRIEDRICH WILHELM VON BERGHOLTZ

Upon his death in 1725, Peter the Great was succeeded by his second wife, Catherine, in what was surely one of the most stunning elevations in the history of monarchy. Indeed, the rise of the former peasant woman to Russia's throne might well have been a fairy tale had it not been absolutely true.

Death did not come easy to Peter the Great. The colossus who had dragged Russia out of its medieval malaise and built an empire by the sheer force of his will now lay convulsing in agony, his eyes filled with fear, as the vital life force that once infused him inexorably drained away. To save his soul, the doomed autocrat acknowledged his sins and repeatedly cried out for absolution. As for the succession, though, Peter was silent.[*] And so he remained through the early morning hours

[*] Legend has it that Peter called for a writing tablet and managed to

of February 8, 1725, when he finally breathed his last. It was thus that the mighty emperor's wishes were buried with him and an heir chosen without his express authority. Perhaps Peter never intended that an uneducated former peasant would come to occupy his throne. On the other hand, he had made this once-lowly creature his wife, then his empress. Certainly that had some significance. Yet again, so did sending her the head of her reputed lover in a jar, just a few weeks earlier.

Only the barest details are known about the early life of the woman who came to rule Russia as Empress Catherine I. She was born Martha Skavronskaya, probably in 1684, to peasant parents in what was then the Swedish province of Livonia.[*] Orphaned as a young girl, she was taken into the household of a Lutheran pastor named Gluck and there served as a maid.[†] With few prospects, Martha's obscurity seemed assured in the small town of Marienburg—until a Russian force swept through during the Great Northern War with Sweden and took her captive in 1702. It was then that the total transformation of Martha Skavronskaya's life began.

The teenage girl was passed around as a spoil of war—wearing nothing but a soldier's cloak to cover her nakedness—until she was finally presented to the fifty-year-old Field Marshal Boris Sheremetev. While serving as the field mar-

---

scrawl, "Leave everything to . . ." before dropping the pen in a sudden fit of tremors.

[*] Livonia is now split between Latvia and Estonia.

[†] According to some accounts, she was married to a Swedish soldier who went off to war shortly after the wedding and was never heard from again.

shal's laundress, or his mistress—perhaps both—she was noticed by Tsar Peter's closest companion and confidant, Alexander Menshikov,[*] who commandeered the girl for himself (and who would come to play an integral role in her eventual accession to the throne).

Though not beautiful in any conventional way, Martha was nevertheless robust and vivacious, with an engaging, generous spirit that immediately attracted the tsar when he first met her at Menshikov's home late in 1703. "He found her clever and ended his badinage with her by saying that when he went to bed she must bring the torch to his room," recalled Peter's aide-de-camp, Captain de Villebois. "This was a decision from which there was no appeal, although it was delivered with a laugh. Menshikov subscribed to it. And the fair one, with the consent of her master, spent the night in the Tsar's room."

Peter the Great's numerous mistresses meant nothing to him—most were mere sexual diversions, easily cast aside (and, in the case of at least one, a source of his gonorrhea). Martha (or Catherine, as she was renamed after her conversion to Orthodoxy) was different, however. She managed to amuse the tsar, sharing his bawdy humor and certainly his

[*] Menshikov came from the humblest origins, some said as a pie seller, but in the world of Peter the Great, a man's background had no bearing—only his talent and potential. The tsar met Menshikov when both were mere boys and was immediately impressed by his great wit and intelligence. The two became instant friends, and, as Robert K. Massie wrote, "Menshikov employed his great charm and his variety of useful talents to make himself one of the wealthiest and most powerful men in eighteenth-century Europe." Even after Menshikov was revealed to be an avaricious plunderer of the state, the normally implacable Peter managed to forgive him. The tsar's grandson, Peter II, would prove to be far less indulgent, however (see footnote on page 63).

SPRINGDALE PUBLIC LIBRARY
405 S. Pleasant
Springdale, AR 72764

fondness for drink, while also encouraging him with her bountiful good sense and eternal optimism. She knew his burdens, and, unlike anyone else, could still his blind rages and convulsive fits.

"The sound of her voice instantly calmed him," observed Count Henning Friedrich von Bassewitz, secretary to the Duke of Holstein, "then she would seat him and hold his head gently stroking it and running her fingers through his hair. This had a magical effect on him and he would fall asleep in just a few minutes. In order not to disturb his rest she would hold his head on her breast and sit motionless for two or three hours. After this he would awake completely refreshed and in good spirits."

But, as biographer Robert K. Massie noted, the tsar's need for her went deeper than simply being nursed: "Her qualities of mind and heart were such that she was able not only to soothe him, play with him, love him, but also to take part in his inner life, to talk to him about serious things, to discuss his views and projects, to encourage his hopes and aspirations. Not only did her presence comfort him, but her conversation cheered him and gave him balance."

Catherine was, simply stated, everything Peter's first wife, Eudoxia (now a nun), was not, and by 1707 the tsar was ready to marry her. It was a secret ceremony, for even a tsar as powerful as Peter the Great would find it difficult to impose a Livonian peasant on the Russian people—at least for the time being. Less than five years later, though, in 1711, that all changed after Catherine played a remarkable role during the Pruth River campaign against the Ottoman Turks.

Peter was in dire circumstances that July, surrounded by an overwhelming enemy force poised to annihilate him. Total and unconditional surrender seemed to be the tsar's only option, but with it came the possibility of losing vast territories not only to the Turks, but to their ally, Russia's most despised foe, the Swedes. Catherine, who accompanied her husband on the campaign and bravely endured the enemy assault by his side, urged the tsar to negotiate with the Turkish grand vizier, Mehemet Baltadji—even if Baltadji's position was so superior that he had to concede nothing. Astonishingly enough, the grand vizier allowed Peter to avoid total destruction with some painful though by no means ruinous concessions.

Legend has it that Catherine had secretly sent her most valuable possessions to the grand vizier as a bribe, which resulted in his relative leniency. Whether or not this was true, the tsar later honored his wife with the new Order of St. Catherine, "instituted to commemorate Her Majesty's participation in the battle with the Turks on the Pruth River, where, in such dangerous circumstances she had proven herself to everyone not as a weak woman, but as a brave man."

Then, seven months after escaping the Pruth River fiasco, Peter married Catherine—again—this time in a splendid ceremony for all the world to witness. "Thus, Cinderella became queen," wrote the Russian historian Evgenii V. Anisimov. "No one had the right any longer to address her in any way other than 'Your Royal Majesty,' and all subjects, regardless of distinction, were considered her slaves and required to bow their heads in her presence."

Although Russians were now required to honor Catherine as tsarina (one monk who failed to do this had his bones broken on a wheel), others were not so obliged. Margravine Wilhelmina of Bayreuth, sister of Frederick the Great, was decidedly unimpressed when Catherine visited Berlin in 1718, and she recorded this most unflattering description:

"The tsaritsa is a small, stumpy, very dark-complexioned, unimpressive and ungraceful woman. It's enough to look at her to see her humble origins. Her tasteless dress seems to have been bought at a junk dealer's: it is old-fashioned, covered with silver and dirt. A dozen orders are pinned on her and the same number of small icons and medallions with relics; all these jingle when she walks so that you have the impression that you are being approached by a pack mule."

For Peter, though, Catherine was perfect. She remained earthy and unpretentious, an oasis of serenity in the tsar's otherwise chaotic life, the mother of eleven of his children (only two of whom survived into adulthood),* and the only true source of comfort and support he had. The numerous letters that passed between the couple when they were apart reflect their mutual tenderness, humor, and understanding.

Though Catherine was Peter's one true love, he remained casually unfaithful to her while she good-naturedly indulged his meaningless affairs. She knew she held the tsar's heart (if not his fly) and was wise enough to recognize that challenging him was a sure way to lose it. This unique facet of their relationship was reflected in an exchange from June 1717, while Peter was undergoing mineral water treatments in Spa:

"There is nothing to write to you about, only that we arrived here yesterday safely, and as doctors prohibit domestic fun [that is, sex] while drinking the water, I have sent my mistress back to you, for I would not have been able to resist the temptation if I had kept her here." In her response, Catherine wryly noted that the mistress was not sent away because

---

* Peter and Catherine's two surviving daughters were Anne of Holstein, mother to the future Emperor Peter III (see Chapter 6), and Elizabeth, who became empress of Russia in 1741 (see Chapter 5).

of doctor's orders but because she had a venereal disease, "and I have no desire (and heaven forbid!) to have this mistress's lover [Peter] come home in the same condition as she."

Catherine's tolerance of the tsar's infidelities was a simple result of her inferior position, but her indulgence may also have been informed by her own reputed extramarital dalliances—one of which would explode into a spectacular scandal. But not before Peter paid Catherine the ultimate tribute and had her crowned as his tsarina.

It was a magnificent event, infused with all the pomp and ceremony Peter normally abhorred. He even dressed for the occasion, replacing the utilitarian work clothes he preferred with a sky-blue caftan embroidered in silver, red silk stockings, and a hat with a white feather. Catherine was even more spectacularly arrayed in a purple gown trimmed with gold, with an ermine-lined brocade mantle around her shoulders, and diamonds shimmering in her hair.

As the bells of Moscow tolled amid thundering cannon fire, the royal couple appeared atop the Kremlin's Red Staircase—sight of the horrors Peter witnessed as a young boy—and proceeded across Cathedral Square to the Cathedral of the Assumption, where Ivan the Terrible was first crowned in 1547. There, in the light of hundreds of candles, they took their places upon two jewel-encrusted thrones. As the elaborate ceremony reached its climax, Peter took the crown—constructed specially for the occasion and consisting of thousands of diamonds, pearls, and other precious stones, including an enormous ruby as large as a dove's egg—and turned to the gathered audience, proclaiming, "It is Our intention to crown Our beloved consort." He then placed the crown upon Catherine's head and handed her the orb. Symbolically, though, he refrained from giving his wife the scepter, the ultimate symbol of royal power.

"One cannot help wondering at God's Providence whereby the empress[*] has been elevated from the lowly position into which she was born and in which she lived to the pinnacle of human honors," noted Friedrich Wilhelm von Bergholtz, a courtier and guest from Holstein.

Peter had indeed raised his stalwart companion high, but what did it signify? Some historians have suggested that he was officially designating Catherine as his heir. All his sons, including the ill-fated Alexis, were dead, and he had already decreed several years before that the traditional rules of succession would no longer apply; that henceforth the tsar would have the absolute power to determine who would rule after him. But, problematically, Peter never explicitly named Catherine as his heir. It was this omission that left biographer Lindsey Hughes to conclude:

In the absence of direct evidence of Peter's intentions on the succession in May, 1724, the coronation should perhaps be taken at face value as what Peter said it was: a ceremony to honour Catherine. In terms of public recognition, it went hand in hand with Peter's creation of a Western-style court for his wife. It was a rebuke to those who muttered about Catherine's unsuitability as an empress and yet another demonstration of Peter's will.

Viewed from another angle, this crowning of a foreign peasant woman as empress was an example of Peter's upside down world, the "mock" universe of his own devising

---

[*] Peter proclaimed Russia an empire in 1721 and he became emperor (a title henceforth interchangeable with tsar). Catherine thus received the title of empress.

which he used to exert his authority and disorientate people.[*]

Whatever Peter's motive in crowning Catherine, he may well have come to regret it, for just weeks later emerged unseemly revelations about the empress's secretary and confidant William Mons—described by the Danish envoy Hans Georg von Westphalen as "among the most handsome and elegant people whom I have ever seen." He was also believed to be Catherine's lover. Mons certainly had a lucrative business selling his influence with the empress, who in turn had the tsar's ear. But was he really sleeping with her? Peter seemed to think so, for after having Mons executed for corruption, he ordered his head preserved in a jar and sent to Catherine—apparently as some kind of perverse keepsake.

Tensions ran high between the royal couple in the wake of the Mons affair. "They almost never talk to each other," reported Jean Lefort in a dispatch to the elector of Saxony; "they no longer eat together, they no longer sleep together." Peter was said to have been so enraged that he smashed a valuable vase.

"Thus will I do to you and yours!" he roared at Catherine, who reportedly replied, "You have just destroyed one of the most beautiful ornaments of your house. Does that give it any more charm?"

The empress herself was devastated by the death of her confidant and possible lover. "Her relations with Mons were common knowledge," reported the French envoy, "and al-

[*] This "mock" universe pervaded much of Peter the Great's reign, where, for example, the autocratic tsar often took a lower rank to his subjects in arenas such as the military and in the "Drunken Synod, where instead of being Prince-Pope, he served as deacon (see previous chapter).

though she tries hard to hide her grief, it is nevertheless evident on her face and in her manner of behavior. All of society tensely awaits what will become of her."

What became of Catherine was entirely unexpected. Instead of falling into disgrace, or worse, she emerged as Russia's next monarch—an empress in her own right, wielding all the power of an autocrat—for shortly after the Mons affair was exposed Peter the Great lay dying.

A great power vacuum loomed and two mighty factions struggled to fill it. On one side were the "new men," many of whom Peter had raised high from the humblest origins. Led by the tsar's close companion Alexander Menshikov (in whose household Peter had found Catherine shortly after her capture), they aimed to maintain power by placing Catherine on the throne. Opposing them were members of the nobility and others who had seen their ancient rights and privileges eroded under Peter's radical regime. Bound by tradition, these men believed the dying tsar's grandson, Peter, son of the doomed Alexis, was the legitimate heir.

Ultimately the decision rested with the Russian Imperial Guard, with whom Peter had replaced the rebellious *streltsy*. "The decision of the Guards is law here," the French envoy accurately reported. And the Guards were with Catherine (the first of a parade of sovereigns they would install—or depose—according to their will). She had accompanied them on many a military campaign, struggling by their side, and in the process earned their loyalty and affection. Now, called by Menshikov and other members of his party, they surrounded the palace where the debate over the succession raged.

Suddenly a loud roll of drums came from the courtyard, drawing the opposing statesmen to the windows. Prince Repnin, president of the College of War and a member of the aristocratic party, reacted furiously, demanding to know why the Guards were there without his order. The commander of the Guard, who had entered the debate chamber, responded coolly, "What I have done, Your Excellency, was by the express command of our sovereign lady, the Empress Catherine, whom you and I and every faithful subject are bound to obey immediately and unconditionally." With that, many of the Guard present tearfully cried out, "Our father is dead, but our mother still lives!"

Seizing the momentum, Menshikov raised his voice above the crowd. "Long live our most august sovereign Empress Catherine!"

"Viva Empress Catherine!" the Guards cheered.

Then, according to Count Bassewitz, "these last words were immediately resounded by all those present, each wanting to appear to the rest as if he were joining in of his own free will, and not merely imitating the example of others."

Thus, on February 8, 1725, the former peasant captive Martha Skavronskaya became Empress Catherine I, autocrat of All the Russias. It was a relatively brief, uneventful reign, with Menshikov in charge and Catherine bombed throughout most of it. The French envoy Jacques de Campredon noted that her "amusements constitute almost daily drinking bouts which take place in the garden and continue the whole night through and well into the next day, and involve persons whose duties require them to always be present at court."

The empress could have been her dead husband in drag, so all-consuming was her taste for alcohol. She even revived Peter's "All-Drunken Synod," and presided over it with a relish that would have made him proud. Catherine was often the last one standing at these booze-filled gatherings, teetering off to bed at dawn, only to wake up and start swilling once again. Her expense ledgers for Hungarian wine, Danzig schnapps, and other libations told their own story of excess. But the empress never paid any attention to expense, or to her health, for that matter—even as the constant drinking took its terrible toll.

Just over two years after ascending the throne, the forty-three-year-old peasant empress was dead.

Chapter 4

Anna (1730–1740):

"A Bored Estate Mistress"

Our sovereign is a fool; you cannot get a decision from her on any matter.

—Artemy Volynsky

Catherine I was succeeded not by either of her two surviving children, Anne or Elizabeth, but by her eleven-year-old stepgrandson, Peter—a boy whose legacy was blackened by the dissipated antics and cruel demise of his father, the Tsarevitch Alexis (see Chapter 2). Orphaned at the age of three and virtually ignored by his grandfather, Peter the Great, the child lived in the shadows for most of his life—no matter that he had emerged as the last Romanov of the male line. When the crown suddenly became his in 1727, Peter II was ready to play. But, after a brief reign of less than three years, marked by indolence and sexual shenanigans that belied his tender age, the boy tsar was dead at age fourteen.

With the throne now vacant, members of the Supreme Privy Council—a regency of nobles that oversaw the affairs of the realm—plotted to make themselves truly supreme. For that, they turned not to the descendants of Peter the Great, but to those of Ivan V, his feeble, mentally challenged half-brother and co-tsar, who, though not capable of much, did at least manage to father three daughters. The Supreme Privy Council arranged for the ac-

*cession of Ivan's middle daughter, Anna, with the understanding
that she would be entirely ruled by them. They were wrong. Anna
retained all her autocratic powers and wielded them in some of the
most bizarre ways imaginable.*

The wedding was gleefully planned by the empress who just
loved her warped amusements. She had paired Prince Michael Golitsyn, a nobleman she had reduced to one of her
court jesters, with a hideous-looking serving wench. Now it
was time for the honeymoon. For that occasion, Anna arranged for a magnificent palace to be built entirely of ice on
the frozen Neva River. Even the minutest details were given
meticulous attention, right down to the ice playing cards that
sat atop an ice table. There were ice trees and shrubs outside,
with an ice elephant guarding the entrance, while inside the
honeymoon suite the couple was provided with a canopied
bed made entirely of ice, along with ice sheets, pillows, and
blankets. A huge crowd joined the grand procession to this
frozen retreat where the unfortunate couple was condemned
to spend the night consummating the marriage neither had
wanted. They emerged the next morning frostbitten and snif-
fling, while the capricious Empress Anna was left howling
with laughter.

Such uproarious fun would have once been unimaginable to
Anna, even a few years previously. Born into a branch of the
Romanov clan with few prospects after the death of her father, Ivan V, she became a political pawn of her uncle Peter
the Great—married as a matter of state to Frederick William,
Duke of Courland, when she was seventeen. While the wedding ceremony did offer a preview of the delights to come

when she was Russia's sovereign—complete with seventy-two dwarfs provided by uncle Peter to amuse the guests (see account in Chapter 2)—Anna was widowed within two months. Rather than allow his young niece to stay home in Russia after her husband's death, Peter forced her to reside in Courland (now part of modern-day Latvia), a region he coveted. It was a bleak existence indeed.

Though Anna was Courland's nominal duchess, her uncle the emperor provided little for her maintenance. Pitifully, she wrote to Peter's successor, Catherine I, begging for assistance: "You, my dear Sovereign, know that I have nothing other than the damask which you had ordered, and if the opportunity were to rise, I have neither suitable diamonds nor laces, neither linens nor a fine dress, and with the revenues from the village I can hardly maintain my home and put food on the table during the course of the year."

Compounding her financial woes, the young widow was lonely and desperately wanted a husband to protect and comfort her. She was thwarted at every turn. The king of Prussia's nephew seemed to be a real possibility and a marriage contract was drafted in 1723, but Peter the Great quickly nixed this match, fearing the influence Prussia would gain in Courland. Then there was Count Maurice of Saxony. Sure he was a wanton philanderer, but he would be Anna's—even if she had to share him. In anticipation of the wedding, Count Maurice was made duke of Courland by the local noblemen. But, alas, someone else had his eye on the ducal seat, and he was a formidable contender indeed: Alexander Menshikov.*

* Peter the Great's favorite (see footnote on page 51) had reached near-royal status during the booze-soaked reign of Catherine I. He "was exercising a perfect despotism," observed General Christoph von Manstein. But the mighty Menshikov eventually met his match with young Peter

"The choice of Maurice is at variance with the interests of Russia," Catherine I wrote sternly, and no amount of pleading on Anna's part would move the empress. Count Maurice was forcibly expelled from Courland, leaving his would-be mate crushed. Lacking a husband, Anna took solace in her lover, Peter Bestuzhev-Ryumin, a skilled diplomat installed in Courland by Peter the Great. The lonely widow subjected herself entirely to this dynamic character, nineteen years her senior, although, like Count Maurice, he was not exactly monogamous. "He lures the ladies-in-waiting outside the court and makes children [with them]," reported one anonymous informer. Needy as she was, Anna overlooked these infidelities, but, in the end, Menshikov ruined that relationship, too. He blamed Bestuzhev-Ryumin for his failure to obtain Courland's throne and the duchess's lover was eventually recalled to St. Petersburg. Anna was inconsolable.

"I humbly request of you, Your Excellency, to intervene for me, a poor woman, before His Serene Highness [Menshikov]," Anna wrote in one of dozens of desperate letters to various court officials. "Be merciful . . . kindly heed the humble appeal of an orphan, give me cause for joy and save me from tears. Have mercy on me, as would God himself. . . . Truly, I live in great sorrow, emptiness, and fear! Do not let me spend the rest of my life in tears! I have grown accustomed to him!"

II, Catherine's successor. If he did nothing else during his brief, lethargic reign, Peter crushed the so-called half-tsar who dared try to control him. (Menshikov had held the new emperor as a virtual captive in his gilded palace, and even tried to perpetuate a personal royal dynasty by betrothing the tsar to his daughter Maria.) "I will show you who is Emperor: Menshikov or me," Peter II angrily exclaimed, right before shipping his nemesis off to Siberia.

Grieved though she was over the loss of Bestuzhev-Ryumin, Anna quickly filled the vacancy in her bed with a new lover, Ernst Johann von Biron—the man who would virtually dominate her ten-year reign when she became empress of Russia in 1730. So what if he was married, with three children. Anna simply made his family her own. In fact, some historians believe that the youngest of Biron's offspring, a little boy named Karl Ernst, was actually Anna's son as well. She certainly kept the child close to her, and awarded him the highest titles and honors when she obtained the crown.

While Anna contented herself with Biron in Courland, the Supreme Privy Council was busy plotting her future in Russia. Peter II was dead and the council—dominated by the powerful Dolgoruky and Golitsyn clans—wanted a compliant successor they could control.* They thought they had the perfect candidate in the late Ivan V's destitute middle daughter, who had shown herself to be entirely submissive in so many matters. Accordingly, they offered her the crown—a glittering prize, to be sure, but one without even a dollop of power, for the council intended to make the sovereign their puppet by assuming all her traditional rights. Feebly, Anna signed the document that sucked the vital essence right out of the autocracy.

But the designated empress would not remain a glorified figurehead for long. A frenzy of discontent arose among the lesser nobility when they learned of the Supreme Privy Council's brazen grasp for power. With an insurrection brewing, once again it fell to the Imperial Guard to determine the fate of the throne—just as it had after the death of Peter the Great. And the Guard liked its sovereign strong. Backed by

---

* Peter the Great's surviving daughter, Elizabeth, was once again rejected as candidate, as were Ivan V's eldest and youngest daughters.

this insurmountable force, Anna ordered the document in which she had signed away her rights and privileges be brought to her. Then she tore it to bits.

The night after Anna received the mandate to rule as she pleased, the sky blazed with scarlet northern lights of unusual intensity, "overspreading the whole horizon," according to one account, "[that] made it appear as if all were drenched in blood." Some saw it as an ill-omen, and the next decade would validate all their fears.

Russia was now in the hands of a petty, suspicious woman with a decided mean streak. And her appearance seemed to match her personality. Burly, with manly features, the empress was by no means a beauty. "Such a *cheek* the pictures give her," the historian Thomas Carlyle wrote, "in size and somewhat in expression like a Westphalia ham!"

Anna was not particularly interested in actually governing Russia, but rather in pursuing her often peculiar pleasures. Like her uncle Peter the Great, the empress delighted in human oddities and surrounded herself with the malformed, disabled, and grotesquely ugly. Even those lacking natural impediments had a place in court, reduced to fools and jesters for Anna's amusement. That's how some noblemen found themselves covered with feathers and forced to sit in a nest clucking like chickens, or spending the night in an ice palace.

An avid hunter like Peter II, Anna brought a unique blood-thirstiness to the sport. Wild beasts from all over Russia were imported to the empress's estates so she could pick them off at her leisure. The animal trophies mounted into the thousands. She even kept guns near the windows inside her palaces so that if a bird happened to fly by she could conveniently shoot it from the sky.

Because of Anna's affinity for it, shooting became all the rage in fashionable society. "The fawning nobility schooled their young daughters by having them shoot at doves," wrote Anisimov. "What else could one expect? If Her Majesty were to take to bathing in a hole cut in an iced-over stream, then all the young and not-so-young countesses and princesses would be obliged to climb into the ice-cold water only to please the crowned naiad."

When she wasn't busy slaughtering animals, Anna kept a keen eye on her subjects—not for their welfare, of course, but to ensure they behaved the way she wanted. Her spies were everywhere, and the torture chambers were packed with those who displeased her. No detail of her subjects' lives—no matter how trivial—escaped the empress's attention. "A bored estate mistress," Anisimov called her. "A superstitious, petty, and capricious mistress, she stood by her Petersburg 'window' and examined her vast yard [Russia] with partiality and keen attention, duly punishing any servants and slaves responsible for any disorder she might happen to see."

Anna sent her agents—particularly her kinsman, Count Semen Saltykov, governor-general of Moscow—to pry into astonishingly inconsequential matters, far more worthy of the neighborhood busybody than the autocratic empress of Russia. Among her many orders to Saltykov:

—"Go to Apraksin's and personally examine his storeroom; look for a portrait in which his father is depicted on horseback, and send it to us; he [Apraksin] is in Moscow, of course, and if he hides it, they, the Apraksins, will be sorry."

—"Let me know if my chamberlain . . . is still married. Here [in St. Petersburg] it is rumored that he is divorced . . . . I am writing to you about this in absolute secrecy so that he will not know about my inquiry."

—"When you receive this memorandum, look for a bride for Davydov. Send her here escorted by a soldier, but do not send any of her relatives, not even her mother."

—"Find out whether Golitsyn's father was really ill, as his son has told us here, or whether he was in good health; if he was ill, then write what kind of illness he had and how long he had been ill."

With such weighty matters to attend to, Anna had little time—and even less inclination—to oversee her *real* responsibilities. "Our sovereign is a fool," complained Artemi Volynsky; "you cannot get a decision from her on any matter." To actually run Russia, well, the empress left that almost entirely to her Courland lover, Biron, described by one contemporary as "haughty, and ambitious beyond all bounds, abrupt, brutal, avaricious, an implacable enemy, and cruel in his revenge." Anna adored him. The couple was almost a single entity, with the empress attuned to her constant companion's every mood and responsive to all his needs.

"Neither one of them could ever completely conceal their feelings," Ernst von Münnich recalled in his memoirs. "If the duke came frowning, the empress immediately took on a worried air. If he was gay, the monarch's face showed obvious pleasure. If someone failed to please the duke, then that someone would immediately detect a marked change in the eyes of the monarch and in the way she received him. All favors were to be sought from the duke, and only after his approval would the empress make her decision."

Made the virtual master of Russia by his mistress Anna, Biron proceeded to make himself thoroughly hated. And so it went for the duration of Empress Anna's decade-long reign. Only her death on October 28, 1740, at age forty-seven, separated the couple at last. The English envoy reported Anna and Biron's final moments together: "Her Majesty, looking up, said to him: *Nie Bois!*—the ordinary expression of this country, and the import of it is: 'Never fear.'"

Yet as it turned out, Biron had much to fear indeed.[*]

---

[*] Biron briefly ruled as regent during the reign of Anna's infant nephew, Ivan VI, before he was ambushed in his bed at the Winter Palace and dragged away—naked as the day he was born. "The noise, shouting, and turmoil of this classic palace coup scene awakened the entire court," wrote Evgenii V. Anisimov, "and only the deceased empress [Anna] showed no sign of interest in what was happening as she lay quietly in her coffin in the palace's state hall [as] Biron was carried out past her bellowing and kicking."

Chapter 5

Elizabeth (1741–1762):

The Empress of Pretense

The secret corners of her heart remain inaccessible even for the oldest and most experienced courtiers, with whom she is never more cordial than when she is stripping them of rank and favor.

—JEAN-LOUIS FAVIER, FRENCH DIPLOMAT

Empress Anna had intended that the Russian throne would remain with the descendants of her father, Ivan V—certainly not with those of her uncle Peter the Great. To that end, she left the crown to her infant great-nephew, Ivan VI. But by then, Peter's only surviving daughter, his adored "Lizetka," had waited in the wings long enough. Disregarded as a silly pleasure seeker, Elizabeth had been bypassed in the succession four times after the death of her father—first in favor of her mother, Catherine I, then by her nephew Peter II, followed by Anna, the cousin who despised her, and finally by Ivan VI. Unfortunately for that infant emperor, after reigning for just over a year, Elizabeth was ready to take his place.

Reports of a coup were mounting and Anna Leopoldovna,[*] Ivan VI's mother and regent of Russia, could no longer afford

---

[*] Anna Leopoldovna was the daughter of Empress Anna's older sister,

to ignore them. She needed reassurance that the throne of her baby son was secure, and, accordingly, decided to confront the person at the center of the rumored uprising: her cousin Elizabeth. Drawing aside the daughter of Peter the Great during a court function, Anna Leopoldovna asked her directly if she was involved in any plot to seize the crown. Given the consequences, it was a question that would have left one less assured flustered and stammering denials, but Elizabeth never flinched.

"[She] was not at all disconcerted," reported General Christoph von Manstein. "She protested to the grand duchess that she had never had the thought of undertaking the least thing either against her or against her son; that she was too religious to break the oath that she had sworn; that all these reports came only from her enemies, who wanted to make her unhappy."

Happily assuaged of her concerns, Anna Leopoldovna joined her cousin in a tearful reconciliation, after which Elizabeth left the palace. Less than a day and a half later she would return, accompanied by armed supporters, to arrest the imperial family and proclaim herself empress.

It was easy to underestimate Elizabeth, as Anna Leopoldovna discovered too late. As a young woman, she was often dismissed as an inconsequential coquette—opinions for which Elizabeth certainly provided plenty of fodder. Her life seemed to consist of little more than perpetual rounds of parties, hunts, and sweaty interludes with a succession of well-formed

---

Catherine of Mecklenburg (see family tree). To help differentiate between the late empress and her niece, Ivan VI's mother is referred to in this chapter with her patronymic, Leopoldovna.

lovers. "The behavior of the Princess Elizabeth gets worse and worse each day," reported the Duke de Liria, ambassador from Spain. "She does things without shame, things that would make even the humble blush."

These impressions of Elizabeth as a lightweight were at least part of the reason why she was so consistently bypassed in the succession to the throne. No one took her seriously. But there was far more to this young woman than people seemed to recognize. While she may have led her nephew Peter II from one mindless diversion to the next (with just a whiff of incest in the mix), she also encouraged his rebellion against the tyranny of Menshikov (see footnote on page 63). Some sensed in Elizabeth this more complex character.

"She has an affability and sweetness of behavior that insensibly inspires love and respect," Lady Rondeau, wife of a British diplomat, wrote in 1735. "In public she has an unaffected gaiety and a certain air of giddiness, that seem entirely to possess her whole mind; but in private, I have heard her talk in such a strain of good sense and steady reasoning, that I am persuaded the other behavior is a feint."

Rather than a disguise, what Lady Rondeau actually saw was two sides of Elizabeth. And there were many more. Indeed, she was an amalgamation of many characteristics, often conflicting and more pronounced after she ascended the throne—a vivacious flirt with a mean streak; a voluptuary with a stout heart when it mattered most; a pious churchgoer prone to promiscuity; a proud Russian with a passion for everything French. All this made her so utterly inscrutable that the soothing assurances of love and loyalty she offered to Anna Leopoldovna before stealing her son's crown were delivered convincingly by a woman who had only to draw the role of devoted cousin from her arsenal of personality traits.

"She resembled her father in a good many ways," wrote biographer Robert Coughlan, "not the least in her ability to meld complex, sometimes opposite, sometimes grotesque character traits into a personage both viable and forceful, and which, bewildering as it often was to others, she was able to carry off with what seemed to be perfect inner assurance."

Such personal resources served Elizabeth well as she navigated her way through four reigns relatively unscathed after the death of her father. Not that matters didn't get a bit harrowing at times, particularly under the rule of her spiteful cousin, Anna. The burly, ill-visaged empress loathed Elizabeth—not the least for her beauty, which was indeed remarkable.

"I have seldom met a woman as beautiful as Princess Elizabeth," the Duke de Liria reported in 1728. "She has a marvelous complexion, beautiful eyes, excellent neck, and an incomparable figure. She is tall and very lively; she is a good dancer and rides a horse without any fear. She is quite intelligent, graceful, and extremely coquettish." In short, everything Empress Anna was not.

The jealous empress went out of her way to make her cousin's life as miserable as possible—slashing her allowance and encouraging malicious gossip—but through tact and abject humility Elizabeth survived. And as Anna's reign gave way to that of the infant Ivan VI, so began a shift in Elizabeth's fortunes. It is unclear what degree of ambition Elizabeth harbored all along. "I am very glad that I did not assert my right to the throne earlier," she later said; "I was too young and my people would never have borne with me."* But as the child

---

* At the time of Peter II's death and the accession of Empress Anna, Elizabeth appeared unready to seek power for herself. "She was having a good time in the country at the time," a French observer reported, "and

tsar lay nestled in his cradle, Elizabeth sensed opportunity. Resentment was running high over the pro-German policies of Anna Leopoldovna's government, and in the midst of widespread discontent, a path to power was opening. In order to clear it entirely, though, Elizabeth needed the Imperial Guard.

She set about the seduction with all her considerable charms. She flattered the men, stood as godmother to their children, reminisced with them about the feats of her mighty father, and, soon enough, had them in her hands. But as Elizabeth's cause gathered momentum, she hesitated. What if her planned coup failed? Then it would be off to the nunnery with her—just like her aunt Sophia*—and as the British envoy wryly noted, there was "not an ounce of nun's flesh about her." As it turned out, the unexpected confrontation by Anna Leopoldovna left her with little choice but to act, immediately.† Donning an armor breastplate over her dress and steeling her strength, Elizabeth made her way to her loyal Guards.

"My friends!" she exclaimed. "Just as you served my father faithfully, in the present situation likewise show your loyalty to me!"

"We will be glad to die for Your Majesty and for our Motherland!" the men shouted in response.

---

even those who were making an effort on her behalf were unable, in view of the circumstances, to get her to come to Moscow."

* See Chapter 1.

† There had been rumors that Anna Leopoldovna planned to consign Elizabeth to a convent. In urging her to act, the future empress's friend and doctor, Jean Armand de L'Estocq, drew a picture for her on a card. On one side was a monarch seated on her throne; on the other was a nun in full habit.

Thus, under cover of darkness in the early morning hours of December 6, 1741, the conquering party boarded sleighs with the Winter Palace as their destination. Arriving at Admiralty Square, Elizabeth got out of her sleigh and started to march on foot the rest of the distance to the palace. But in the rush, she got tangled in her skirts and mired in the snow. Without hesitating, the grenadiers lifted her up on their shoulders and carried her along the rest of the way.

The palace sentries were asleep in their barracks when Elizabeth came. "Wake up, my children, and listen to me!" she announced. "You know who I am, and that the crown belongs to me by right. Will you follow me?" With the sentries behind her, Elizabeth ordered the palace secured and then went to Anna Leopoldovna's chambers, where she found the regent asleep in bed with her friend Julie Mengden. "Awake, my sister," Elizabeth said, gently shaking her rival. Anna Leopoldovna had only to look around at the guards filling her room to know it was all over. It was a bloodless coup, but in an instant Ivan VI went from emperor to prisoner. Taking the baby up to her breast, Elizabeth said to him, "You are not guilty of anything, little one!" She then handed him off to a horrible fate.[*]

---

[*] The ex-emperor and his family were sent to a series of increasingly isolated prisons until 1744, when four-year-old Ivan was cruelly snatched away. He was never to see his parents or siblings again, although, for a period, he was kept in a gloomy cell right next to them—entirely unaware that they were on the other side of the thick wall that separated them. The extreme isolation to which Ivan was subjected over the years, being deprived of every childhood joy and mercilessly tormented by his guards, gradually made itself manifest in the boy, who began to show signs of mental damage—particularly after he was moved at age fifteen to the notorious island prison of Shlisselburg. As one guard reported, "his articulation was confused to such a degree that even those who constantly saw and heard him could understand him [only] with difficulty. . . . His

As baby Ivan VI and his family were escorted away, the Age of Elizabeth began. The jesters and malformed unfortunates so favored by Empress Anna gave way to gilded palaces filled with sumptuous French furniture and fine arts to reflect the glory (and good taste) of the new empress. And in these great palaces there were plenty of mirrors so she could admire herself from every angle—for if ever vanity had a name, it was Elizabeth.

The empress loved to showcase herself at masquerades and other frequently held diversions. Sometimes she dressed as a man, which, with her figure and bearing, she carried off to great effect.* But when she was feeling feminine, she adorned herself with flashing diamonds and rich French gowns— never worn twice and often changed several times a day. In fact, after her death in 1762, an astonishing fifteen thousand dresses were reportedly found in her wardrobe, along with "two chests filled with silk stockings, several thousand pairs of footwear, and more than one hundred untouched lengths of splendid French fabric."†

---

mental abilities were disrupted, he had not the slightest memory, no ideas of any kind, neither of joy nor of sorrow, and no special inclinations." Through three reigns Ivan lived in this dank prison. Peter III even came to visit him shortly before he was deposed. But it was under Catherine the Great that he finally perished. The empress had ordered that if any attempt were ever made to free the royal prisoner—referred to as "the nameless one"—he should be killed immediately. And when one misguided officer tried to do just that in 1764, Ivan VI met his end.

* The empress took particular pleasure in occasionally ordering men to dress as women and women as men. Unlike her, though, few could carry off these gender-bending directives without looking absolutely ridiculous.

† This report of the empress's vast wardrobe is attributed to Jacob von Staehlin, tutor to Elizabeth's successor, Peter III.

"She danced with perfection and had a particular grace in all that she did, whether dressed as a man or a woman," recalled Elizabeth's eventual successor, Catherine the Great. "One would have liked to be always looking at her, and only regretfully turned the gaze away, because no object could be found to replace her."

Elizabeth was at the center of her own universe, and she insisted those who orbited around her to reflect her magnificence. Accordingly, there were strict standards of dress and decorum. Gentlemen had to be dashing, and ladies were expected to emulate their sovereign and never wear the same dress twice. To ensure this, gowns were marked or tagged during a ball to ensure they would not be seen again. Yet while guests at the empress's affairs had to look good, they had better not look *too* good. If one did inadvertently outshine the empress, the penalty often proved dear—for Elizabeth could wield a pair of scissors as ferociously as her father. The future Catherine II, who was fortunate enough on one occasion merely to be ordered to change an offending dress, recorded the plight of several other women who perilously tipped the beauty scale:

> My dear aunt was very prone to petty jealousies, not only in relation to me, but to all the other ladies as well. She had an eye particularly on those younger than herself, who were continually exposed to her outbursts. She carried this jealousy so far once she called up Anna Naryshkina ... who, because of her beauty, her glorious figure, superb carriage, and exquisite taste in dress, had become the empress's pet aversion. In the presence of the whole court, the empress took a pair of scissors and cut off the trimming of lovely ribbons under Madame Naryshkina's neck. Another

time, she cut off half the front curls of two of her ladies-in-waiting on the pretext that she did not like their style of hair dressing. Afterwards, these young ladies said privately that, perhaps in her haste, or perhaps in her fierce determination to display the depth of her feelings, Her Imperial Majesty had cut off, along with their curls, some of their skin.

On one occasion Empress Elizabeth was having a hellishly bad hair day—so bad, in fact, that after a botched dye job, she had to have her head shaved. "Under these conditions, how could she tolerate in her wake all those women with their arrogant heads of hair?" wrote Henri Troyat. "No, the duty of good subjects was to imitate their sovereign in everything." That came as an order: All the other women of the court had to have their locks shorn as well, replaced by ill-fitting black wigs.

With or without hair, an endless cycle of balls, soirees, theatrical performances, and masquerades were scheduled for nearly every night of the year. And while the elite were expected to indulge in all of these entertainments with enthusiasm equal to the empress's, most lacked her unlimited resources. Indeed, the costs to the nobility to maintain what Catherine the Great termed the "contrived coquetry" demanded by Elizabeth were so staggering that some were driven to bankruptcy.

For most, though, it was far better to be broke than banished from the imperial presence. It was ironic, then, that the most favored of Empress Elizabeth's subjects—the ones who shared her bed—started off as the poorest, or at least the most humble. First and foremost among them was Alexis Razumovsky, a rough, handsome Ukrainian with a marvelous singing voice. Elizabeth became smitten with this peasant shepherd when she first met him in 1731, and took him from the court choir to the highest echelons of power when she came to the throne a decade later. Unlike other royal bedmates—like Empress Anna's Biron, or Catherine the Great's fleet of young paramours (see Chapter 7)—Razumovsky eschewed the privileges and lofty positions Elizabeth lovingly bestowed on him. "Your Majesty may create me a field marshal if you so desire," Razumovsky once told her, "but I defy you or anybody else to make even a tolerable captain out of me."

Because of his influence on the empress, and, of course, his place in her boudoir, people took to calling Razumovsky the "Night Emperor," and it was even rumored that the couple secretly wed.* But, like that of her eventual successor, Catherine II, Elizabeth's sexual appetite was voracious. So when she decided to replace Razumovsky with a new, younger lover—her page Ivan Shuvalov—the good-hearted "Night Emperor" graciously stepped aside.

Busy as she was with her multiple amusements, in and out of the bedroom, Empress Elizabeth did manage to squeeze in a little time for statecraft when she woke up in the afternoon. Her cultural contributions vastly improved a nation that had so sorely lacked them. It was she who funded many of Russia's most enduring architectural treasures, while the arts flourished under her patronage. The empress also took some interest in foreign policy, always keeping Russia's best interests at

---

* No definitive evidence of this supposed marriage has ever been produced. Elizabeth was earlier engaged to Prince Karl Augustus of Holstein-Gottorp, who happened to be Catherine the Great's maternal uncle, but he died soon after.

heart, and she did her best to rule in the progressive spirit of her father*—even if lacking entirely Peter the Great's vigor. Elizabeth was, in fact, essentially a loafer.

Important papers sat on her desk for weeks without being read or signed, which sent her ministers into fits of frustration. "If the empress would give to government affairs only one one-hundredth of the time [Austrian empress] Maria Theresa devotes to them, I should be the happiest man on earth," remarked Alexis Bestuzhev-Ryumin, vice chancellor of foreign affairs.

The future empress Catherine II, herself a model of industry, observed that "laziness had prevented [Elizabeth] from applying herself to the cultivation of her mind." Instead, Catherine continued, "flatterers and gossip-mongers succeeded in surrounding this princess with such an atmosphere of pettiness that her daily occupations consisted of a tissue of caprices, religious observances, indulgence; lacking all discipline, never occupying her mind intelligently with any serious or constructive matters, she became bored during the last years of her life and the only escape open to her from depression consisted in spending as much time as possible in sleeping."

Ultimately, Empress Elizabeth's only real interest in governance was sustaining her own power. Foolish or inattentive as she may have sometimes seemed, all her actions—or, often, inaction—had at their core one defining principle: she was

---

* And this spirit was not always a benevolent one. As biographer Evgenii V. Anisimov noted, "This charming beauty, who had always demonstrated in her decrees a natural maternal magnanimity, unwaveringly sent a pregnant woman to the torture chamber and wrote a directive in this regard to the head of the Secret Chancery in the same curt, severe, and cruelly businesslike tones that her father had once used when writing to his chief of political investigations."

the autocrat and nothing would be allowed to diminish that. Whether she appeared rigid or wavering, capricious or kind, Elizabeth was always weighing the effect on her sovereignty—"that was her principle of government," wrote Anisimov, "and simple as it was, it proved sound in practice."

Elizabeth liked to present herself as Mother Russia, lovingly tending to her people as she would her own children. It was an image somewhat supported by her displays of mercy and the promise she made never to execute any of her subjects (though torture was another matter entirely). Still, there was another aspect to the ever enigmatic empress.

"Through her kindness and humanness one can frequently see her pride, arrogance, sometimes even cruelty, but most of all her suspiciousness," the French diplomat Jean-Louis Favier reported later in Elizabeth's reign. "Being highly jealous of her great status and supreme power, she is easily frightened by all that might threaten to lessen or divide that power. On more than one occasion she proved to be extremely ticklish concerning this point. To make up for it Empress Elizabeth has mastered perfectly the art of pretension. The secret corners of her heart remain inaccessible even for the oldest and most experienced courtiers, with whom she is never more cordial than when she is stripping them of rank and favor."

There was one thing Elizabeth feared losing almost as much as her power, and that was her looks. She did not age well—or gracefully—and every new wrinkle or sign of bloating drove her to the depths of despair. She "is still fond of wearing fancy clothes, and with each passing day she becomes even more particular and fastidious in this respect," Favier reported. "No woman has had a more difficult time reconciling herself to the loss of youth and beauty. It often happens that, having spent a good deal of time at the dressing-table, she becomes angry with the mirror, and gives orders to remove the headpiece and other articles of clothing which she had put on, cancels the theatrical performance or dinner she had planned on attending, and locks herself in her room refusing to see anyone whoever it might be."

The increasingly reclusive Elizabeth lived in terror because the march of time had one inevitable conclusion, and the multiple illnesses she suffered in her later years only served to magnify her dreaded mortality. "Her health is becoming worse and worse with each passing day," the French diplomat Lafermière wrote in May 1761, "there is little hope that she will live long. But no one more meticulously conceals this from her than she conceals it from herself. Nobody has ever feared death as much as she does. The word is never spoken in her presence. She cannot stand the very thought of death. Anything which might remind her of death has been removed."

Loath as she was to even think of the world without her, Elizabeth did at least provide for the succession. Two decades earlier, she imported from Germany her nephew Peter Ulrich, son of her late sister Anne of Holstein. It was an unfortunate choice of heir, and when in 1762 the fifty-three-year-old empress finally met the end she couldn't face, an imbecile stood ready to take her place.

Chapter 6

Peter III (1762): "Nature Made Him a Mere Poltroon"

Never did two minds resemble each other less.

—EMPRESS CATHERINE II ON HER HUSBAND PETER III

Soon after her accession to the Russian throne in 1742, Empress Elizabeth sought to secure the dynasty by bringing to Russia the last of Peter the Great's grandsons, also named Peter, from the German duchy of Holstein. Alas, the young man—son of Elizabeth's late sister Anne—was nothing like his esteemed namesake. Rather, he was a stunted simpleton with a loathing of all things Russian who would one day be usurped by the wife Elizabeth selected for him, the future empress Catherine the Great.

The late empress Elizabeth, dressed regally in one of her fifteen thousand gowns, lay motionless in her coffin, her painted face a mask of perfect impassivity, as her fool of a successor, Peter III, created a spectacle of himself right in front of her. He "made faces, acted the buffoon, and imitated poor old ladies," his mistress's sister noted. And that's when Peter even bothered to interrupt the raucous celebrations of his newfound power to pay tribute to his deceased aunt like the rest of Russia. His asinine behavior only grew more pronounced during the funeral procession, as Peter entertained himself with a little game, described by his wife Catherine:

"He loitered behind the hearse, on purpose, allowing it to proceed at a distance of thirty feet, then he would run to catch up with it as fast as he could. The elder courtiers, who were carrying his black train, found themselves unable to keep up with him and let the train go. The wind blew it out and all this amused Peter III so much that he repeated the joke several times, so that I and everybody else remained far behind and had to stop the ceremony until everybody had caught up with the hearse. Criticism of the Emperor's outrageous behavior spread rapidly and his unsuitable deportment was the subject of much talk."

Soon enough, talk would turn into action, and Peter III would no longer be laughing. His wife made certain of that.

In the annals of rotten royal marriages, of which there were legion, that of Peter and Catherine would surely rank among the most miserable. Although both spouses—second cousins—were born in Germany and imported to Russia as teenagers, that's about all they had in common. He was a sniveling, underdeveloped nincompoop—even if his worst qualities may have been a bit exaggerated by Catherine in her *Memoirs**—while she was an avid student of the Enlightenment, with ambitions that extended far beyond her designated role as a royal baby breeder. It was a toxic pairing that would end triumphantly for one and rather grimly for the other.

---

* There is a certain level of a usurper's self-justification in Catherine's *Memoirs*. Nevertheless, the unflattering portrait of her husband she presents is echoed in quite a number of other contemporary accounts.

Peter came to the marriage with quite a few deficits, not the least of which was the brutal upbringing that warped him immeasurably. His mother, Peter the Great's elder daughter Anne, died just three months after giving birth to him, and his father, Charles Frederick, Duke of Holstein, showed very little interest in the boy before dying himself when Peter was eleven. Deprived of any parental love or affection, the young prince was raised instead by a borderline sadist, Otto Brümmer, who terrorized the small, sickly child. Whenever Peter failed in his studies or any other task, which was often enough, Brümmer was quick to humiliate him by making him wear the picture of an ass around his neck, or depriving him of food, or applying one of his favorite methods of torture, which was to make the boy kneel for hours on hard dried peas. The inevitable product of this hideous regime was an emotionally stunted, deceitful boy with a lifelong aversion to learning and a penchant for torturing animals.

Already damaged beyond repair, Peter was fourteen when his aunt, Empress Elizabeth, beckoned him to Russia in 1742 to become her adopted heir. As she quickly discovered, he was not a promising choice. Scrawny, with protuberant eyes and no chin, Peter was, alas, as dumb as he looked. Appalled by her nephew's ignorance, Elizabeth promptly retained Professor Jacob von Staehlin of the Imperial Academy of Sciences to tutor him. "I see that Your Highness has still a great many pretty things to learn," she gently said to Peter, "and Monsieur Staehlin here will teach them to you in such a pleasant manner that it will be a mere pastime for you."

But it was no use. Peter was "utterly frivolous" and "altogether unruly," Staehlin reported. He also steadfastly refused to become Russianized, disdaining the language and customs of the country he was destined to rule. Upon his grudging conversion from Lutheranism to Orthodoxy, Elizabeth raised her nephew to the rank of Imperial Highness and granted him the title of grand duke. She also made him a lieutenant colonel in the elite Preobrazhensky Guards, founded by his grandfather, Peter the Great. None of this made a bit of difference, however. Young Peter's heart was in Holstein and there it would remain. The best the empress could hope for was that her nephew would produce an heir to carry on the Romanov dynasty. And for the unenviable task of mating with him, she brought to Russia Peter's German cousin—the future Catherine the Great.

She was born Sophia Augusta Fredericka, the daughter of Prince Christian Augustus, ruler of the tiny German duchy of Anhalt-Zerbst, and his socially ambitious wife, Princess Johanna Elizabeth of Holstein-Gottorp. Sophia wasn't warmly welcomed into the world on May 2, 1729—at least by her mother, who made no effort to disguise her epic disappointment that the little princess wasn't the son she wanted and expected after a life-threatening delivery.

"My mother did not pay much attention to me," Sophia (eventually rechristened Catherine) wrote in her *Memoirs*. "A year and a half later, she gave birth to a son whom she idolized. I was merely tolerated and often I was scolded with a violence and anger I did not deserve. I felt this without being perfectly clear why in my mind."

It was not just her daughter's sex that aggravated Johanna, but her looks as well. She deemed Sophia ugly, a genuine liability when one hoped to advance their standing through the European royal marriage market. Neither did she give the girl credit for her lively intelligence and engaging personality. In fact, these attributes were dismissed as arrogance. Yet despite all the deficits she perceived in her daughter, Johanna did drag Sophia along on her endless rounds of visits to the other royal families of Germany, including her own, hoping to make some kind of advantageous match for her. She only dared dream that it would be someone as illustrious as the grandson of Peter the Great.

When the unexpected call came from Russia requesting fourteen-year-old Sophia's presence there, Johanna was ecstatic. How this union between her daughter and the Russian heir would add to her own luster! Wasting not a minute, she immediately heeded the invitation to her glorious future—undeterred by the winter conditions that would make the journey to Russia treacherous, nor by the pesky fact that this trip really wasn't about her.

Before embarking, Johanna was asked by Frederick II of Prussia to visit him in Berlin. The king, then at war with Austria, had promoted the match between Sophia and Peter with the hope that it would help keep neighboring Russia neutral in the conflict. He was eager, therefore, to meet the young princess upon whom a key part of his foreign policy depended. But Johanna arrived at King Frederick's court unaccompanied by Sophia, who, she feared, might dim her own star. It was not until the king finally insisted that Johanna relented and brought her daughter along. Frederick was enchanted.

"The little princess of Zerbst combines the gaiety and spontaneity natural to her age with intelligence and wit surprising in one so young," the king, known to history as Frederick the Great, wrote to his fellow monarch, Empress Elizabeth.

Much to her delight, Johanna wasn't completely ignored in the equation. Frederick gave the self-important princess the mission to be his secret agent at the Russian court, and to undermine as best she could Elizabeth's staunchly anti-

Prussian vice chancellor, Alexis Bestuzhev-Ryumin, who vigorously opposed the proposed marriage of the German Sophia to the German Grand Duke Peter. It was a task Johanna relished, but one that would end disastrously for her and nearly ruin her daughter.

After an arduous wintertime trek across Russia—made, by the empress's command, with their identities and purpose concealed, only a bare staff of servants to support them, and relegated to increasingly squalid accommodations along the way—Johanna and Sophia finally arrived in St. Petersburg in February 1744, to a thunderous welcome. "Here everything goes on in such magnificent and respectful style that it seemed to me . . . as if it all were only a dream," Johanna wrote to her husband, Prince Christian, who had not been invited to Russia.

Johanna was clearly in her element, but for Sophia, her future was at that moment miles away in Moscow, where Empress Elizabeth and Grand Duke Peter had departed several weeks earlier and now awaited her. It was suggested to Johanna and Sophia that it would be pleasing to the empress if they timed their arrival in Moscow to coincide with Peter's upcoming sixteenth birthday, on February 21. Accordingly, they set off in a grand cavalcade of thirty sledges.

Peter seemed genuinely pleased to see his German relatives when they arrived at Moscow's Golovin Palace, greeting them with a goofy grin and chatting incessantly. He then took Johanna by the arm, while the Prince of Hesse-Homburg took Sophia's, and led them through a series of glittering passages to meet the empress.

Mother and daughter were awed by the tall, robust figure standing before them in her silver gown, shimmering in diamonds, with a black feather perched at the side of her head—

such a contrast to the puny, pale-faced heir. Elizabeth greeted her visitors warmly, visibly moved by the sight of Johanna, who so closely resembled her brother, the empress's deceased fiancé, Charles Augustus of Holstein. And she seemed delighted with Sophia, the young princess upon whom all her hopes for the future rested. She showered the girl with gifts and embraced her—at least for a time—with the kind of maternal love Sophia had never known. Peter, on the other hand, was decidedly less enamored. Sophia would suit him well as a playmate, but he was not at all interested in having her as a wife.

"I was in my fifteenth year and he showed himself very assiduous for the first ten days," Sophia wrote in her *Memoirs*. "In that short space of time I saw and understood that he cared but little for the nation over which he was destined to rule, that he clung to Lutheranism, that he had no affection for those about him and that he was very much a child. I kept silent and listened, which helped to gain his confidence. I remember he told me among other things that what he liked most in me was that I was his second cousin and in that capacity, as a relative, he could talk freely with me; after this he confided that he was in love with one of the Empress's ladies-in-waiting who had been expelled from Court . . . he would have liked to marry her, but he had resigned himself to marrying me as his aunt wished it. I listened to these disclosures with a blush, thanked him for his premature confidence, but privately observed with astonishment his imprudence on a number of matters."

Sophia willingly joined with Peter in his silly games. She was still a child herself, after all, so these simpleminded pastimes with her future spouse were not too troubling. Plus, she wanted to please Peter. It was an imperative emphasized to her by her father before she left Germany, and one upon which she believed her future ambitions absolutely depended. "I was the confidante of his childish nonsense," she wrote, "and it was not for me to correct him; I let him do and say what he pleased." Thus, when the odious Otto Brümmer, who had accompanied Peter to Russia and continued to torment him, asked Sophia to intervene and guide the grand duke to nobler pursuits, she refused. "I told him that it was impossible for me to do so, and that if I tried, I would become as hateful to him as all the others around him."

Indulging her future spouse in all his inanities was one thing, but Sophia was wise enough to recognize that she also had to please Empress Elizabeth, as well as the rest of the nation. To that end, she set out to make herself thoroughly Russian. Unlike Peter, who stubbornly resisted learning the language and rejected the national religion, Sophia became an avid student. Indeed, she worked so hard that her health declined and she came down with a case of pneumonia that nearly killed her. Yet it was an illness that turned into a triumph.

The doctors tending Sophia insisted she be bled to alleviate her symptoms. But to this Johanna strenuously objected. Her brother had died after being bled while suffering from smallpox and she was terrified of the procedure—not to mention how her daughter's death might adversely affect her own prospects. "There I lay with a high fever between my mother and the doctors arguing," Sophia wrote. "I could not help groaning, for which I was scolded by my mother who expected me to suffer in silence." It was then that Empress Elizabeth intervened, berating Johanna for daring interfere with her own doctors and kicking her out of the sickroom. Elizabeth then nursed Sophia herself, tending to her with the kind of maternal devotion that Johanna seemed incapable of providing.

At one point, when it looked as though Sophia might die, Johanna insisted that a Lutheran minister be brought to her. But the ailing princess requested an Orthodox priest instead. "This raised me in the eyes of the Empress and of the whole Court," she recalled.

While Sophia basked in the approbation she received for her diligent efforts to become Russian—and especially her reliance on an Orthodox rather than Lutheran confessor during her time of peril—her mother nearly ruined everything. Almost as soon as Johanna arrived in Russia earlier that year, she had begun conspiring against Bestuzhev-Ryumin with the French and Prussian ambassadors, just as King Frederick II had instructed. It was a fool's endeavor, which Bestuzhev-Ryumin quickly uncovered through intercepted letters and duly reported to the empress. Elizabeth was wild with rage at this scheming, ungrateful woman whom she had welcomed so generously and even granted membership in the prestigious Order of St. Catherine. Johanna was in disgrace, and it looked like her daughter was as well.

Sophia was sitting with Peter, laughing at something he had said, when the empress's French physician and friend L'Estocq burst into the room. "This horseplay will stop at once," he shouted. Then, turning to Sophia, he snarled, "You can go pack your bags. You will be leaving for home immediately." It was a stunning declaration for both Sophia and Peter, neither of whom was aware of Johanna's machinations, or that she had just been trapped. It was only when the empress entered the room to reassure Sophia that she did not hold her responsible for her mother's treacherous behavior that the young princess could breathe again. But she had also become aware in those anxious moments that her intended spouse cared nothing for her. Looking at him while her fate remained uncertain, she later wrote, "I saw clearly that he would have parted from me without regret."

Even if Peter didn't love her, so be it. Nothing would deter Sophia from her destiny. The young couple was formally betrothed on June 29, 1744, in a formal ritual at the Kremlin's Cathedral of the Assumption, where Russian tsars had been crowned for generations. The day before, Sophia was formally converted from Lutheranism to Orthodoxy and given the new name of Catherine, as well as the title of Imperial Highness and the rank of grand duchess. The former German princess had made a significant step on her way to becoming a Russian royal. Marriage, however, would have to wait.

Peter was still sexually underdeveloped at the age of sixteen and incapable of siring an heir. Thus Elizabeth was urged to postpone his nuptials in order to give the grand duke more time to mature. Though impatient to secure the dynasty, the empress reluctantly agreed. Then, later that year, came disaster. Following a bout with the measles, the heir to the throne was stricken with the far more dangerous smallpox. Unexpectedly, given the risks to her life and, even more important, to her looks, it was the empress who lovingly tended to her nephew as he suffered the near-lethal effects of the contagious disease. And though Peter survived, he emerged from his sickbed looking almost monstrous. Catherine was barely able to contain her revulsion after seeing her future husband in this condition for the first time.

"The sight of the Grand Duke filled me almost with terror," she wrote; "he had grown very much in stature but his face was unrecognizable—his features were coarser, his face was still swollen, and one could see beyond doubt that he would always remain deeply pockmarked. His head had been shaven and he wore an immense wig which disfigured him all the more. He came up to me and asked whether I found it difficult to recognize him. I stammered a few wishes for his convalescence, but in fact he had become horrid to look at."

Some historians attribute Peter's subsequent treatment of Catherine to her reflexive recoil at seeing him in such a state, but given his disposition, as well as his previously demonstrated attitude toward her, it seems inevitable that he would have made a vile spouse either way. Still, a deeper chasm did develop in the aftermath of the grand duke's illness. "This was the end of all the Grand Duke's attentions for me," Catherine wrote. "I understood perfectly how little he wanted to see me and how little affection he bore me."

It was in the thick of this frost that the empress, eager as ever, set a wedding date for the toxic couple. As she bustled about planning the festivities, which she insisted must be more extravagant than any ever seen in Europe, Elizabeth was blithely indifferent to the hostility her nephew had for his intended. She was also unaware of his woeful ignorance about the opposite sex, nor of the physical limitations that would make fully appreciating a woman almost impossible for him. Sure, Peter vaguely understood the mechanics of sex, relayed to him in the crudest way possible by his drinking pals, but that was the extent of it. And as for intimacy, the grand duke could never be taught that. In fact, about the only thing Peter grasped about marriage was what one of the servants relayed to him: that a husband should keep his wife submissive, and, if necessary, slap her around a bit should she forget her place. It was this lesson that Peter, "about as discreet as a cannonball," delighted in passing along to Catherine.

Although her love life would later become legendary (see Chapter 8), Catherine was, at the time, actually more naïve about sex than Peter was. Several weeks before the wedding, the sixteen-year-old went to her mother for guidance about the opposite sex and was severely scolded for her sauciness.

Catherine may have been kept ignorant about what would actually happen when she went to bed with Peter, but she was wise enough to sense what was in store for her otherwise. "As my wedding day came nearer, I became more melancholy, and very often I would weep without quite knowing why," she wrote. "My heart predicted little happiness; ambition alone sustained me. In my inmost soul there was something that never for a single moment allowed me to doubt that, sooner or later, I would become the sovereign Empress of Russia in my own right."

On August 21, 1745, all of Empress Elizabeth's meticulous planning came to fruition in a splendid wedding ceremony. "Of all the pompous shows in Russia," reported one English observer, "the appearance made upon the [grand] duke's marriage, in clothes and equipage, was the most magnificent." Bride and groom were both dressed to dazzle, although the effort was wasted somewhat on Peter. "The sumptuous apparel only made him look more like a monkey," as biographer Henri Troyat so artfully put it. It was all a glittering show that delighted the empress but disguised something essentially rotten. Then came the wedding night.

Catherine was undressed by her ladies and put to bed. There she waited for two hours before Peter arrived, drunk, and declared how amused the servants would be to see them in bed together. She awoke the next morning still a virgin. And so she would remain for the next eight years.

Her new husband had no interest in sleeping with her, nor, for that matter, was he capable. Though he certainly liked to crow about his prowess with other women, really all that interested the grossly immature grand duke was carousing with his low-level servants, playing with his toys, and indulging his obsession with all things military. There was no room for his wife, unless, of course, he was putting her through military drills. Stuck in this loveless rut, Catherine wrote, "I yawned and yawned with boredom." She also came to a quick conclusion about Peter:

> I should have loved my new husband if only he had been willing or able to be in the least lovable, but in the very first days of my marriage I made some cruel reflections about him. I said to myself: "If you love that man, you will be the most wretched creature on earth; it is in your nature to want to be loved in return; that man scarcely even looks at you, practically all he talks about is dolls, and he pays more attention to any other woman than to you." . . . This first impression, made on a heart of wax, remained, and I never got these reflections out of my head.

In the midst of her lonely marriage, Catherine found comfort with the most unlikely of persons: the woman who berated her unmercifully and competed with her for attention at court: her mother. Yet Johanna was in disgrace and her days in Russia were numbered. Empress Elizabeth had allowed the woman she now despised to remain at court long enough to see her daughter married, but soon after the wedding

Johanna was unceremoniously sent back to Germany. "At that time," Catherine wrote, "I would have given much if I could have left the country with her."

Empress Elizabeth had for some time presented herself as a benevolent second mother to Catherine, lavishing expensive gifts upon her and tenderly nursing her during her illness. "My respect for the empress and my gratitude to her were extreme," Catherine wrote. "And she used to say that she loved me almost more than the Grand Duke." But Elizabeth was every bit as mercurial as her father had been, and, soon enough, Catherine was subjected to the darker, more capricious side of the empress.

There were petty slights, like sending Catherine's best friend away for no reason, or making her change her dress because she looked too pretty in it. The empress assaulted the girl she once seemed to adore for the debts she had accumulated, and when Catherine's father died in 1747, Elizabeth ordered that she limit her mourning to a week, "because, after all, your father was not a king." The empress's capacity for cruelty now seemed boundless. "She did harm gratuitously and arbitrarily," Catherine recalled, "without the shadow of reason."

Yet Elizabeth's wrath wasn't reserved just for Catherine. Peter shared in the abuse as well, and for much better reasons. "My nephew, Devil take him, is a monster!" she declared. On one occasion, when the empress found that the grand duke had secretly drilled a hole in a chamber wall to spy on her, she stormed into Peter's apartment and, as Catherine wrote, "let fly at him with the most shocking insults and abuse, displaying as much contempt as anger. We were dumbfounded, stupefied and speechless, both of us, and, though this scene had nothing to do with me, it brought tears to my eyes."

Though she had plenty of reasons to scorn Peter, much of Elizabeth's rancor was rooted in the couple's persistent infertility—and for that she blamed Catherine. In one particularly nasty scene, the empress confronted the hapless grand duchess directly on the issue. "She said . . . that it was because of me that my marriage had not yet been consummated," Catherine wrote. "She began to revile me, to ask me if it was from my mother that I had received the instructions which guided my conduct: she said that I was betraying her for the King of Prussia, that she knew all about my cunning tricks and double-dealing, that she knew everything."

And now the empress was in full fury. "I could see the moment coming when she would strike me," Catherine wrote, "I knew that she beat her women, her servants and even her gentlemen-in-waiting sometimes when she was angry; I could not save myself by flight because I had my back against a door and she was directly in front of me." The only option was abject humility, which seemed to appease Elizabeth's wrath.

Peter and Catherine's unproductive marriage had serious consequences for both of them. The empress's policy was to isolate the couple, which, in her mind, would give them the alone time they clearly needed to reproduce. And this corresponded well with the agenda of Elizabeth's anti-Prussian chancellor, Bestuzhev-Ryumin, who was wary of the German-born pair and fiercely opposed their marriage in the first place. All of Peter and Catherine's closest associates were gradually sent away, and a decree was issued governing the couple's behavior.

One person of distinction would watch over Peter to "correct certain unseemly habits of His Imperial Highness, such as . . . emptying the contents of his glass over the heads of those serving him at table, accosting those who have the honor to approach him with rude remarks and indecent jests and disfiguring himself in public by continually grimacing and contorting his limbs." Considering the behavior described, Catherine's ordered role in the marriage would seem near impossible: "that Her Imperial Highness, by her reasonable behavior, her wit and virtue, should inspire sincere love in His Imperial Highness and win his heart, so that there may be produced the heir so greatly desired for the Empire and the scion of our illustrious house."

To enforce the couple's isolation, as well as to inspire them with their own fruitful marriage, a cousin of the empress, Maria Choglokova, and eventually her husband, Nicholas, were appointed as watchdogs. She was "uneducated, malicious, and full of self-interest," as Catherine described Maria, while he was "an arrogant and brutal fool . . . stupid, conceited, malicious, pompous, secretive, and silent, with never a smile on his lips . . . an object of terror to everyone." Together, the Choglokovs made life for Catherine and Peter a perpetual torment, with the added horror of forcing them closer together. For Catherine, that was the height of misery.

"Never did two minds resemble each other less," she wrote. "We had nothing in common in our tastes or ways of thinking. . . . There was no amusement, no conversation, no kindness or attention to help alleviate this boredom for me. My life became unbearable."

Peter became entirely dependent on his wife, even if he didn't care for her. She was his sole confidante and playmate, a role Catherine found increasingly burdensome. "Often I was very bored by his visits, which would last for hours," she wrote, "and even exhausted by them, for he never sat down, and I always had to walk up and down the room with him. . . .

He walked quickly, taking long strides, so that it was hard for me to keep up with him and at the same time maintain a conversation about the most minute military details, a subject which he was always eager to talk about and upon which, once launched, he would hold forth interminably."

The marriage bed remained as inactive as ever, at least when it came to lovemaking. Peter filled it instead with his own childish diversions. "Often I laughed," Catherine wrote, "but more often still I was exasperated and even made uncomfortable, the whole bed being covered and filled with dolls and toys, some of them quite heavy." Even playing cards with her husband was an ordeal. "I would deliberately lose to avoid his tantrums."

One regrettable hobby Peter picked up during his enforced isolation was dog training, which, Catherine noted ruefully, was an unwelcome addition to his vain attempt to become a violinist—especially since he decided to keep the hounds in the apartments they shared. "So," she wrote, "from 7 o'clock in the morning until late into the night, either the discordant sound which he drew very forcefully from the violin or the horrible barking and howling of the five or six dogs, which he thrashed throughout the rest of the day, continually grated on my core. I admit that I was driven half mad. . . . After the dogs I was the most miserable creature in the world."

The only relief Catherine found was in reading, which she pursued voraciously, and horseback riding, her "dominant passion." But in 1751 she found a new, more enticing diversion in a charming young nobleman who would relieve her not only of her deep loneliness, but of her virginity as well. His name was Sergei Saltykov.

Love was an alien feeling for Catherine: She had known little of it growing up, and had certainly not found it in her marriage. But that all changed when, after a year's wooing, Saltykov finally managed to seduce her. He was "as handsome as a god," Catherine wrote, "not lacking either in wit or in the sort of worldly knowledge, manners and savoir faire which one acquires in the best society and especially at court. He was twenty-six years old. All in all, by reason of his birth and his many other qualities, he was a distinguished gentleman." He was also a rascal, a wily seducer who would eventually leave her devastated. "His chief interest in life was winning a lady's heart, laying siege to her virtue and demolishing it," wrote biographer Henri Troyat. Nevertheless, while the affair lasted, Catherine found true passion for the first time. She also found herself pregnant—a rather inconvenient state for a woman with a reputation to maintain and a husband who had not yet slept with her after eight years of marriage.

Some historians believe Peter's inability to have sex was due to an affliction of the penis known as phimosis, in which the foreskin is so tight that it causes extremely painful erections. The remedy is circumcision, and, according to the French diplomat Jean-Henri Castéra, it was Saltykov who, perhaps seeking insurance against any unwelcome potential paternity questions, convinced the grand duke to undergo the procedure. Whether or not Castéra's account is accurate, it was around this time that Madame Choglokova, under pressure from the empress, arranged through one of Peter's valets to have a young widow by the name of Madame Groot introduce the virginal grand duke to the carnal pleasures of which he had long been deprived. Now, either freed of his physical impediment or his inhibitions (perhaps both), Peter, at age twenty-five, could finally bed his wife. Not that either one of them particularly enjoyed the experience.

While the grand duke was being initiated by Madame Groot, Catherine's affair with Saltykov appeared to be receiving some kind of imperial sanction. It seemed abundantly evident that Empress Elizabeth would have her heir, no matter how Catherine managed to conceive him.

After two miscarriages, Catherine was pregnant again early in 1754. But in April of that year Nicholas Choglokov died. It was quite a blow for Catherine, as her keeper had become far more humble and pliable, especially after the supposedly virtuous guardian had been caught having an affair. "He was dying just at a time when, after many years of trouble and pain, we had succeeded in making him not only less unkind and malicious, but even tractable," Catherine wrote. "As for his wife, she was now sincerely attached to me, and she had changed from a harsh and spiteful guardian to a loyal friend."

Unfortunately, Madame Choglokova was dismissed after her husband's death, and the vacancy left by the couple was filled by persons Catherine found far more formidable: Count Alexander Shuvalov and his wife. It was not just Shuvalov's position as the head of the feared secret police that disconcerted Catherine, but the "convulsive movement" that sometimes distorted half his face. "It was astonishing," she wrote, "how this man, with so hideous a grimace, could have been chosen to be the constant companion of a pregnant young woman. Had I been delivered of a child having this same unfortunate tic, I think the Empress would have been greatly vexed."

As her pregnancy progressed, Catherine was becoming increasingly miserable. She was stuck with a ferocious new watchdog; a lover who, having conquered her, was growing increasingly distant; and, of course, a simpleton husband, who, though now sexually mature, nevertheless remained an emotionally disturbed child with a drinking problem. One day, Catherine walked into Peter's room and found a rat hanging, "with all the formality of an execution," she wrote, from a makeshift gallows. The rodent had committed treason, the grand duke explained, having devoured two of his toy soldiers made of starch. And there it would remain "for three days, as an example."

On October 1, 1754, Catherine gave birth to a son, Paul, the paternity of whom remains a mystery. Was he Saltykov's child, or did Peter actually manage to impregnate his wife?[*] As far as the empress was concerned, the father was of no consequence. Neither was the mother, for that matter. Indeed, as soon as Catherine delivered the baby, Paul was whisked away by the triumphant Elizabeth, who intended to raise the boy herself. As for Catherine, Troyat wrote, "she was only a womb emptied of its contents. She was no longer of interest to anyone. In an instant her room was deserted."

Exhausted by her prolonged labor, Catherine was left alone on the mattress upon which she had given birth. Her pleas for fresh linen and something to drink went unanswered for hours. "I was dying of fatigue and thirst," she wrote. "I had been in tears ever since the birth had taken place, particularly

---

[*] Historians are torn on this issue, which has never been resolved. Certainly Paul grew up to behave much like Peter III, and his rather repulsive appearance as an adult could possibly argue against the dashing Saltykov being his father. On the other hand, the aversion Peter had for Catherine in the bedroom—and the possibility that smallpox had made him sterile—might indicate that he never impregnated her. And Catherine herself implies in her *Memoirs* that Saltykov was Paul's father.

because I had been so cruelly abandoned. . . . Nobody worried about me. . . . At last they placed me in my own bed, and I saw no other living soul all that day, nor did anyone send to inquire after me. As for the Grand Duke, he did nothing but drink with anyone he could find, and the Empress busied herself with the child." Catherine would not see her baby again for well over a month. And Saltykov, conveniently sent away on a diplomatic mission to Sweden (ironically to announce the birth of the boy who may have been his son), was gone for good.

Alone and in despair, Catherine retreated to a small, drafty room where she would remain through the winter, nursing her sorrow while the rest of the world celebrated the birth of her son. "This was the worst, cruelest, indeed the most devastating period of her whole life," wrote her biographer Robert Coughlan. "During it she arrived at the edge of emotional collapse and perhaps even of lifelong emotional invalidism. She survived. And in surviving became a different person."

Catherine emerged from isolation transformed indeed. No longer would she be the compliant, eager-to-please young woman she had been, but instead a fierce advocate of her own interests and an instrument of her own advancement. "I drew myself up," she wrote. "I walked with my head held high, more like the leader of a great faction than like one humiliated and crushed."

For too long Catherine had endured Peter's folly and neglect. Now the two were emerging as mortal enemies. Still, the grand duke continued to consult his wife on many matters—from wooing his mistresses to ruling his duchy of Holstein from afar. "Madam Resourceful," he called her. "No matter how angry or sulky he might be with me," she wrote, "if he was in distress on any point whatever, he would come running to me as fast as his legs would carry him, as was his wont, to snatch a word of advice and, as soon as he had it, would run off again as fast as he had come."

Yet despite his reliance on "Madame Resourceful," Peter ignored her counsel when it came to his overt allegiance to his native Holstein. At one point he even imported into Russia a large contingent of soldiers from his native land, which only served to antagonize his future subjects, especially the army, and added to the mounting evidence that he would serve only German interests when he became tsar.

"The Grand Duke had an extraordinary passion for the little corner of the earth where he was born," Catherine wrote. "It constantly occupied his mind though he had left it behind at the age of thirteen; his imagination became heated whenever he spoke of it, and, as none of the people around him had ever set foot in what was, by his account, a marvelous paradise, day after day he told us fantastical stories about it which almost put us to sleep."

Peter's pro-German proclivities were becoming an increasing liability, particularly after Russia went to war with Prussia in 1756. Recognizing her own fortunes were inexorably tied to her foolish husband's, Catherine began to forge secret political alliances—including one with her erstwhile enemy Chancellor Bestuzhev-Ryumin—that would better position her for the future should Peter succeed in completely destroying his own credibility, which he seemed determined to do. "It was a question of either perishing with him or through him," she wrote, "or else saving myself, my children and perhaps the State, from the shipwreck that was foretold by every moral and physical attribute of this Prince."

Catherine's concerns took on a new urgency when Empress Elizabeth suffered a series of strokes and her survival appeared uncertain. Disaster loomed in the person of her husband, and her political maneuvering reflected the profound ambition she had long maintained to rule Russia without him, whatever the cost. "There is no woman bolder than I," she declared to a French diplomat. "I have the most reckless audacity." Yet it was just this quality that nearly destroyed her.

Meanwhile, though preoccupied in the forging of her own destiny, Catherine didn't neglect her love life. She began an affair with the young protégé of her political ally the British ambassador Sir Charles Hanbury-Williams. His name was Count Stanislaus Poniatowski, and unlike his predecessor Sergei Saltykov, he was entirely in love with his mistress, particularly since it was she who first introduced him to sex. "My whole life was devoted to her," he wrote, "much more sincerely than those who find themselves in such a situation can usually claim."

The affair took a rather awkward turn when Peter caught Poniatowski, in disguise, sneaking into the palace. The cuckolded husband wasn't in the least bit angry, however. Rather, he took a perverse delight in dragging his wife out of bed and insisting that she and her lover join him and his mistress for dinner. This was followed by more intimate soirees among the four, during which Peter developed an attachment to his wife's bedmate—just as he had earlier with Saltykov. "Nature made him a mere poltroon," Poniatowski wrote of Peter. "He was not stupid, but mad, and as he was fond of drink, this helped to addle his poor brains even further."

During her affair with Poniatowski, Catherine found herself pregnant. And once again, the paternity of the child she was carrying was in question. "Heaven alone knows how it is that my wife becomes pregnant," Peter exclaimed. "I have no idea whether this child is mine and whether I ought to recognize it as such."[*]

Though Catherine's affair with Poniatowski, and the pregnancy that may have resulted, ultimately had few consequences (save for the tedious occasions the couple had to spend with Peter), her political dabbling had far more significant ramifications when some of her allies, including Bestuzhev-Ryumin, began to topple. Trouble began when one of Catherine's known associates, General Stefan Apraksin, commander of the Russian forces against Prussia, suddenly retreated after an impressive victory over Frederick II's army. Treason seemed to be afoot, and, as an investigation was pursued, Catherine fell under suspicion. After all, she had written to Apraksin, despite the fact that such correspondence was strictly forbidden her.

Feeling a noose tightening around her neck, Catherine made a bold move. She wrote a letter to the empress, "making it as moving as I could," in which she expressed sentiments quite the opposite of what she really desired—which was to remain in Russia and ultimately rule: She asked to be sent home.

When her letter failed to get a response, Catherine intensified the pathos, feigning illness and calling for the empress's own confessor, who promised he would go to Elizabeth right away and urge her to receive the unfortunate young woman. On April 13, 1759, the fateful meeting took place. Catherine performed brilliantly, summoning the perfect mixture of de-

[*] Catherine delivered a baby girl named Anne, who lived only three months.

spair and servility while spiritedly defending her loyalty to the empress. Peter, who had been watching the proceedings from behind a curtain, popped out at one point and began to cruelly berate his wife, which served only to make Catherine seem all the more sympathetic. All the while, Elizabeth's anger slowly melted away.

"I could see that my words made a strong and favorable impression on her," Catherine wrote. "Tears stood out in her eyes and to conceal how much she was moved, she dismissed us."

Catherine's *Memoirs* stop abruptly as she begins to relate the details of a second, more private interview with the empress. Nevertheless, it is clear that while she emerged chastened, she was unbroken. Now all she had to do was survive the rest of Elizabeth's reign, and her husband's malevolent hatred.

On January 5, 1762, Empress Elizabeth died of a massive stroke at the age of fifty-three. Peter was now emperor, and, as such, immediately set about alienating his new subjects. After six years of bloody warfare, Russia was poised to finally crush the Prussian forces of Frederick the Great. But Peter III wasn't about to let his idol Frederick go down in such ignominious defeat. Instead, he simply canceled the war, snatching certain victory away from his own armies. It was an outrage, compounded by the new emperor's insistence that the elite Guard units start wearing Prussian-style uniforms.

Having essentially routed his own military, Peter began an assault on the Orthodox faith—one of the pillars of Russian society. Although he had officially converted upon being designated as Elizabeth's heir, the emperor held the Russian religion in total contempt, clinging stubbornly to the Lutheran tradition with which he had been raised. In a move almost perfectly designed to estrange himself from the Orthodox hierarchy, he ordered sacred icons removed from places of prayer and even went as far as to confiscate church property.

"Do you know that your emperor must be mad as a hatter?" a foreign diplomat remarked to a lady of the court. "No man could behave as he does otherwise."

Peter III was making powerful enemies with his galling behavior, but perhaps none greater than his own wife. The couple had grown to truly loathe each other, and the emperor made no secret of his desire to rid himself of his detestable wife and marry instead his ugly mistress, Elizabeth Vorontzova.* He installed Elizabeth in his own apartments and made her head of the household while relegating Catherine to a distant side of the palace. As an additional humiliation, he ordered his wife to attend a public ceremony in which he awarded to his mistress one of Russia's highest honors for women, the Order of St. Catherine, created by Peter the Great in tribute to his wife Catherine's heroism during the Pruth River campaign against the Turks in 1711 (see Chapter 3). The bestowal of such an award to Elizabeth Vorontzova had a certain menacing significance, since it was given automatically to those who married into the royal family.

Peter's malignant feelings toward Catherine were made vi-

---

* "She has a dull mind," the French ambassador Baron de Breteuil wrote of Elizabeth Vorontzova in January 1762. "As for her face, it is the worst possible. In all respects she resembles an inn servant of the lower sort." Another correspondent provided an even less flattering portrait of Peter's mistress: "She swore like a trooper, had a squint, stank, and spat when she talked." According to some reports, she also liked to beat up her boyfriend when they drank.

ciously apparent during a banquet celebrating a treaty with Prussia, in which the two nations, only recently enemies, agreed to ally themselves in an ill-advised war against Denmark. The emperor proposed a toast "to the imperial family," after which all the guests rose, except Catherine. When Peter sent an adjunct to his wife's end of the table to inquire why she remained seated, Catherine sent word back explaining that as a member of the imperial family being toasted, it would be improper for her to stand. For some reason this enraged the emperor. "Fool!" he screeched at his wife from across the table, shocking those in attendance into silence. A drunken Peter ordered Catherine's arrest, but he was finally dissuaded from this course by the unhappy couple's mutual relative, Prince George of Holstein, whom the emperor had placed in command of the Russian army.

"Peter III's barbarous, senseless ferocity made it seem quite possible that he intended to eliminate his wife," the French chargé d'affaires wrote afterward. The emperor was in essence declaring war upon Catherine, but in this he woefully underestimated his enemy.

"The Empress [Catherine] is in the most cruel situation and is treated with the most marked contempt," the French ambassador Baron de Breteuil wrote to the French foreign minister, the Duc de Choiseul, early in 1762. "I have told you, Monseigneur, that she sought to fortify herself with philosophy, and I have said how ill this nourishment consorted with her character. I have learned since, beyond any doubt, that she is already very impatient with the Emperor's conduct toward her and of the arrogance of Mademoiselle Vorontzova. Knowing as I do the courage and violence of this Princess, I cannot imagine that she will not sooner or later be moved to some extreme. I know that she has certain friends who are trying to calm her but who would risk everything for her, if she required it."

Indeed, while the emperor was charting his own self-destructive course, Catherine had been nourishing this circle of devoted allies. Among them was her new lover, Gregory Orlov, a handsome, battle-hardened Guards officer whose child Catherine secretly carried,* along with his four brothers—all of whom were well respected in the Russian military and would be instrumental in garnering its support. Catherine even had on her side the sister of her husband's mistress, who had valuable contacts in the government and a shared revulsion to Peter III's policies.

The scorned, mistreated wife certainly had plenty of support, but she and her backers, biding their time, had no real plan of attack—that is, until one of their number, Captain Passek, was arrested on June 27, 1762, after drunkenly disparaging the emperor in public. With the very real danger that he might betray them under torture, the plotters leapt to action. Meanwhile, the unwitting emperor, who left St. Petersburg several weeks before to prepare his troops for the upcoming war against Denmark, had ordered his wife to take up residence at the palace of Peterhof, where, he informed her, he would arrive on June 29, to celebrate his name day. No one knew what else he might have in store for Catherine.

Thus, in the early morning hours of June 28, Gregory Or-

* After carefully concealing her pregnancy, Catherine's son by Gregory Orlov was born in secret in April 1762. To distract Peter while she was in labor, the empress's faithful valet, Vasili Shkurin, burned down his own home, knowing that the firebug emperor would race off to watch the excitement. The child was given the name Alexis Gregorovich Bobrinsky: the patronymic for his father, Gregory Orlov, and the surname for the estate where he was raised.

lov's brother Alexis arrived at Mon Plaisir, a summerhouse on the grounds of Peterhof, where Catherine was staying. Urgently, he roused her out of bed. "It's time to get up," he said. "Everything is ready to proclaim you Empress." With barely time to dress, Catherine was hustled out into a waiting carriage that immediately raced off toward St. Petersburg.

At just past seven in the morning, Catherine arrived at the headquarters of the first of three Guards regiments. The Orlovs had already prepared her way, and the reception she received there was rapturous. "Hurrah for our Little Mother Catherine!" the ranks cheered, with some kneeling before her and kissing the hem of her skirt. Also kneeling was the commander of the regiment, Cyril Razumovsky (brother of Empress Elizabeth's lover), who proclaimed Catherine sovereign and, in the name of all the soldiers, swore allegiance to her. The group, now swelled by elated officers and soldiers riding along with Catherine's carriage, next proceeded to the second Guards regiment, where the new empress was welcomed with equal enthusiasm. Finally, after a tense period of uncertainty, Peter the Great's elite Preobrazhensky unit rose up for Catherine as well.

All of St. Petersburg seemed to turn out in celebration as the smiling empress made her way first to the Church of Our Lady of Kazan, where she received the priests' blessings amid holy icons and pealing bells, then to the Winter Palace to be greeted by the various ranks of Russian society who wished to pay homage. It had been a heady day, for sure, yet there remained the problem of Peter III, who still remained at large, with a formidable force at his disposal.

After securing St. Petersburg and issuing a manifesto that detailed Peter's crimes against Russia, as well as her justification for usurping his crown, the empress rode out on horseback to Peterhof, there to confront whatever forces her husband had managed to rally (which were none, as it turned out). Dressed smartly in the uniform of one of the Guard regiments, sword in hand, her hair flowing freely under an oak leaf crown she had fashioned around her hat, Catherine was the very image of the warrior queen leading her loyal troops into battle. It was an awesome sight that left all who witnessed it cheering wildly for her success.

As his wife was being proclaimed in St. Petersburg, the fallen emperor—having no idea that he had in fact fallen—arrived at Peterhof as planned, mistress in tow. But, of course, Catherine wasn't there. Incensed by her defiance of his orders, Peter began a frenzied search for his recalcitrant spouse, checking under beds and inside closets. Then he received word of what had happened that morning in the capital. It was a crippling blow, but rather than rally himself to confront Catherine, Peter collapsed in despair.

"Courage, Majesty! Courage!" one of his ministers counseled the sobbing ex-sovereign. "One word from you, one imperious glance, and the people will fall on their knees before the Tsar! The men of Holstein are ready! This moment we march on St. Petersburg!"

But there would be no such movement. Peter was a frantic mass of indecision. Between fainting spells, gasping sobs, and heaping gulps of brandy, he issued desperate orders and limpid manifestos, all without accomplishing anything. The ministers he sent to St. Petersburg to confront Catherine never returned, either joining her cause or put under arrest.

With few options remaining, the deposed emperor was finally persuaded to sail to the island fortress of Kronshtadt, from where he might be able to rally those forces still loyal to him. But there was no succor to be found there. Catherine's delegate, Admiral Talysin, had already persuaded the fortress's commander that Peter III was no more. Accordingly, booms were set up to block his way.

"It is the emperor," Peter cried out upon reaching the blockade.

"There is no emperor," came the response from the fortress; "there is only the empress!"

Peter might have courageously forged on, as his officers urged him to do, but instead he joined the ladies aboard the schooner in their pitiful wails. He then ordered the ship to set sail for his summer residence, Oranienbaum, where, depleted, he fell into bed with Elizabeth Vorontzova—and left himself to the mercy of Empress Catherine II.

The ex-emperor was taken to Peterhof, but Catherine refused to see him. She had already obtained what she wanted from him, which was Peter's signature on the letter of abdication she had drafted. It read: "During the brief period of my absolute rule over the Empire of Russia [six months], I have recognized that my strength was not sufficient to bear such a burden. . . . For this reason, after mature reflection, I solemnly declare, of my own free will, to all Russia and to the entire universe, that I renounce the government of the said Empire for as long as I shall live." As it turned out, that would be a week.

Peter had allowed himself to be dethroned, King Frederick II later wrote, "like a child being sent to bed." Now all he wanted was mercy, the company of his dog and mistress, as well as a ticket back to Holstein. And for that, the onetime commander of all those toy soldiers—stripped of his uniform, decorations, and sword—fell to his knees and groveled. The sight of Peter the Great's grandson in such a pathetic state was too much for Count Nikita Panin, one of Catherine's co-

conspirators, who later wrote, "I consider it one of the greatest misfortunes of my life to have been obliged to see Peter at that moment!"

Ultimately it was decided that the former emperor would be sent to the island fortress of Shlisselburg, where the deposed Ivan VI still languished (see footnote on page 75) and where, ironically, Peter III had only recently gone to visit him. But while his accommodations at Shlisselburg were being prepared, Peter was sent to a summer estate at Ropsha. There he spent the last week of his life, writing a series of pitiful letters to his estranged wife, now celebrating her glorious triumph in St. Petersburg.

In his first missive, Peter wrote: "I beg Your Majesty . . . to have the kindness to remove the guards from the second room, because the room I am in is so small I can hardly move in it, and as Your Majesty knows that I always walk back and forth in the room, that will make my legs swell. Also I beg you to not order the officers to remain in the same room [with me]; since I must relieve myself, that is impossible. Moreover, I beg Your Majesty to treat me [less] like the greatest criminal, not knowing to have offended you ever. Commending myself to Your Majesty's magnanimous thoughts, I beg Your Majesty to let me [go] as soon as possible with the person mentioned [his mistress Elizabeth Vorontzova] to Germany. God will surely repay Your Majesty for it and I am your very humble servant."

Peter followed this woebegone letter with another: "Your Majesty, if you do not absolutely wish to kill a man who is already wretched enough, then have pity on me and leave me my only consolation, which is Elizabeth [Vorontzova]. By that you will do one of the greatest works of charity of your reign. Moreover if Your Majesty was to see me for an instant, I would have attained my dearest wish."

Empress Catherine never responded, but a week into Peter's captivity she received news from Ropsha that would haunt her for the rest of her reign. Her husband was dead, either killed deliberately by his captors, or, as Alexis Orlov claimed, accidentally during a drunken quarrel. Clearly the former emperor's demise was convenient for the new regime, but there is little indication that this is what Catherine wanted. Indeed, it was a blot on her reputation just as she was embracing her new sovereignty.

"My horror at this death is inexpressible," the empress confided to a friend. "This blow strikes me to the earth!" That may have been true, but few believed the official line that it was an acute hemorrhoidal attack that carried Peter away. Even fewer really cared.

Chapter 7

Catherine II (1762–1796):

"Prey to This Mad Passion!"

It is my misfortune that my heart cannot be content, even for one hour, without love.

—EMPRESS CATHERINE II

Catherine II certainly ranks among the most impressive of Russian sovereigns, standing firmly beside Peter I, the visionary monarch after whom she modeled herself and with whom she shares the laudatory appellation "the Great." The accomplishments of her thirty-four-year reign were remarkable, from subduing the Turks and annexing the Crimea to her energetic leadership in fully incorporating Russia into the political and cultural life of Europe— all hallmarks of the German-born empress's fierce pride in her adopted homeland. Voltaire and Diderot adored the autocrat for her liberalizing spirit (though the realities of internal revolt and revolution abroad greatly dimmed her initial zeal for reform), while the great courts of Europe alternately envied, admired, and feared her. Still, no matter what glories Catherine the Great managed to attain, her legendary love life remains her most enduring legacy. It was a busy one indeed, though never inclining toward the equine, as many still believe.

The empress was startlingly candid when she recounted in her *Memoirs* how as a young girl she would straddle her pillow at night and ride it vigorously, trying to satisfy some yearning yet to be defined. The pillow would eventually be replaced by a long procession of lovers, starting with Sergei Saltykov, who finally showed the future sovereign what real passion was after she had endured eight years of virginal marriage to a dolt. And though Saltykov turned out to be a cad, abandoning Catherine (after perhaps siring her son Paul) and bragging to the world about his royal conquest, the sexuality he awakened in her remained an essential component of her being. It invigorated and intoxicated her—sometimes to the point of foolishness, especially as the empress grew older and tricked herself into believing that the handsomely rewarded young men she took to her bed were there because they loved her, even if she had grown heavy and was missing most of her teeth. Certainly Catherine's carnal desires carried no shame for her, and she made no apologies for them. Each young man to whom she devoted herself had as prominent a place at court as he did in her bed—until he was replaced. And even then, the gaps between lovers never lasted too long. "It is my misfortune," she declared, "that my heart cannot be content, even for one hour, without love."

After Saltykov's cruel betrayal, Catherine found comfort in the arms of Stanislaus Poniatowski, who, unlike his predecessor, was entirely enchanted by his married mistress. Years later, he still rhapsodized about "her black hair, her skin fair but of the liveliest coloring, her very eloquent big blue eyes and long dark lashes, her Grecian nose, her mouth which seemed to ask for kisses, her perfect arms and hands, her dignified and noble bearing, and a laugh as gay as her humor." It was Catherine who initiated the virginal Pole, two years her junior, into the bedroom pleasures she herself had discovered only recently. "I cannot deny myself the pleasure of noting even the very clothes I found her in that day," Poniatowski recalled of their first sexual interlude: "a little gown of white satin with a light trimming of lace, threaded with pink ribbon for its only ornament." Though Poniatowski was eventually forced to leave Russia when Catherine's political maneuverings were revealed, she did make him king of Poland when she became empress—then proceeded to devour a huge chunk of his kingdom. Still, Poniatowski's love was enduring, even if it was no longer reciprocated.

The vacancy left by Poniatowski's untimely departure was filled by Gregory Orlov, the dashing adventurer who, along with his four brothers, had helped Catherine seize the throne of her husband Peter III. In recognition of the pivotal role he played in her rise, as well as a testament to her love, Catherine heaped vast riches upon her favorite and made him the most powerful man in the empire. Yet this wasn't enough to satisfy Orlov's grand ambitions; he wanted to make the autocratic empress his wife—*his* subject. As biographer Robert Coughlan wrote, he was "a natural daredevil full of self-assertiveness and male pride; a predatory rough-and-ready man's man to whom it would be altogether unnatural and impossible to be a woman's man—any woman's. Not that he was a brute. He was capable of love, sentiment, tenderness, and even constancy. But it was an intrinsic part of this masculine love that he be the possessor, protector, and giver, not the possessed, protected, and receiver. Before and during the coup he had filled a role that entirely suited him, a man working and taking risks on behalf of the woman he loved. But in helping to make her Empress, he had made himself her subject, no longer her bold, possessing lover but her imperial 'favorite.'"

There is some evidence that Catherine was not opposed to the idea of marrying Orlov. In fact, one account has it that she even went as far as to investigate the possible precedent for such a union by sending her chancellor, Michael Vorontzov, to the home of Alexis Razumovsky—the late Empress Elizabeth's so-called Night Emperor (see Chapter 5)—to see if he might have any documentation proving that Elizabeth had secretly married him, as many believed she had. But Razumovsky disliked Orlov and mistrusted his motives. Thus, according to the story handed down by Chancellor Vorontzov's descendants, the old man went over to a cabinet, withdrew a faded parchment tied with a pink ribbon, and, without saying a word to Vorontzov, tossed it into the fire.

Even if Razumovsky had not destroyed whatever possible evidence there was that an empress had once made a lowly subject her husband, there was still plenty of political opposition to Catherine wedding Orlov—a man whom many among the Russian nobility and gentry considered to be an uncouth, greedy upstart who, with his brothers, harbored dangerous ambitions to wield imperial power. "The Empress can do what she wishes," declared her foreign minister, Count Nikita Panin, "but Madame Orlov will never be the Empress of Russia."

Deprived of his ambition to share Catherine the Great's power as her husband, Orlov sulked bitterly that he remained little more than the empress's service stud, albeit a very well compensated one. "The larger her figure loomed on the political horizon, the more he shrank in her shadow," wrote biographer Henri Troyat. "She sought his kisses and silenced him as soon as he expressed an opinion on public affairs." Like a bored mistress, Orlov lashed out at his lover, who, consumed as she was with managing the empire, often had little time left for him. The triumphs of his past had been long since subsumed by a life of indolence, and as the breach with Catherine widened, Orlov sought fresh conquests in other women—*lots* of other women. Yet this was not enough to revive him, or give his gilded life much meaning. And still Catherine the Great dominated him.

Orlov hoped to prove himself in battle against the Turks like his brother Alexis, but the empress wouldn't hear of it. After all, someone needed to keep her bed warm. However, another opportunity for glory arose when an epidemic of plague swept through Moscow in 1771 and resulted in violent eruptions of public disorder. Orlov asked to be sent to take control of the dangerously unsettled city and Catherine, her ardor having cooled somewhat, agreed to let him go. It was a magnificent success for the favorite, accompanied by the great acclaim he craved, and on the heels of it the empress sent him as her representative to a peace conference with the Turks in Moldavia.

A flush of her old feelings for her longtime lover seemed to have overwhelmed Catherine as Orlov prepared to depart for the conference—proud, handsome, and literally shining in the diamond-studded jacket she had given him as a gift. "My angels of peace are now on the spot, I think, and face to face with those ugly bearded Turks," the empress wrote to her friend Madame de Bielke. "Count Orlov, who, without exaggeration, is the handsomest man of his time, must really look like an angel compared to those louts; his retinue is brilliant and select. . . . But I would wager that his person eclipses everyone around him. He is such a remarkable personage, this ambassador; Nature has been so extraordinarily liberal with him from the point of view of face, mind, heart and soul!"

As it turned out, any revived passion Catherine may have felt for her fading favorite was only temporary. Soon enough she began to receive reports of his strutting arrogance at the peace conference, coupled with his striking incompetence as a negotiator. And while he was making a buffoon of himself in Moldavia, Orlov's enemies at home gleefully informed the empress of his many excursions outside her bedroom. That news was little more than a knife in a corpse, though, because after more than ten years with this turbulent lover, Catherine was ready to move on anyway.

For her next paramour, the empress had in mind a virile, highly charismatic officer with only one eye (the other reportedly lost in a brawl with Orlov's brother Alexis). His name was Gregory Potemkin, and Catherine admired not only his many talents, energy and wit, but his hulking physique as well. Unfortunately, Potemkin was otherwise occupied with military matters when the empress needed a fresh new body by her side, and so she settled for the services of a strapping young guardsman by the name of Alexander Vasilchikov, who happened to be nearly half her age. "I was only a kept woman," he later said of the relationship. "I was treated as such." But Vasilchikov did his duty, and apparently did it well—even if, out of bed, Catherine found him unbearably boring. "The Empress writes Monsieur Vasilchikov the most burning letters," reported Sabatier de Cabre, the French chargé d'affaires, "and constantly gives him presents that know no bounds."

When Orlov received word that his place at court had been usurped by young Vasilchikov, he immediately abandoned his post as Catherine's representative at the peace negotiations and raced back toward St. Petersburg to reclaim it. But he was intercepted along the way and ordered to his summer palace at Gatchina. There was no menace in Catherine's command, only fear of what her brash former lover might do in the face of his demotion. "You don't know him!" the empress told friends. "He is capable of killing me!"

To placate her erratic ex-lover, Catherine sent him a steady stream of lavish gifts, and even conferred upon him the title of prince. Orlov, however, took all this as an indication that he had been restored to favor and so returned to court without permission. The empress received him coolly, but did not send him away. Instead, she simply continued to bed Vasilchikov. Prince Orlov did not handle this well. Frozen from the empress's affections, he turned to drinking and whoring to soothe the deep bruises of his precipitous fall, and his crass behavior seemed to reflect this diminished stature. He acted "like a man who wants to resume his old way of life or to have himself locked up," observed Sabatier de Cabre.

As Orlov unraveled, and his replacement Vasilchikov— "his head stuffed with hay"—remained unrelentingly dull, the empress once again set her sights on Potemkin, the one-eyed giant who so intrigued her with his extraordinary mixture of vigor and mysticism, brawn and intelligence. After coaxing her desired one back from the front lines in 1774, Catherine happily plunged into what became one of history's more storied romances. As she wrote to her friend and confidant Friedrich Melchoir Grimm, "I have parted from a certain excellent but very boring citizen [Vasilchikov], who has been immediately replaced, I know not how, by one of the greatest, oddest, most amusing and original personalities of this iron age."

The forty-five-year-old empress, ruler of vast domains and literally the most powerful woman in the world, became positively giddy when it came to Potemkin, for whom she lovingly conjured an arsenal of pet names: "golden cock," "dear plaything," "my darling pet," "my twin soul," "my dearest doll," "tiger," "little parrot," "infidel," "my little Grisha," "my golden pheasant," "lion of the jungle," "wolfbird," "my marble beauty," "my beloved whom no king on earth can match."

"Darling," she wrote, "what comical stories you told me yesterday! I can't stop laughing when I think of them. . . . We spend four hours together without a shadow of boredom, and it is always with reluctance that I leave you. My dearest pigeon, I love you very much. You are handsome, intelligent, amusing."

An overwhelming passion consumed Catherine as she reveled in Potemkin's rough, dominating sexuality. And the avalanche of love notes with which she inundated him gave free expression to it. A few choice excerpts:

—"There is not a cell in my whole body that does not yearn for you, oh infidel!"

—"I thank you for yesterday's feast. My little Grisha fed me and quenched my thirst, but not with wine."

—"My head is like that of a cat in heat."

—"I will be a 'woman of fire' for you, as you often say. But I shall try to hide my flames."

There were times when Catherine seemed to marvel at the intensity of her own feelings. "Oh, Monsieur Potemkin!" she wrote. "What a confounded miracle you have wrought to have so deranged a head that heretofore in the world passed for one of the best in Europe! . . . What shame! What a sin! Catherine the Second a prey to this mad passion! 'You will disgust him with your folly,' I tell myself."

As the empress made abundantly evident in her feverish expressions, sex with Potemkin was spectacular. But there was far more to her "golden cock" than just a hulking body to keep her company at night. This was a man whom Catherine the Great considered to be her equal—an utterly dynamic character with the same energy, vision, and zeal for living that she possessed, yet with a bundle of contradictions tossed in to make him all the more alluring.

"He is the most extraordinary man I have ever met," reported the Prince de Ligne. "He gives the appearance of laziness and yet works incessantly . . . always reclining on his couch yet never sleeping, day or night, because his devotion to the sovereign he adores keeps him constantly active. . . . Melancholy in his pleasures, unhappy by virtue of being happy, blasé about everything, quickly wearied of anything, morose, inconstant, a profound philosopher, an able minister, a sublime politician and a child of ten . . . prodigiously wealthy without having a sou; discoursing on theology to his generals and on war to his archbishops; never reading, but probing those to whom he speaks . . . wanting everything like a child, capable of dispensing with everything like a great man. . . . What then is his magic? Genius, and then genius, and then more genius!"

In recognition of her partner's manifold gifts, the empress granted him unlimited powers in addition to the vast riches her other lovers enjoyed. Potemkin became in essence her co-sovereign, and together the pair spent endless hours planning Russia's further greatness through the subjugation and incorporation of new territories. In all likelihood, he also became her secret husband, as much evidence suggests. Certainly Catherine's letters and notes to Potemkin seem to confirm such a status. She often referred to him as "my beloved spouse," or "my dearest husband," and to herself as "wife." There was one piece of correspondence in which she wrote, "What is the good of believing your morbid imagination rather than the facts, all of which confirm the words of your wife? . . . Have I not been, for two years, bound to you by the most sacred ties? . . . I remain your faithful spouse who loves you with an eternal love."*

Although Catherine's political partnership with Potemkin would endure until his death in 1791, the intimate side of their relationship was doomed from the beginning. Jealousy was the source of the problem; Potemkin was consumed by it. When he first arrived at court and found Vasilchikov still installed as the favorite, he retreated in a huff to a monastery and only reluctantly emerged after the empress's repeated assurances that he was the only one she wanted. Even then, Potemkin remained obsessed with his predecessor and his own place in Catherine's heart. "You have not the least reason to be afraid," she wrote soothingly. "I burned my fingers badly with that imbecile Vasilchikov. . . . You can read in my soul and in my heart. . . . My love for you is boundless."

But it was not only Vasilchikov who provoked such monumental insecurity in Potemkin. It was every man with whom Catherine had ever slept—a legion of lovers he believed to number fifteen. As a sop to his sensitivities, the empress went so far as to write what she called "A Sincere Confession," in which she detailed the circumstances of the *four* affairs she

---

* Then there was that kind of comfortable intimacy shared by married couples. "I have some diarrhea today, but apart from that, I am well, my adored one," the empress shared. "Do not be distressed because of my diarrhea, it cleans out the intestines." This was ancillary evidence of a marriage, to be sure, but certainly not the language of lovebirds caught up in the anticipatory blush of a budding romance.

had actually conducted prior to Potemkin's entry into her life. It was a stunning act of humility and devotion—one that few other absolute monarchs would ever deign to provide a subject—yet it wasn't enough.

Potemkin was tortured not only by the previous men in Catherine's life, but by irrational fears of his own status with her. Was he really her enduring partner, or would he be replaced on a whim? The doubts that gnawed at him often made him moody and quarrelsome, which exasperated the empress. Thus, between passionate lovemaking and the pursuit of statecraft, there were furious fights that erupted almost daily—started by Potemkin and usually smoothed over by Catherine:

—"If your stupid ill humor has left you, kindly let me know. . . . You are a wicked Tatar!"

—"Truly, it is time for us to live in perfect harmony. Do not torment me by mistreating me. Then you will not see my coldness."

—"My little soul, I have a piece of string to one end of which I have attached a stone and, to the other end, all our quarrels, and I have thrown the whole thing into a bottomless pit. . . . Good day, my beloved! Good day, without quarrels, without discussions, without disputes."

"There is no reason to be unhappy," the empress wrote in one of her many conciliatory notes. "But no, it's time to stop giving you assurances. You must be most, most, most certain by now that I love you. . . . I want you to love me. I want to appear desirable to you. . . . If you want, I shall paraphrase this page for you in three words and cross out all the rest. Here it is: I love you."

Each passing storm was followed by a brief interlude of serenity before the next roared in, beginning anew the endless cycle of recriminations, doubts, and sulking, followed by the empress's perpetual efforts to placate her tempestuous lover. After two and a half years of such upheaval, the relationship was becoming strained beyond endurance. "Your foolish acts remain the same," Catherine wrote; "at the very moment when I feel safest a mountain drops on me. . . . To a madcap like you . . . tranquility is an unbearable state of mind*. . . . The gratitude I owe you has not vanished and I suppose there has never been a time when you haven't received signs of this. But now you take away all my force by tormenting me with new fabrications. . . . Please tell me whether I should be grateful to you for that. Until now I always thought that good health and restful days were esteemed for something in this world, but I would like to know how this is possible with you."

The volcanic intensity of Catherine and Potemkin's passion quickly exhausted itself, and by 1776 they were no longer lovers. Nevertheless, they remained devoted partners (or perhaps spouses), ruling Russia together in restored harmony. And Potemkin still managed to maintain some kind of sexual authority over the aging empress by essentially pimping his replacements in her bed. Deftly separating her regal self from her vigorous love life, Catherine happily flitted from one virile youngster to the next—each of whom paid Potemkin a

---

* Potemkin was indeed subject to fits of black despair, even when things seemed ideal. On one occasion, after his nephew commended him for his good spirits, he replied, "Could any man be happier than I? All my hopes, all my desires have been fulfilled as if by magic." Then, after elucidating all the manifold bounty he enjoyed, Potemkin smashed a valuable plate, stormed off to his room, and locked the door behind him.

handsome fee for the privilege of sleeping with her, and, of course, reaping the enormous bounty that came with such services.

Each in the succession of well-formed favorites was similar: young, handsome, rapturously extolled by the empress, and then, after a year or two of passion (in the case of most of them), sent away. Potemkin made certain of that. "Of course he did not for a moment contemplate resuming his place in Catherine's bed," wrote Troyat, "but he would not allow an intruder to claim her attention for longer than the duration of a caprice."

According to irresistible legend, after procurement by Potemkin, candidates for Catherine's bed were thoroughly vetted—first by her doctor, to ensure they were free of sexually transmitted disease, then by the empress's confidante, Countess Bruce, who reportedly took them on an intimate test drive of sorts, just to make sure their performance would measure up to some rather exacting standards.*

And so the servicemen came and went for two decades, each adored by the aging but still lustful empress until they were replaced. When her friend Voltaire gently chided Catherine for her inconstancy in love, she responded that she was, on the contrary, "absolutely faithful."

"To whom?" she continued. "To beauty, of course. Beauty alone attracts me!"†

---

* Some of Catherine II's biographers—including the more scholarly among them, such as John T. Alexander and Isabel de Madariaga—have dismissed this as legend (much like her supposed equine proclivities), conjured by the empress's French detractors.

† The empress further elucidated on love, lust, and desire in her *Memoirs:* "For to tempt, and to be tempted are closely allied, and, in spite of

The first of the post-Potemkin bedmates was a young Ukrainian by the name of Peter Zavadovsky, who, though relished by the empress, could never quite escape the shadow of the giant who had recommended him and still remained at his mistress's side. As Zavadovsky noted with a mixture of admiration and frustration, "In all the centuries rarely had God produced a person so universal as that which is Prince Potemkin: he is everywhere and everything." After about a year— just as the American colonies were declaring their independence from Britain—Catherine asserted hers in 1776. Zavadovsky was sent away, but not without ample reward for his services.

"He has received from Her Majesty fifty thousand rubles, a pension of five thousand, and four thousand peasants in the Ukraine, where they are worth a great deal," the Chevalier de Corberon, the new French chargé d'affaires, reported to his brother. "You must agree, my friend, that it's not a bad line of work to be in here."[*]

No sooner was Zavadovsky out the door than he was replaced by Simon Zorich, known among the court ladies as "the Adonis." The Chevalier de Corberon duly reported the latest development: "[Potemkin], who is in higher favor than ever, and who now plays the same role that the Pompadour did with Louis XV toward the end of her life,[†] has presented

---

the finest moral precepts, no sooner is feeling excited than we have gone vastly further than we are aware of. And how is it possible to prevent one's feelings aroused I have yet to learn. . . . All that can be said in opposition must seem prudery quite out of harmony with the instincts of the human heart; besides, no one holds his heart in his hand, tightening or relaxing his grasp at pleasure."

[*] Zavadovsky later reemerged as state secretary in Catherine's government.

[†] Madame de Pompadour, chief mistress of King Louis XV of France, wielded great influence behind the scenes.

to [the empress] one Zorich, a major in the Hussars, who has been made lieutenant colonel and inspector of all the light troops. This new favorite has dined with her. They say that he received 1,800 peasants for his trial effort! After dinner, Potemkin drank to the Empress's health and knelt before her."

Like his predecessor, Zorich resented the looming presence of his procurer. Unlike Zavadovsky, however, the brash young lover—as his position began to inevitably totter—actually dared to challenge Potemkin's supremacy. "Zoritz [sic] is prepared for his dismission [sic]," reported the new British ambassador, James Howard Harris, "but I am told he is resolved to call his successor to an account. 'Of course I know that I'm going to be sacked, but by God I'll cut off the ears of the man who takes my place,' were his words, in talking the other day on the subject."

The fading favorite made a violent scene, but his insignificance was such that Potemkin contemptuously dismissed his invitation to a duel. Soon enough, Catherine dismissed Zorich as well—her lavish parting gifts no doubt assuaging his impotent fury. "Last night I was in love with him," the empress wrote candidly; "today I cannot stand him anymore."

Catherine was a forty-nine-year-old grandmother when, in 1778, she was presented with her next paramour, Ivan Rimsky-Korsakov, who was half her age. The Chevalier de Corberon wrote of the empress's latest love, "He was the model of conceit, but conceit of the pettiest kind, the sort that would not be tolerated even in Paris." He was pretty, though, and really that's all Catherine cared about. When her friend Grimm teased her about being "infatuated" with Rimsky-Korsakov, the empress responded, "Infatuated, infatuated! Are you aware that that term is entirely inappropriate when one is speaking of Pyrrhus, King of Epirus, who defies the skill of painters and is the despair of sculptors? It is admiration, Monsieur, enthusiasm, that the masterpieces of nature inspire in us."

Catherine's enthusiasm for this particular work of art was diminished somewhat when she found him in bed with her lady-in-waiting, Countess Bruce. Thus, if there was any truth at all to the countess serving as the empress's "tester," she obviously liked this applicant so much that she went back for a more thorough examination. Both were dismissed as a result. Replacing the countess was Anna Protasova ("*l'Eprouveuse*" in Byron's *Don Juan*);* the new lover was Alexander Lanskoy.

Though Catherine the Great was old enough to be the mother of any one of her later lovers, she had genuine maternal feelings for the unassuming Lanskoy, whose virtues were praised even by those hostile to the empress. "He is a model of kindness, humanity, civility, modesty and beauty," wrote Charles Masson. "A lover of the arts and a friend to talent, he is humane, benevolent." And Lanskoy seemed to reciprocate Catherine's lavish attentions, which, in his case, extended beyond the bedroom. "Relations could not be more trusting between a mother and son," the empress's private secretary noted.

It was touching (albeit a tad creepy) how Catherine, whose own son Paul was such a disappointment (see following chapter), sought to groom this eager young man, this surrogate, for something greater—perhaps as a new Potemkin. They read and studied together, enjoyed the arts, and simply enjoyed each other's company. With his good humor, the empress

---

* Byron probably used the memoirs of Charles Masson, a chronicler hostile to Catherine, as his source for the term "l'Eprouveuse," which has a near translation in French as "an apparatus formerly used to test the strength of gunpowder."

wrote, Lanskoy made Tsarskoe Selo (the Tsar's Village) "into the most charming and pleasant of places where the days passed so quickly one did not know what had become of them."

After four years, "cheerful, honest, gentle" Lanskoy's tenure had already outlasted all previous lovers except Orlov. And there appeared to be no end to it. "I hope that he'll become the support of my old age," Catherine shared in a letter to Grimm. Ten days later, however, the young man fell ill, probably of diphtheria, and on June 25, 1784, he died.

"When I began this letter I was happy and joyful, and my thoughts sped so quickly that I knew not what became of them," the empress wrote in the missive she had been composing to Grimm. "It is no longer so; I am plunged in the keenest grief and my happiness has fled. I almost died myself from the irreparable loss I have just sustained, a week ago, of my best friend. . . . He applied himself, he learned much, he had acquired all my tastes. He was a young man whom I was educating, who was grateful, sweet-tempered and gentlemanly, who shared my troubles when I had any and rejoiced in my joys. In brief I have the misfortune to tell you, sobbing as I write it, that General Lanskoy is no more. . . . My bedroom, which used to be so pleasant to me, has become an empty cave in which I drag myself about like a shadow. . . . I cannot set eyes on a human face without being choked with sobs so that I cannot speak. I can neither sleep nor eat. It wearies me to read, and to write is beyond my strength. I know not what is to become of me, but I do know that never in all my life have I been so wretched as since my best, kind friend has abandoned me. I opened my drawer, I found this sheet begun, I have written these lines, I cannot go on."

In her grief, Catherine waited nearly a year—a relative eternity—she before felt ready to plunge into another affair, this time with a thirty-one year-old nonentity named Alexander Ermolov. Like Zorich before him, Ermolov was stupid enough to tangle with Potemkin. Aligning himself with the powerful prince's enemies, the foolish favorite accused him of misappropriating funds. Catherine was understandably incensed, but Potemkin maintained his grip over her. He bluntly denied the charges without deigning to explain himself and, to show his own displeasure, stormed out of the palace.

"Don't worry," he said to the Count de Ségur, "a child isn't going to topple me, and I don't know who dare. . . . I scorn my enemies too much to fear them." Supremely confident of his value to the empress, Potemkin eventually barged into her apartments with an ultimatum: "Madame, you must choose between Ermolov and me and dismiss one or the other; so long as you keep that white Negro I shall not step foot in your palace." There was really no choice, and the inconsequential Ermolov was sent off with the usual compensatory riches.

Potemkin was quick to replace him three days later with a smarter, better-looking Guards officer named Alexander Mamonov. Catherine, now fifty-seven, was smitten with her new man (whom she referred to as "the redcoat" because of the scarlet uniform he liked to wear to bring out his dark eyes) and wrote of him with the same frenzied ecstasy she always did in the first flush of fresh romance: "This Redcoat is so admirable, so witty, so gay, handsome, obliging and well-bred that you would do well to love him without knowing him."

But by this time in her life, Catherine's girlish passions were making her look increasingly silly; the snickering behind her back grew bolder and more abusive, but the empress seemed not to notice. Emperor Joseph II of Austria, who accompanied Catherine and her young lover on an extended river tour of the freshly conquered Crimea,* was bewildered by his fellow sovereign's undignified behavior. "What I do not understand," he remarked, "is how a woman who is so proud and so careful of her reputation can show such a strange weakness for the caprices of her young aide-de-camp Mamonov, who is really nothing but a spoiled child."

Though the empress was thoroughly besotted with Mamonov, he was stultified by her, which was entirely understandable. After all, behind all the glitter and prestige that came with being the favorite, Mamonov was still a vigorous young man forced to follow around and bed an increasingly fat, wheezing older woman who found it difficult to make it up a flight of stairs. As one of his friends reported, "[He] considers his life a prison, is very bored, and supposedly after every public gathering where ladies are present, the Empress attaches herself to him and is jealous."

To escape his clingy mistress, Mamonov began to ignore her nocturnal beckoning by pleading illness and instead launched a secret affair with someone closer to his own age—whom he then impregnated. Catherine was devastated, of course, and humiliated as well. Still, she played the magnanimous sovereign and blessed the union of the young couple. Behind the scenes, though, she raged.

"I have suspected him for eight months!" she exclaimed to her secretary. "He was avoiding me. . . . It was always because

---

* It was along the river route of this Crimean tour that Potemkin allegedly set up the legendary "villages" for Catherine's edification: elaborate façades in front of which cheerful residents of the newly annexed territory supposedly stood and waved to their new monarch.

he was having difficulty breathing that he had to keep to his room! Then lately he took to talking about qualms of conscience that pained him and made it impossible for him to continue our life together. The traitor! It was this other love, his duplicity that was suffocating him. But since he could not help himself, why didn't he admit it frankly? . . . He cannot imagine what I have suffered."

Potemkin, whose advice to the betrayed empress was "spit upon him," quickly distanced himself from his protégé. "I never had any illusions about him," he declared of Mamonov. "He is a mixture of indolence and egotism. This later trait made him the ultimate Narcissus. Thinking only of himself, he demanded everything without paying anything in return."

Once the ex-favorite settled into the dull routine of marriage and fatherhood, he realized life in the empress's gilded prison wasn't quite so bad after all. He begged for his old place back, but by then Catherine II was preoccupied with her very last lover.

Physically, Platon Zubov was typical fare for the empress— "supple, muscular and well proportioned," as Masson described him. But he wasn't Potemkin's man. Indeed, while the great prince was off fighting the Turks, the strikingly shallow, immensely greedy twenty-two-year-old Zubov slithered in, on his own initiative, and seduced the empress, thirty-eight years his senior. Soon enough, he would eclipse Potemkin entirely—not because he exceeded him in talent, for Zubov had precious little of that—but through the indulgence of an adoring empress in her dotage, who, for the first time, allowed statecraft to be entirely subordinated to pleasure. "I have come back to life like a fly that has been numbed by the cold," she gleefully wrote to Potemkin of her new discovery. ("A big fly of sixty," wrote Troyat, "restless, buzzing and hungry.")

The strutting new favorite—"resplendent in his new uniform, with a great plumed hat on his head," as Masson reported—immediately began lording his new status, imposing his will, and shamelessly brokering his influence. The flatterers flocked to him. "Every day, starting at eight o'clock in the morning, his antechamber was filled with ministers, courtiers, generals, foreigners, petitioners, seekers after appointments or favors," reported Count Langeron. "Usually, they had to wait four or five hours before being admitted. . . . At last the double doors would swing open, the crowd would rush in and the favorite would be found seated before his mirror having his hair dressed, and ordinarily resting one foot on a chair or a corner of the dressing table. After bowing low, the courtiers would range themselves before him two or three deep, silent and motionless, in the midst of a cloud of powder."

After their interminable wait outside his chambers, the seekers were fortunate if they were acknowledged by anything more than Zubov's capuchin monkey, which ran screaming through the room and rummaging through their hair. "The old generals, the great men of the Empire, did not blush to ingratiate themselves with the least of his valets," wrote Masson. "Stretched out in an armchair in the most indecent, careless attire, with his little finger in his nose and his eyes fixed vaguely on the ceiling, this young man with his cold, vain face, scarcely deigned to pay attention to those around him."

And yet the infatuated empress believed that Zubov—or "the child," as she called him—was a precious cherub. He has "the most innocent soul," Catherine wrote to Potemkin, and is "without malice or treachery, modest, devoted, supremely grateful." Clearly Potemkin knew better, and as news of Zubov's dangerous ascendency reached him, he abruptly left the front lines for St. Petersburg.

"Prince Potemkin arrived here four days ago, more handsome, agreeable, witty and brilliant than ever, and in the gayest possible humor," Catherine wrote to Grimm; "that's what a fine and glorious campaign does for a man, it puts him in a good mood." The prince's spirits darkened, though, when he realized that the reports of Zubov's sensational rise were entirely accurate. And though the empress continued to show her "lion of the jungle" proper respect and esteem, the one-eyed giant was no longer master of Russia. He had been supplanted by "the child."

In what was either a futile attempt to reassert his position, or a formal farewell to the empress he had loved and helped become "the Great"—perhaps both—Potemkin threw an extravagant ball at his Tauride Palace in the spring of 1791, the opulence of which had rarely been seen in the capital before. It was a grand success, in that the empress stayed until two in the morning, but at the end of the night it was Zubov trailing behind her as she left.

Dejected, Potemkin returned to the front, where he at least hoped to pursue an aggressive policy against the Turks. However, he arrived to find that Catherine had overridden all his designs and, following Zubov's own policy, had ordered an immediate cessation of hostilities. Now the once-invincible prince was broken entirely, his proud spirit replaced by weakness and doubt. "The Prince was destroying himself," reported Count Langeron. "I have seen him, during an attack of fever, devour a ham, a salted goose, and three or four chickens, and drink kvass, klukva [cranberry liquor], mead, and all sorts of wines."

With no real sense of purpose, Potemkin left the peace conference, writing to Catherine, "Little Mother, gracious sovereign, I can no longer endure my torments. The only chance remaining for me is to quit this city [Jassey]; I have given orders that I be taken to Nikolayev [the town he founded in the Ukraine]. I do not know what will become of me. Your very faithful and very grateful subject—Potemkin."

It was while traveling to Nikolayev in October 1791 that Potemkin fell ill again. He asked to be taken out of the carriage and laid in the grass to rest. And there he died, essentially in a ditch: the conqueror of new territory, the builder of cities, the man of genius who served an empress as lover, possible husband, and virtual co-sovereign.

"Once again, a terrible, crushing blow has fallen on my head," Catherine wrote to Grimm in a long, despairing letter. "I regard Prince Potemkin as a very great man, who did not accomplish half of what he was capable of." Yet no matter how powerfully she felt about the man she had just lost, Catherine's tributes to him would have to remain private—on that Zubov insisted, no doubt keenly aware of how insignificant a specimen he really was compared to the great Russian he had replaced. Thus was Potemkin quietly laid to rest. "What is most extraordinary is that he has already been completely forgotten," Count Feodor Rostopchin later wrote. "The generations to come will not bless his memory."

With the towering prince gone, his pale shadow emerged more powerful than ever. "Count Zubov is everything here," reported Rostopchin. "There is no other will but his. His power is greater than that of Potemkin. He is as reckless and incapable as before, although the Empress keeps repeating that he is the greatest genius the history of Russia has known."

Indeed, Catherine remained enchanted with this colossal

ninny. At his insistence, she put him in charge of all foreign affairs,* and decorated him with so many awards that Masson was prompted to quip that he looked like "a hawker of [ribbons] and trinkets at a fair." The empress also turned over Potemkin's apartments to Zubov, but there was little she could do to transfer his achievements.

"Potemkin owed almost all his greatness to himself," wrote Masson; "Zubov owed his only to Catherine's decrepitude. We watched him wax in power, wealth, prestige, in proportion as Catherine waned in activity, vigor and understanding. . . . He was obsessed with the desire to do everything, or seem to do everything. . . . His haughtiness was equaled only by the servility of those who hastened to prostrate themselves before him. . . . Everyone crawled at Zubov's feet; he stood erect and thought himself great."

So arrogant had Zubov become that he even had the audacity to hit on the wife of Catherine's grandson, the future emperor Alexander I. And there was not much the royal couple could do about it. "My wife behaves like an angel," Alexander confided to a friend. "But you must admit that it is exceedingly awkward to know how to conduct oneself toward Zubov. . . . If you treat him well, it is as if you approved of his love, and if you treat him coldly to discourage him, the Empress, who is ignorant of the situation, may be offended that

---

* In one of Zubov's more glaring blunders in this capacity, he arranged the marriage of Catherine's thirteen-year-old granddaughter Alexandra to the young king of Sweden, Gustav IV. Only he neglected to settle the vital question of religion before King Gustav came to officially court the Russian princess. The Swedes thought it essential their queen become Lutheran. The empress, on the other hand, would not countenance the girl's conversion from Orthodoxy. It all ended in a humiliating debacle when it became apparent too late that neither side was prepared to budge on the issue.

you are not sufficiently honoring a man whom she favors. It is extremely difficult to keep the middle course, as is necessary, especially before a public as malicious and as ready to do spiteful things as ours."

What Zubov apparently failed to recognize as he preened and swaggered in the glow of imperial favor was the inescapable fact that his mistress's remaining time was limited. And without her protection, he was nothing. Thus, when Catherine II was felled by a stroke in 1796, Zubov was in "despair . . . beyond comparison," as one witness described him. With his power slipping away as quickly as the empress's life, he stood by her bed sobbing uncontrollably.

Then, on November 17, 1796, Platon Zubov found himself the subject of a new sovereign—one he had been foolish enough to scorn and mock. (In one very public scene, for example, the future emperor Paul voiced his agreement with a point Zubov made one night at dinner. To this the favorite responded contemptuously, "What? Have I said something silly?")

Just when it seemed severe retribution was in order, though, Emperor Paul showed himself to be rather magnanimous. He made a personal visit to the now-helpless Zubov and raised a toast to him. "I wish you as many happy days as there are drops in this glass," Paul declared. It was a cruel ruse. Soon after, the emperor confiscated all Zubov's property and sent him into exile. But Catherine the Great's "child" would have the last laugh against her half-mad son.

Chapter 8

Paul (1796–1801):

"He Detests His Nation"

There is no one who does not daily remark on the disorder of his faculties.

—GRAND DUCHESS (LATER EMPRESS) MARIA FEODOROVNA

After her death in 1796, Catherine the Great was succeeded by her son Paul, whose father was either the late empress's murdered husband, Peter III, or, more likely, her first lover, Sergei Saltykov. Though questions of paternity lingered, Paul believed he was Peter's son and honored him accordingly—by imitation, alas, which ultimately resulted in the two emperors sharing the same ghastly fate.

Catherine II was dead, and now it was time for her son and successor, Paul, to rectify some wrongs. Certainly he would bury with all due honor the mother he so feared and despised. But she wouldn't be alone. The new emperor ordered that the skeletal remains of his putative father, Peter III, be disinterred from his vault at the Alexander Nevsky Monastery and, with much ceremony, carried to the Winter Palace and laid in state next to Catherine's coffin. Thus, after thirty-four years, the husband and wife who loathed each other in life were reunited in death as their former subjects shuffled by to pay homage. Paul was pleased with this bit of macabre handi-work, but he still had more planned. During the funeral procession that followed, he arranged for the architect of his father's murder, the now aged and decrepit Alexis Orlov, to carry the dead emperor's crown on a cushion, while other surviving conspirators were designated pallbearers. Then, amid the incense and solemn chants at the Cathedral of St. Peter and St. Paul, Catherine II and Peter III were interred together forever.

The bond between the baby Paul and his mother had been broken at a most critical time, when the infant was whisked away by Empress Elizabeth immediately after Catherine delivered him in 1754. The new mother was only allowed to see her son occasionally, and then for just the briefest visits. Paul was a child of the state, and the state, in the person of the empress, literally smothered him.

"He was kept in an excessively warm room," Catherine wrote, "swaddled in flannel, and laid in a cradle lined with black fur; he was covered with a counterpane of pink satin, lined with wadding, and another one above it, lined with black fur. I saw him many times often lying so, with sweat running down his face and his whole body, and so it was that when he grew older, the least breath of air chilled him and made him ill. In addition, he was surrounded by a bevy of ignorant old crones, who, by dint of their senseless means of management, did him infinitely more harm than good, both physically and mentally."

While Catherine was always concerned about the welfare of the baby snatched away from her by Elizabeth, her husband showed no such inclination. Perhaps Peter doubted whether

Paul really was his child, or, just as likely, there was little room in his disordered mind for much paternal sentiment. Indeed, the only real interest Peter ever showed in the boy was when he insisted at Paul's birth that he receive the same financial reward his wife did when she delivered the child. (To satisfy this petulant demand, Elizabeth, her treasury nearly empty at the time, had to ask Catherine to temporarily return her bequest so the empress could pay off Peter.) Yet despite his father's near-total indifference, it would be Peter III whom Paul would come to emulate.

Even as a boy, the future emperor was demonstrating some of Peter's more unsettling characteristics—evidence, perhaps, that they were indeed father and son after all. He was often restless and agitated, with a mania for all things military, and possessed of a disturbing capacity for cruelty. "With the best intention in the world," the boy's tutor warned him, "you will make yourself thoroughly hated."

Once, during a theatrical performance when he was ten, Paul was so outraged when some members of the audience dared applaud before he had himself indicated his reaction to the play that he asked his mother—now empress—to exile the offenders. Of course Catherine ignored this impudent demand, but she couldn't ignore the emerging character deficits in her son that were so frighteningly reminiscent of her late, demented spouse. They left her cold.

"He is believed to be vindictive, headstrong and absolute in his ideas," the French chargé d'affaires Sabatier de Cabre reported of Paul when he was fourteen. "It is only to be feared that by virtue of having his wings clipped, a potentially decided character may be rendered obstinate, that it may be replaced by duplicity, repressed hatred and perhaps pusillanimity, and that the high-mindedness which might have been developed in him may be stifled at last by the terror that his mother has always inspired in him. . . . It is true that the Empress, who is careful of appearances so far as everything else is concerned, observes none of them in relation to her son. For him she always has the tone and manner of a sovereign, and this attitude is often combined with a coldness and neglect that disgust the young prince. She has never treated him as a mother treats her son. Therefore the Grand Duke [Paul] behaves with her as if he stood before a judge."

Catherine II did indeed have a difficult time loving her son, who in his adolescence was becoming increasingly unstable as he seethed with suspicion and paranoia—especially toward the empress he was beginning to suspect had murdered his father. "The mere sight of her made him think of death," wrote biographer Henri Troyat; "the breath of the tomb hung about her." Once, after finding a few tiny shards of glass in his food, Paul, wild with fury, ran screaming through the palace and accused his mother to her face of trying to kill him. Even his appearance started to reflect his temperament. The features of the once-charming, fair-haired boy with his pert turned-up nose became grossly distorted as he grew—with thickened lips, facial tics, and flattened nostrils resembling those of a bulldog. Worst of all, Paul was beginning to pose a threat to his mother's throne.

"This young Prince gives evidence of sinister and dangerous inclinations," reported the French diplomat Bérenger. "A few days ago, he was asking why they had killed his father and why they had given his mother the throne that rightfully belonged to him. He added that when he grew up, he would get to the bottom of all that. People are saying . . . that the child allows himself too many remarks of that sort for them not to reach the ears of the Empress. Now, no one doubts that that

Princess will take all possible precautions to prevent him from putting words into action."

Catherine hoped that marriage might divert Paul from some of his more malignant passions, and, even better, produce an heir she could mold in her own image to carry on the policies her own son seemed to despise. Accordingly, she turned to Frederick the Great (the Prussian monarch who had helped arrange her own marriage to the future Peter III) to find Paul an eligible German bride—hopefully one possessing the same qualities the empress admired so much in herself.

Frederick immediately thought of the three youngest daughters of the Landgrave of Hesse-Darmstadt. But, unable to choose which one, he decided to send all three princesses to Russia for Catherine's inspection and Paul's approval. The grand duke was immediately taken by the eldest, Wilhelmina, who also captured the fancy of his best friend Andrei Razumovsky as he accompanied her by ship from Germany. For Wilhelmina, Paul represented the prize—future sovereignty over Russia—but his person left much lacking. "The distinction of which the heir to the throne has made her the object does not seem to be disagreeable to her," Wilhelmina's mother wrote to the empress, with a notable lack of enthusiasm.

Like young Princess Sophia had all those years ago, Wilhelmina was to be thoroughly Russianized, converted to Orthodoxy, and rechristened Natalia. She would also cheat on her husband with his best friend Razumovsky, although, unlike her mother-in-law, she wouldn't wait nearly a decade to stray. And it wouldn't be from a spouse who despised her.

Paul was in fact smitten with his bride; Catherine not so much. "The Grand Duchess loves extreme in all things," the empress wrote to her friend Friedrich Melchoir Grimm. "She will listen to no advice, and I see in her neither charm, nor wit, nor reason." Natalia spent most of her time either conspiring with her husband against his mother, or carrying on with his friend. And to help facilitate those extramarital romps, the two lovers often dosed Paul with a little opium to put him to sleep, and, as the Count d'Allonville put it, "reduce their trio to a single tête-à-tete."

The heir to the throne appeared to be the only one at court oblivious to his wife's infidelity. But any thought Catherine may have had in squelching the affair evaporated when Natalia became pregnant. She was carrying the future sovereign, even if the child may not have been Paul's. In the end, it didn't matter, as Natalia died while delivering a stillborn son. Her cuckolded husband went mad with grief, smashing the furniture in his apartments and threatening to hurl himself out a window. He even refused to have Natalia buried because he believed she might still be alive.

The empress finally put an end to this nonsense when she told her son the cold truth about his dead spouse and presented as proof the love letters from Razumovsky that she found in Natalia's desk. Thus, having crushed Paul's sentiments toward his beloved wife, or at least confused them, the empress presented him with the plans she had for a replacement.

"I have wasted no time," she wrote to Grimm. "At once, I put the irons in the fire to make good the loss, and by so doing I have succeeded in dissipating the deep sorrow that overwhelmed us."

The German princess Catherine had in mind to sacrifice to her son was sixteen-year-old Sophia Dorothea of Württemberg, with Frederick the Great once again serving as matchmaker. Paul was sent off to Berlin to inspect his potential mate, and, fortunately for his mother, who hoped to strengthen ties with Prussia, he instantly fell for the girl. "I found my intended to be such as I could have dreamed of," Paul wrote to his mother. "She is tall, shapely, intelligent, quick-witted, and not at all shy."* And the fact that Sophia Dorothea came recommended by Frederick only added to her luster, for Paul, like Peter III, idolized the Prussian monarch. King Frederick, on the other hand, was less than impressed by the Russian heir.

"He seemed proud, haughty, and violent, which made those who knew Russia apprehend that he would have no little trouble maintaining himself on the throne," the king wrote of Paul. "He would have to fear a fate like his unfortunate father."

On September 26, 1776—less than a year after his first wife's burial—Paul married Sophia Dorothea, who, after her required conversion to Orthodoxy, was given the name Maria Feodorovna. Catherine the Great adored her new daughter-in-law. "I confess to you that I am infatuated with this charming Princess, but literally infatuated," the empress wrote to a friend. "She is precisely what one could have wished: the figure of a nymph, a lily-and-rose complexion, the loveliest skin in the world, tall and well built; she is graceful; sweetness, kindness and innocence are reflected in her face."

And, for once, the empress and her estranged son were in

---

* Shockingly, the young princess seemed to be equally attracted to the pug-faced prince. "I am more than content," she wrote after meeting Paul. "Never, dear friend, could I be happier. The Grand Duke could not be more kind. I pride myself on the fact that my dear bridegroom loves me a great deal, and this makes me very, very fortunate." After their engagement Sophia Dorothea wrote to Paul: "I cannot go to bed, my dear and adored Prince, without telling you once again that I love and adore you madly."

complete accord—at least when it came to Maria. "She has the art not only of driving out all my melancholy thoughts," Paul wrote of his new bride, "but even of giving me back the good humor that I had completely lost over these last three unhappy years." Unfortunately, Maria was not able to drive out the demon that tormented her new husband most: his mother.

Catherine consumed Paul's thoughts as an evil entity bent on destroying him, just as she had the man he believed to be his father. Yet it was this same enmity that only served to alienate the empress further. More and more she came to see her son as unfit to succeed her, and instead placed all her hopes and ambitions for the future on the next generation. Thus, when Grand Duchess Maria gave birth to a boy, the future Alexander I, in 1777, Catherine immediately swooped in to make the child her own—just as Empress Elizabeth had done to her decades earlier when she delivered Paul.

"I am making a delicious child of him," Catherine wrote to Grimm with great satisfaction. "It is astonishing that, although he cannot talk yet, at twenty months he knows things that are beyond the grasp of any child at the age of three. Grandma does what she likes with him."

And Grandma did the same with the next child,* Constantine, who she dreamed would one day rule over the yet-to-be-conquered Byzantine Empire. These little boys were to be the very personification of Russian greatness. Their father, on the other hand, was to be superfluous—merely a sire for the glorious offspring. Alexander "is going to become an *excellentissimo* personage," the empress declared, "if only the *secondaterie* [Paul] doesn't hold me back in his progress."

---

* Paul and Maria would have ten children in all, including the future emperor Nicholas I.

Rendered impotent as a parent—and in every other official capacity, for that matter—Paul wrote to a friend in frustration, "I am already thirty years old, and I have nothing to do." The heir's only real diversion was to pursue his obsession with Prussian-style militarism at his estate of Gatchina, where he maintained an army of two thousand men, and, as one visiting foreign royal noted, "distinguished [himself] by incomprehensible strangeness and foolishness." Given his disposition, there were many who feared the time when this vile-tempered, paranoid drillmaster's domain would extend beyond the borders of his fortified estate and consume all of Russia. "Woe to his friends, his enemies, his allies and his subjects!" wrote Prince Charles de Ligne. "He detests his nation."

Paul's wife, Maria, though she managed to love him, was nevertheless aware of what was being said about her husband. "There is no one who does not daily remark on the disorder of his faculties," she confided. And she was right. There was in fact a litany of dire assessments regarding the heir's character, sanity, and fitness to rule:

—The English ambassador: "[He has an] acrimony of disposition which already renders the Great Duke an Object dreadful to those who look forward to a future reign."

—The Austrian ambassador: "With a Prince of his character, one cannot count on the stability of his sentiments."

—The French ambassador: "They are going so far as to say that his mind is deranged."

—The Swedish ambassador: "Grand Duke Paul continues to behave very badly and to lose ground not only in the minds of the great but in the minds of the people as well."

Perhaps the most detailed, and frightening, account of Paul's behavior during this period was provided by Count Feodor Rostopchin, who became the grand duke's confident—a role to which he was apparently most unwillingly consigned. "Next to dishonor, nothing could be more odious to me than Paul's good will," he wrote. "The Grand Duke's head is filled with phantoms, and he is surrounded by such people that the most honest man among them would deserve to be hanged without trial." Rostopchin continued:

"It is impossible to observe what the grand prince does without shuddering and pity. [It is] as if he seeks out every means of making himself hated. He is obsessed with the idea that people do not respect him and that they scorn him. Proceeding from that [assumption], he fusses over everything and gives orders indiscriminately. . . . On Wednesdays, he holds maneuvers, and every day he is present for the changing of the guard and also for punishments, when they take place. The slightest tardiness, the slightest contradiction put him beside himself, and he is inflamed with rage. It is remarkable that he is never aware of his own mistakes and continues to be angry with those he has offended. . . . He is destroying himself and contriving the means of making himself hated."

Of course no one was more concerned about Paul's fitness to wear the Russian crown than the empress herself. "I see into what hands the empire will fall when I am gone," she once remarked gloomily. Catherine II had long cherished the idea of disinheriting her unworthy son in favor of her hand-raised grandson, Alexander, and it was widely believed that she was prepared to issue a manifesto to that effect at the beginning of 1797. Fate intervened, however, when the empress was felled by a stroke and died in November 1796. Paul immediately ordered his mother's office sealed, thus ensuring that if a document barring him from the succession did exist, he had plenty of opportunity to destroy it—just as he would attempt to do with the rest of his despised mother's legacy. And so began the mad reign of Emperor Paul.

After orchestrating the ghoulish exhumation and reburial of Peter III next to his mother, Paul turned his unsteady gaze toward the Russian empire he now ruled. In a frenzy of legislomania, the emperor began to assert his control over the minutest aspects of his subjects' lives. A new dress code was instituted, for example, and those who failed to follow it often found themselves under assault by government troops who were known to shred banned clothing while it was still being worn and to confiscate unsanctioned shoes. Women were now legally obliged to prostrate themselves, even in the mud, whenever Paul happened to pass by in his carriage, and houses could only be painted in state-approved colors. Printing presses were shut down, imported books and music banned, and, in deference to the emperor's abhorrence of the French Revolution, such incendiary words as *citizen* were stricken from the language.

Count Golovkin lamented the woeful state of St. Petersburg under the new regime: "This beautiful capital, in which people used to move about as free as air, which had neither gates nor guards nor customs officers, is transformed into a vast prison surrounded by guard posts; the palace has become the seat of terror, before which one may not pass, even in the absence of the sovereign, without taking off one's hat; these fine, broad streets have become deserted, the old nobility being unable to go to perform their functions at court without showing police passes seven times over."

The new emperor's domestic tyranny coincided with a bizarre foreign policy, which was perhaps best illustrated by one of his more inspired diplomatic overtures. Seeking to resolve all conflicts in Europe once and for all, Paul publicly challenged his fellow monarchs to face one another in a series of duels.

But the emperor was undoubtedly the most capricious when it came to the Russian military, which, fulfilling the dream of Peter III, he reinvented in the style of his idol Frederick the Great—reducing the proud force into what one bitterly called "Prussian monkeys," and punishing them mercilessly. Any missed goosestep or unpolished button would result in ferocious imperial wrath, and officers were known to carry extra money with them should they suddenly find themselves hauled off to Siberia.

"In general," one diplomat reported, "the slightest mistake committed by an officer on parade, a small irregularity in saluting . . . is punished either by transferring the regiment to the provinces . . . by cashiering it at once from service, or sometimes by reducing it to the rank of simple foot soldiers. . . . Petersburg has become the domicile of Terror."

Even the emperor's family feared him and grew increasingly disturbed by his erratic policies. His son Alexander, whom Catherine the Great dreamed of making her successor, had shown proper deference to his father when the empress died, eschewing any thought of challenging him for the throne. He even appeared at Catherine's deathbed in the Prussian-style uniform so favored by Paul—a move designed to please. But soon enough the loyal son grew disgruntled.

"Everything has been turned upside down all at once," Alexander wrote to his former tutor in 1797, "and that has only increased the confusion of affairs, which was already too great.

The military waste almost all their time on parades. In other areas, there is no coherent plan. An order given today will be countermanded a month hence. No remonstrance is ever tolerated until the damage has already been done. In short, to speak plainly, the happiness of the State counts for nothing in the governing of affairs. There is only one absolute power, which does everything without rhyme or reason. It would be impossible to enumerate to you all the mad things that have been done. . . . My poor country is in an indescribable state: the farmer harassed, commerce obstructed, liberty and personal welfare reduced to nothing. That is the picture of Russia."

Alexander's wife, Grand Duchess Elizabeth, had an equally low opinion of her father-in-law, which she expressed in a letter to her mother. "It is always something to have the honor of not seeing the Emperor," she wrote. "In truth, Mama, I find that man *widerwartig* [disgusting], just to hear him mentioned, and I find his society even more so. . . . In any case, he doesn't care if he is loved so long as he is feared, he has said so himself. And his wish is generally fulfilled, he is feared and hated."

After four years of maniacal rule, Emperor Paul had thoroughly alienated his subjects, many of whom believed him to be actually insane. "The fact is, and I speak it with regret, that the Emperor's literally not in senses," the English ambassador reported in 1800. "This truth has been for many years known to those nearest to Him, and I myself had frequent opportunity of observing it. But since He has come to the Throne, his disorder has gradually increased, and now manifests itself in such a manner as to fill everyone with the most obvious alarm."

To save Russia from its rabid monarch, a band of conspirators colluded to force his removal. Count Peter Pahlen, governor of St. Petersburg and Paul's close confidant, headed the group, which also included Catherine the Great's last lover, Platon Zubov—primed to avenge the humiliation he had endured under Paul—and his brothers. Before they could proceed, however, the plotters needed the support of the emperor's son and heir, who would take his father's place on the throne. Though Alexander had previously shuddered at the very idea of participating in an act of such magnitude, now Paul was looming as an increasing threat to him.

On one occasion, while Alexander was reading Voltaire's tragedy *Brutus,* his father burst into the room, seized the book, and shook with rage as he read the last line, "Rome is free; that is enough. . . . Let us give thanks to the gods." Without a word, the emperor left his son's apartments, returned to his own, and pulled from his library a life of Peter the Great. He then opened the book to the passages detailing the death by torture of the tsar's disobedient son and had it sent to Alexander with instructions to read the illustrative part. The message was clear, and so with Pahlen's assurance that his father would not be harmed in the planned coup, merely sent away into honorable retirement, Alexander gave his tacit approval to the scheme. He refused, however, to actually participate in it.

The date set for deposing Paul and forcing his abdication was set for mid-March 1801. In the meantime, however, the emperor was growing suspicious. After being warned of a possible plot against him, he abruptly summoned Pahlen to his study and demanded to know if any members of the imperial family might be involved. As if prepared for such a confrontation, the leader of the forthcoming coup laughed and replied merrily, "But, Sire, if there is a conspiracy, I am part of it. I hold the strings of everything and nothing escapes my knowledge. Set your mind at ease; no conspiracy is possible without me. I'll stake my life on that."

Paul was only partially reassured by Pahlen's soothing deception and remained broody and snappish—particularly toward his family. "Our existence is not cheerful," Empress Maria confided to a friend, "because our dear master is not at all so. In his soul there is underlying sorrow that preys upon him; his appetite suffers; he no longer eats as before and rarely has a smile on his lips." Even the relentlessly rainy weather seemed to reflect the sense of gloomy foreboding. "It is always dark," one wrote at the time, "weeks pass without our seeing the sun; one has no desire to go out. Besides, one does not go out without danger. It is as if God had turned away from us."

It was only on the last day of his life that the emperor's spirits seemed to lift a little. Whereas at dinner the night before he sat stewing, disconcerting his guests and reducing his wife to tears, Paul now beamed with affability during his last supper at the recently constructed Mikhailovsky (or St. Michael's) Castle. But just as soon as the meal was concluded the emperor abruptly got up and left the room without saying a word. Then, at the entrance to his private apartments, he angrily confronted the commander of the Horse Guards regiment and accused the sentries posted at his rooms of being subversives. "I know what's what," Paul declared to the commander. "Dismiss your men." As the soldiers marched away, the emperor summoned two castle lackeys to replace them. And, with that, he went into his bedroom, followed by his little dog Spitz—never to emerge again.

Meanwhile, at around ten o'clock that night, the band of fifty or so conspirators—representing nearly every branch of the military—gathered at the regimental barracks of the Preobrazhensky Guard adjacent to the Winter Palace. "We are among ourselves, gentlemen," Pahlen declared, "and we understand one another. Are you ready? We are going to drink of champagne to the health of the new sovereign. The reign of Paul I is over. We are not guided by a spirit of revenge, but we wish to put an end to the outrageous humiliations and the shame of the motherland. We are Romans. We all know the significance of the Ides of March. . . . All precautions have been taken." When one of the gathered asked what would happen if the emperor resisted, Pahlen replied, "You all know, gentlemen, that to make an omelet one must break eggs."

Flush with alcohol and patriotic fervor, the men made their way to Mikhailovsky Castle and slipped inside. They were surprised to find not a regiment of sentries there, but the two lackeys, one of whom was quickly dispatched while the other fled in terror. Now that the path was clear, though, the enormity of what they were about to do struck some of the conspirators and they retreated. The remainder proceeded into the apartments. There they found an empty bed. "The bird has flown!" Zubov exclaimed furiously. But upon feeling the sheets, another concluded, "The nest is still warm, the bird cannot be far off!" And that's when they saw two bare feet poking out from beneath a screen.

Behind it was the quivering emperor in his nightclothes. "What do you want of me?" he stammered in terror. "What are you doing here?" Paul was told he was under arrest, to which he replied, "Under arrest? Under arrest? What does that mean?" Zubov then interrupted him. "We come in the name of the motherland to beg Your Majesty to abdicate," he announced. "The security of your person and suitable maintenance are guaranteed to you by your son and by the State." Another of the leaders, General Bennigsen, added: "Your

Majesty can no longer govern millions of men. You make them unhappy; you should abdicate. No one wants to make an attempt on your life; I am here to defend you. Sign the act of abdication." With that, the emperor was pushed toward a table upon which the document was spread, and an officer held out a pen. Paul resisted. "No, I will not sign this!" he shouted.

An uproar then erupted among the agitated men as the emperor remained obdurate. A scuffle broke out and the single candle lighting the room was tipped over. Now, in the semidarkness, the conspirators fell upon Paul, who fought back ferociously. Finally, a sash was drawn around his neck and tightened until the breath finally left him. Hearing the commotion, Empress Maria rushed to the room, but her passage was blocked. *"Päulchen, Päulchen!"* the horrified woman screamed in German. She was perhaps the only one left who still cared about the mad monarch.

While Paul met his end upstairs, his son Alexander waited anxiously downstairs in his own apartments to learn what the night had wrought. Pahlen found him clinging to his wife, their foreheads touching in tender uncertainty. Then, when he was told what had transpired, the new emperor burst into sobs—stricken by the fact that he had passively participated not only in parricide, but regicide as well. Pahlen addressed him sternly: "That's enough childishness. Go reign. Come show yourself to the Guards!" His wife Elizabeth exhorted him as well.

"It was a night," she wrote, "that I shall never forget."

Chapter 9

Alexander I (1801–1825):

Napoleon's Conqueror

One of us—either he, Napoleon, or I, Alexander—
must lose his crown.

—EMPEROR ALEXANDER I

*To Russians, it is known as the Patriotic War of 1812—the great
struggle that inspired Tolstoy's* War and Peace *and Tchaikovsky's*
1812 Overture. *But behind all the bloodshed and misery that accompanied France's ill-fated invasion of Russia, the war was also
a personal confrontation between two emperors: the seemingly invincible upstart Napoleon and the fourteenth Romanov of the
line, the brooding, duplicitous Alexander I.*

It was the opening salvo of an epic clash. And it came in the
form of an insult—a stinging barb delivered by Napoleon
Bonaparte, the potbellied Corsican who was about to proclaim himself emperor of France, and aimed right at the heart
of the Russian sovereign, Alexander I.

In 1804, the French leader had ordered the abduction and
subsequent execution of the Duke d'Enghien, a member of
France's deposed Bourbon dynasty. Alexander was appalled
that the base-born Bonaparte would dare lay hands on a per-

son of royal blood. Yet with Russia in no position to respond militarily to such "revolting high-handedness," all the emperor could do at the time was order a week's mourning for the murdered prince and erect a memorial cenotaph in St. Petersburg dedicated to the victim "of a Corsican Monster, the Terror of Europe, the Scourge of Mankind."

Alexander also issued a tepid protest. Napoleon's response, however, was anything but: Were the murderers of Emperor Paul ever arrested? he asked belligerently through his foreign minister, Talleyrand, while sharply reminding Alexander that France had never protested against *that* regicide and suggested the Russian emperor similarly restrain himself now.

The staggering punch was published in a widely read newspaper, which made excruciatingly public what had privately tormented Alexander since his father's murder three years before. Not only did Napoleon give lie to the official story that Paul had died of apoplexy; he also drew unwelcome attention to the fact that the dead emperor's son had stood by and allowed the killers to escape justice.

Thus, while Alexander I had politically opposed Bonaparte and his expansionism in Europe, the Russian emperor's opposition now became a personal vendetta against the man he described as "one of the most famous tyrants that history has produced."

The very idea of Napoleon in his assumed role of a royal personage offended Alexander, who, though educated with certain egalitarian principles, certainly knew what an emperor was. And the raw greed with which the Corsican upstart eyed his neighbors made him all the more odious. "This man is insatiable," the emperor exclaimed. "His ambition knows no bounds; he is the scourge of the world. He wants war, does he? Very well, he shall have it, and the sooner the better."

Though Russian interests were not directly compromised as Napoleon gobbled up neighboring territory, Alexander nevertheless allowed himself to be drawn into a coalition with Britain and Austria to halt his outsized ambitions. It was a moral imperative for the emperor; the first step in what he idealistically hoped would result in a harmonious union of civilized nations, where conflicts would be arbitrated to avoid bloodshed and "the sacred rights of humanity" would triumph. As historian Adam Zamoyski wrote, "He had assumed the role of knightly defender of a Christian monarchical tradition against the onslaught of the barbarism as represented by Napoleon." Plus, like any young man steeped in martial tradition and training—yet who had never seen war—the emperor longed to test his mettle in actual combat.

Napoleon, who saw no purpose or gain from war with Russia, tried to dissuade Alexander from the alliance, but the emperor was unmoved. In fact, in his haughty rejection of Bonaparte's peace overture, he addressed him as "the Head of the French Government," so insufferable did he find Napoleon's recent adoption of the imperial title. Yet while Alexander avoided addressing his adversary as *emperor,* he could not escape that quality most closely associated with Bonaparte: military genius. Soon enough, he would see it for himself at Austerlitz.

Proud and splendid, Alexander I rode out to confront his enemy at Wischau (now part of the Czech Republic) on November 25, 1805—the first Russian monarch to do so since Peter the Great. It was a minor victory for the Russians and their Austrian allies, who now became more convinced of their superiority. "We are certain of success," proclaimed the emperor's aide-de-camp, Peter Dolgoruky; "we have only to go forward, as we did at Wischau." But then, ten days later, came Austerlitz. It was an overwhelming rout, one that decimated the ranks and sent them fleeing for their lives. Twenty-five thousand soldiers were killed—"only a drop of blood" for Russia, as the Sardinian ambassador Joseph de Maistre noted—but one that devastated Alexander nonetheless. "A deep sorrow could be read on his face," General Alexis Ermolov said later; "the remnants of all the regiments were passing before him and he had tears in his eyes." Indeed, that evening the crushed sovereign, once so certain of victory, sat under a tree and sobbed.

Napoleon, meanwhile, was jubilant. "I have defeated the Austro-Russian Army commanded by two emperors," he crowed in a letter to his wife, Josephine. "The battle of Austerlitz is the finest of all I have fought." Invigorated by his triumph, which forced Austria out of the coalition and sent Alexander home in shame, Bonaparte gave no thought to peace. And therein victory was the seed of his ultimate destruction: All Europe was now aroused against him. Thus, as his biographer Alan Schom noted, "The Austerlitz campaign was to prove one of the greatest mistakes of his career."

The Napoleonic rampage through Europe continued. Soon after Austerlitz, he dissolved the centuries-old Holy Roman Empire in Germany and essentially took over most of it. Alexander watched in dismay, but with his army depleted and bled dry, there was little he could do except try to ensure the security of his own borders through flaccid negotiation.

"The Emperor is still the same," wrote his foreign minister; "fear and weakness are still at their height. We are afraid of everything, we are incapable of making a firm decision; it is even impossible to advise him, for fear that the advice will not be accepted.... He is a combination of weakness, uncertainty, terror, injustice, and incoherence that drives one to grief and despair."

But with a plea from the Prussian king, Frederick William III, Alexander I became more resolute. "Tell me, Sire, I beseech you," Frederick William wrote in August 1806, "if I may hope that your troops will remain within reach to come to my aid and if I may count on them in case of aggression." Though the Prussian king had proven to be an inconstant friend, allying with Napoleon after the Russian defeat at Austerlitz, Alexander gave his fellow sovereign all the assurances he needed to officially demand the removal of all French troops from his kingdom. Bonaparte, of course, responded with an invasion.

Prussia was quickly and easily subdued in October, its king and queen forced to flee. But now Alexander picked up Frederick William's broken sword. Having apparently learned little from his ignominious defeat at Austerlitz, the emperor's armies confronted Napoleon's first at Eylau—"It was not a battle but a slaughter," Bonaparte remarked—then at Friedland, where Alexander once again found himself defeated and humiliated by the enemy's superior forces.

"Sire," his brother Constantine said to him, "if you don't want to make peace with France, well, give a loaded pistol to each of your soldiers and ask them to blow their brains out! You will achieve the same result as you will obtain from another and final battle which will unfailingly open the gates of your empire to the French troops, who are experienced in combat and always victorious!"

Constantine's blunt assessment was conclusive: Alexander would have to come to terms with "the Corsican ogre." And he would do it face-to-face. The historic first meeting between the monarchs was a grandiose affair, just as Bonaparte intended it. A raft was set up in the middle of the Nieman River, upon which were two white tents, the larger of which was embellished on one side with the letter N and on the other side, A. The two sovereigns were rowed out to the raft from opposite banks of the river and, upon arrival, greeted each other heartily.

Physically, they were in vivid contrast: Alexander, tall and slender, with powdered chestnut hair and luminous blue eyes—the very portrait of grace and elegance, dressed in the resplendent green uniform of Peter the Great's own Preobrazhensky regiment. Beside him was the diminutive Bonaparte, only recently royal—coarse, rather pasty, with a protruding stomach and steely eyes. Yet it was he who held the upper hand; the military master who gradually seemed to entrance the Russian emperor.

While Alexander knew there was little he could do to preserve his unreliable ally Prussia, he believed that Napoleon simply wanted to be left alone to dominate central Europe, and, in exchange, would not interfere with Russia's ambitions at the expense of Turkey. To some extent, Bonaparte indicated as much. But as negotiations continued amid glittering festivities in the town of Tilsit, Napoleon, "by slow degrees . . . pulled the covers over to his own side of the bed," as biographer Henri Troyat wrote. Alexander was left to sign a rotten treaty that, among other conditions, hobbled Russia's expansion, left open the question of Polish hegemony, and, perhaps worst of all, obligated the tsar to participate in an economically ruinous blockade of British trade.

"Russia had been pushed into a loveless and unequal marriage with France," wrote Zamoyski, "and soon adopted the sullen resentment of the unhappy wife. Sooner or later, she would be unfaithful, and Napoleon would have to go to war again in order to bring her back to bed." But for the time being, the appearance of contentment was maintained as medals and honors were exchanged in ceremonious brotherhood.

Both emperors left Tilsit with conflicting impressions of the other. "My dear," Napoleon wrote to Josephine, "I have just seen the Emperor Alexander; I was very pleased with him; he is a very handsome, good young emperor; he is cleverer than commonly thought. . . . He is a hero out of a novel. He has all the manners of an agreeable Parisian." Later, though, he commented, "No one could have more intelligence than the Emperor Alexander, but I find that there is a piece missing in his character, and I cannot discover what it is."

Similarly, the Russian tsar made lauding public pronouncements about his erstwhile enemy. "I shall confess to you that no one ever had more prejudices against a person than I had against [him]," Alexander said to Napoleon's envoy, General Savary; "but after three-quarters of an hour of conversation with him, they all disappeared like a dream and I never remembered them, so deeply was I struck by what he said to me."

But dissembling was second nature to Alexander I. He needed peace with Napoleon, certainly, but he still cordially hated him. "Fortunately, with all his genius, Bonaparte has a vulnerable side," the emperor wrote to his mother: "It is vanity, and I have decided to sacrifice my pride for the salvation of the empire." And in a private message to the king of Prussia: "Have patience. We shall take back what we have lost. He will break his neck. In spite of all my demonstrations of friendship, and my external actions, at heart I am your friend and I hope to prove it to you by acts."

Still, no matter his secret motives, in the minds of his subjects Alexander had shaken hands with a monster. "The dissatisfaction with the Emperor is increasing, and the remarks one hears on all sides are frightening," reported the Swedish ambassador. "It is only too true . . . that in private gatherings and even in public assemblies there is often talk of a change of reign and that people so far forget their duty as to say that the whole male line of the reigning family should be proscribed."

The emperor's close advisor, Nicholas Novosiltsev, was so concerned about the mounting hostility that he dared whisper in Alexander's ear, "Sire, I must remind you of the fate of your father."

"Good heavens," the emperor responded, "I know, I see that, but what can I do against the destiny that is leading me?"

Alexander's wife, the gentle, lovely, and much-betrayed Empress Elizabeth, expressed grave reservations about her husband's apparent rapprochement with Napoleon. But what galled the empress even more was her own mother-in-law's fierce stance against Alexander's policy of appeasement.

"The Empress who, as a mother, should support and defend the interests of her son, from thoughtlessness, from pride (and certainly for no other reason, for she is incapable of evil intentions), has succeeded in becoming like a leader of an insurrection," Elizabeth reported to her mother; "all the malcontents, of whom there are a great number, rally around her, praising her to the skies, and never has she attracted so many people to Pavlovsk [the dowager empress's palace] as this year. I cannot express to you how indignant it makes me."*

The emperor hoped to distract the people from their outrage over his ill-received truce by expelling the Swedes from the Baltic, as Napoleon had suggested at Tilsit. ("The lovely ladies of St. Petersburg must not hear from their palaces the cannons of Sweden," the French emperor said at the time. "Sweden is your geographical enemy.") But even the annexation of Finland was greeted with indifference. And the question of Poland began to loom ever larger. Napoleon coveted it as a reconstituted kingdom under French control, but for Alexander, that would be an unthinkable hazard to Russia's border security. "Poland is the only question on which I shall never compromise," he declared. "The world is not big enough for us to reach an accommodation on the affairs of that country."

With relations unraveling yet again, a second meeting between the emperors was scheduled for September 1808, at Erfurt. It was what Alexander had to do to buy time. "There is no room for the two of us in Europe," he wrote to his sister. "Sooner or later, one of us will have to bow out." In the meantime, though, he had to appear amenable. Still, the prospect of another shameful accommodation horrified his mother. "Alexander, stay away from it!" she pleaded. "You will ruin

---

* While her son disdained all the ceremony and glitter of sovereignty, and opted to live quietly, his haughty, cold, and categorical mother, Dowager Empress Maria, reveled in her royal position. "The Empress Mother is the one who displays her imperial state," Savary reported to Talleyrand. "Every external honor, every homage is directed to that point. . . . The great personages of St. Petersburg are careful not to let two weeks pass without making an appearance at the Empress Mother's. [Empress] Elizabeth [Alexander's wife] almost never appears there, but the Emperor dines there three times a week and often sleeps there."

your empire and your family. Turn back, there is still time. Listen to the voice of honor, to the prayers and supplications of your mother. Stop, my child, my friend."

The emperor tried to reassure the dowager empress by explaining his rationale. "Let us not hasten to declare ourselves against him," he wrote; "we would run the risk of losing everything. Rather, let us appear to consolidate the alliance so as to lull him into a sense of security. Let us gain time and prepare. When the time comes, we shall look on serenely at Napoleon's downfall."

The encounter at Erfurt, once again arranged by Bonaparte, took on an entirely different tenor than at Tilsit, although with the same superficial cordiality. "I have much affection for the Emperor Napoleon and I shall prove it to him at every opportunity," Alexander said disingenuously to Marshal Jean Lannes, who greeted him. Then, with gritted teeth, the Russian tsar proceeded to play the part of Napoleon's willing ally. The emperors amicably dined together and showed each other every courtesy during the formal ceremonies of the summit meant to permanently bind them.* There was even a bit of fraternal bonding one night at a theatrical performance, when the randy Russian emperor showed particular interest in the "actress" Antoinette Bourgoin, known as "the goddess of joy and pleasures."

"I do not advise you to make advances to her," Napoleon warned.

"You think she would refuse?" Alexander responded.

---

* Napoleon's courtesy did not extend to the monarchs of the various German kingdoms he now controlled. Indeed, they were treated as mere ornaments. During one formal dinner, King Maximilian Joseph raised his voice a little too loud for the French emperor, who snapped, "Hold your tongue, King of Bavaria!"

"Oh no!" said the French emperor. "But tomorrow the post leaves, and in five days all Paris would know the details of Your Majesty's figure from head to toe.... And then, I take an interest in your health. So I hope you will be able to resist temptation."

Beneath the bonhomie, however, Napoleon found a far more intractable Alexander than he expected. With urgent business in rebellious Spain (which Bonaparte had annexed), the French emperor was eager to secure the Russian tsar's promise that he would fight with his forces if Austria became aggressive during his absence. Alexander hedged. "Emperor Alexander is as stubborn as a mule," Bonaparte exclaimed in frustration. "He plays deaf to whatever he doesn't want to hear. This confounded business in Spain is costing me dear!"

At one point Napoleon became so irate that he threw his hat down on the floor and stomped on it. "You are violent, I am stubborn," Alexander remarked coolly in response to the tantrum. "So anger will get you nowhere with me. Let us talk, let us reason, or I shall leave."

While the French emperor insisted on Russian assistance with Austria, Alexander had a few demands of his own—not the least of which was France's evacuation of Prussia. Napoleon was stunned: "Is it my friend, my ally who proposes that I abandon the only position from which I can threaten Austria's flank if she attacks me while my troops are in southern Europe, four hundred leagues from home? . . . It is a system of weakness that you are proposing to me. If I agree to it, Europe will soon be treating me like a little boy."

It was during these tense negotiations that Alexander was secretly approached by Napoleon's recently resigned foreign minister, Talleyrand, who seemed to have treason on his mind. "Sire," he said, "what did you come here for? It is up to you to save Europe, and you will succeed in doing that only if you hold your ground against Napoleon. The French people are civilized, their sovereign is not. The sovereign of Russia is civilized, his people are not. The sovereign of Russia should therefore be the ally of the French people. The Rhine, the Alps, the Pyrenees are conquests of France. The rest is the conquest of the Emperor, France doesn't care about it."[*]

Talleyrand's confidence reassured Alexander that his position was stronger than anyone, especially Napoleon, believed. An agreement was reached, and though it provided for Russia's assistance against a bellicose Austria, the tsar really had no intention of ever fighting his former ally. "Bonaparte claims that I am only a fool," he wrote to his sister. "He laughs best who laughs last. As for me, I place all my hope in God."

With false promises made, the summit was concluded as genially as it began. "Everything is going well," a placated Napoleon wrote to Josephine. "I am pleased with Alexander. He must be pleased with me! If he were a woman, I think I would make him my sweetheart."

But since Alexander was most decidedly not a woman, Napoleon was determined to make the tsar's sister his wife. He informed the Russian emperor of his plan to repudiate his wife, Josephine, "so as to consolidate his work and found his dynasty." Marriage to a Russian grand duchess would give the next generation of Bonapartes the perfect royal pedigree. To avoid such a calamity, the emperor's sister Catherine was hur-

---

[*] There had long been concerns in France that Napoleon was too intoxicated by power and ambition. "The Emperor is mad, completely mad," Minister of the Navy Denis Decrès declared; "he'll bring ruin upon himself and upon us all."

riedly engaged to the Duke of Oldenburg. He was not particularly attractive, but then anybody would be better than the odious Corsican.

Not to be deterred, Napoleon simply proposed that a younger sister, Anne, become his bride—never mind that she was only thirteen. Dowager Empress Maria was understandably aghast at the prospect of her little girl replacing "the whore" Josephine in Napoleon's bed. Yes, it would be dangerous for Russia to deny Napoleon his underage prize. But so be it.

Though Alexander tried to soften the blow of his rejection by assuring Napoleon the matter could be revisited when Anne actually hit puberty, the French emperor wasn't fooled. And the insult he felt was only aggravated by the lavish wedding of his first choice, Catherine, to the Prince of Oldenburg—a celebration that included his vanquished enemies, the king and queen of Prussia. Bonaparte would get his revenge by eventually attacking Oldenburg. "It's like a public insult," exclaimed Alexander, "a slap in the face of a friendly power." Plus, Napoleon never bothered to wait for Anne— which, though a relief, was also a slap at Russian honor. Instead, he married Marie Louise of Austria, which prompted the Prince de Ligne to quip, "Austria has sacrificed a beautiful heifer to the Minotaur."

But these marital travails became insignificant after Austria declared war on France in 1809. By the terms of the treaty signed at Erfurt, Alexander was now obligated to aid his enemy. And he made every effort to pretend to do so. "If you make a move, I will march [on France's side]," the emperor warned the Austrian envoy Prince Schwarzenberg, in what was really a bit of theater. "You will set fire to Europe and you will fall victim to that fire."

Privately, though, Alexander was far more conciliatory. "The Emperor assured me that nothing would be neglected that was humanly possible to think of to avoid striking blows at us," Schwarzenberg reported; "he added that his position was so strange that although we found ourselves in opposite camps, he could not help wishing for our success."

The tsar proved good to his word, if not to Napoleon, then to the Austrians. His forces barely touched theirs in the ensuing battles. "I am loath to accuse the Russian generals of such perfidy," Prince Poniatowski reported to Napoleon, "but I cannot conceal from Your Majesty that there is perfect concert between them and the enemy." Russia's limp partnership did little to hamper the French, however, and Austria was decisively crushed. "You have been colorless," Napoleon ranted at Count Nicholas Rumiantsev. "The saber was not drawn a single time."

The spoils of victory were commensurate with Russia's efforts in the conflict. The French emperor tossed his "ally" a scrap of territory in Poland. "Napoleon has humiliated Alexander," wrote the journalist Nicholas Gretsch, "by giving him, out of the lands taken from Austria, not some province but 400,000 souls, the way our tsars used to reward their accomplices." Worse, Alexander's greatest fear was realized when Poland was almost entirely reconstituted under French protection. And despite Napoleon's empty assurances that he was ready to "eliminate the words *Poland* and *Poles* not only from all political transactions, but also from history," Russia's vital buffer from invasion was breached.

A decisive clash was now all but inevitable. Simply put, Bonaparte could not afford to retreat and leave his conquered territories exposed, and Alexander could not tolerate having him so close by. Thus both emperors prepared for the war neither really wanted. But first there was posturing on both sides. Napoleon later admitted that they had got themselves "into the position of two blustering braggarts who, having no wish to fight each other, seek to frighten each other."

"Before two months are out, Alexander will sue for peace," the French emperor confidently declared. "A shattering blow dealt at the heart of the empire on Moscow the great, Moscow the holy, will deliver me in one instant that whole blind and helpless mass." The Russian tsar was equally belligerent. "If once the war be fairly entered upon," he told the French ambassador, "one of us—either he, Napoleon, or I, Alexander, must lose our crown."

Napoleon's threatening presence actually had the effect of buoying the once-wavering Russian emperor. "Irresolute at first, he would let himself be driven back and forth between opposite solutions for a long time," wrote his biographer Henri Troyat; "then, like a marble that has found a groove, he would never deviate from his path. It was as if his stubbornness were the natural consequence of the difficulty he had experienced in coming to a decision. His strength was born of weakness, his persistence was the result of previous vacillation."

Alexander had no illusions about what war would bring. "It is going to cause torrents of blood to flow," he said, "and poor humanity is going to be sacrificed again to the ambition of a man who seems to have been created for its misfortune." But he was ready. Napoleon, on the other hand, seemed somewhat less certain on the eve of his invasion. "The Emperor, who was ordinarily so gay and so full of ardor at times when his troops were executing a major maneuver, remained very serious and preoccupied for the rest of the day," reported Napoleon's close advisor (and former ambassador to Russia) Armand de Caulaincourt. Some interpreted his somber mood as a foreboding of disasters to come. But none could have possibly imagined just how dreadful the Russian expedition would be.

On June 24, 1812, Napoleon made his fateful passage across the Nieman River into Russian territory. It was his long-dreaded declaration of war. But there would be no battle. Alexander's troops had amassed around the Lithuanian town of Vilna, but given Bonaparte's surprise crossing and the vast size of his Grande Armée, a tactical decision was made to burn Vilna and retreat. Bonaparte was about to receive a foretaste of what was to come in Mother Russia.

"Six hundred thousand men of all the European nations politically subject to Napoleon were marching in two columns, without stores, without rations, in a country [Lithuania] impoverished by the continental system [blockade] and only recently ruined by heavy requisitions," wrote Countess Tiesenhausen. "In the town and in the countryside, unheard of disorders. Churches looted, the sacred vessels, even the cemeteries were not respected, the unfortunate women outraged. . . . The looters were shot [by order of Napoleon]. They went to execution with incredible insouciance, their little pipes in their mouths. What difference did it make to them if they died now or later. . . . The army had been without bread for three days. At Vilna they gave the soldiers bread that was not properly kneaded or baked, a kind of biscuit; there was no fodder for the cavalry, and they fed the horses with wheat cut in the fields at the end of June. They were dying like flies and their carcasses were thrown in the river."

And so it went for the rest of the summer as Bonaparte's

Grande Armée plunged deeper and deeper into the heart of Russia—either finding ruined villages and scorched fields in their path, or leaving them in their wake. Nature did the rest.

"The heat in this part of the world at this time of year is nothing like the heat of southern Europe," wrote one French soldier. "It was not just the heat of the sun we had to bear, but the vapors emanating from the baking earth. Our horses kicked up a cloud of burning sand as fine as dust, with which we were so covered that it would have been difficult to distinguish the color of our uniforms. This sand, which got into our eyes, subjected us to excruciating pain."

And still, other than a few skirmishes and a fruitless assault on the fortress town of Smolensk,* the French soldiers had yet to engage decisively in the arena that most favored them: the battlefield. Indeed, all they encountered was a perpetual Russian retreat. "This is no way to fight," one disaffected Georgian prince exclaimed. "We are going to lead them to the very gates of Moscow."

In fact, it was outside Moscow, around the town of Borodino, that the fleeing Russian bear finally bared its claws. It was a vicious, bloody battle, after which both sides claimed victory. "My dear," Napoleon wrote his new wife, Marie Louise, "I write you from the battlefield of Borodino. Yesterday I beat the Russians, their whole army. . . . The battle was hot . . . I had many killed and wounded." At the same time the Russian commander Prince Michael Kutuzov was reporting to

---

* Virtually nothing was accomplished by the assault on Smolensk, which the Russians abandoned and burned, except utter annihilation. "One had to walk over debris, dead bodies and skeletons which had been burned and charred by fire," recalled a French officer. "Everywhere unfortunate inhabitants, on their knees, weeping over the ruins of their homes, cats and dogs wandering about and howling in the most heart-rendering way, everywhere only death and destruction."

his wife, "I am well, my dear, and I am not beaten: I have won the battle with Bonaparte."

But if the Battle of Borodino itself was not conclusive, the aftermath was. Rather than engage the enemy again, Kutuzov decided to abandon one of Russia's proudest, most sacred cities. "You are afraid of the retreat through Moscow," he told his associates, "but for my part I consider it providential, because it will save the army. Napoleon is like a torrent that we cannot yet stop. Moscow will be the sponge that absorbs it. . . . I feel that I shall have to pay the piper, but I sacrifice myself for the good of my country. I order retreat." That night Kutuzov could be heard quietly weeping in his bed.

A massive exodus from the old capital commenced, reducing the population of Moscow from 250,000 to 15,000—mostly invalids, wounded soldiers, and freed prisoners. The Grande Armée then poured in, mixing freely with the looters and scavengers who remained. "Soldiers, *vivandieres* [women attached to French regiments], convicts, and prostitutes ran through the streets," recorded Captain Eugene Labaume, "entered the deserted palaces and snatched everything that could gratify their greed. Some covered themselves with stuffs woven of gold or silk; others put over their shoulders, without choice or discernment, the most highly prized furs; many covered themselves with women's and children's pelisses, and even the convicts hid their rags beneath court garments. The rest, flocking to the cellars, broke down the doors and drinking the most precious wines, staggered off with their immense booty."

Within a short time, the great city, built mostly of wood, was in flames. Some believed the Russians started the fires themselves, to obliterate anything useful to the enemy; others said it was the Antichrist, Bonaparte himself, who created the apocalypse. The inferno raged for days, and the eerie red glow it produced could be seen for miles around; the sound was like a hurricane. "It was the most grand, the most sublime, and the most terrific sight the world has ever beheld," Napoleon reminisced.

"So now the horde of barbarians is lodged in the ruins of that beautiful capital," Empress Elizabeth wrote to her mother. "They acted there as they have done everywhere else. Our people began to set fire to the object of all their affections rather than let it fall undamaged into the hands of the enemy, and the *great nation* [the French] will not stop sacking, looting, and destroying so long as there is anything left to destroy. In the meantime, our army has gone around Moscow and is posted in the vicinity of the road by which the enemy came and is already beginning to disrupt his communications. When Napoleon entered Moscow he found nothing of what he hoped for. He was counting on a public, there no longer was one, everyone had left; he was counting on resources, he found almost nothing; he was counting on the moral effect, the discouragement and prostration he would cause the nation, he has only aroused rage and the desire for vengeance.... Every step that [Napoleon] takes in Russia brings him nearer to the abyss. We shall see how he endures the winter!"

While there may have been a tactical advantage in sacrificing Moscow, for many it was as if the very soul of the nation had been ripped out. "I regard Russia as lost forever," Rostopchin wrote to his wife. And in their agony and grief, the people blamed their emperor. Roxanne Stourdza, a lady-in-waiting to Empress Elizabeth, witnessed the dark mood when she accompanied Alexander to the celebration of his coronation anniversary in St. Petersburg:

"Our windowed carriages moved slowly through the immense crowd whose very silence and angry faces contrasted with the festive occasion. So long as I live I shall never forget the moment when we ascended the steps of the cathedral, between two ranks of common people who uttered not a single cheer. One could have heard the sound of our footsteps, and I have never doubted that one spark would have been enough, at that moment, to produce a general conflagration. A glance at the Emperor told me what was going on in his mind and I felt my knees buckle under me."

"You are openly accused of having brought disaster upon your empire," the emperor's sister Catherine wrote to him, "of having caused general ruin and the ruin of private individuals, lastly, of having lost the honor of the country and your own personal honor. . . . You need not fear a catastrophe of the revolutionary sort, no! But I leave it to you to judge the state of affairs in a country whose leader is despised. . . . The idea of peace, fortunately, is not widespread; far from it, for the feeling of shame following the loss of Moscow gives rise to the desire for revenge."

"Of course there are things that it is impossible to imagine," Alexander responded. "But be persuaded that my resolve to struggle is more unshakable than ever; I should rather cease to be what I am than compromise with the monster who is the curse of the world. . . . I place my hope in God, in the admirable character of our nation, and in my steadfast determination not to bow under the yoke."

Meanwhile, Bonaparte brooded in the Kremlin, hoping for some change in fortune. After all his efforts, he possessed only a ruined city, surrounded by enemies, and without supplies. "Suddenly Napoleon felt as if in Russia he was faced with another Spain," Troyat wrote, "this one gigantic, fierce, Asiatic, polar." Still, he somehow had to save face; his ego absolutely demanded it. But that could only come with an accommodation from the Russian emperor. "I want peace, I need peace, I must have peace!" he insisted to one of his emissaries. "Just save my honor." Alexander, however, had lost too much to even consider his adversary's increasingly desperate entreaties.

"All the news that you will receive from me, all my exhortations, all the ukases [imperial orders] addressed to you, in a word everything convinces you of my firm resolve," the emperor wrote to Kutuzov: "at the present time no proposal from the enemy will persuade me to cease combat and, by so doing, to fail the sacred obligation to avenge the offended motherland."

There was perhaps no concept as alien to Napoleon Bonaparte as retreat. Through years of glorious campaigns and conquests, he rarely had to face it. Now, just four months after crossing the Nieman, the ignominious prospect he had long avoided became his only option. So, on October 23, 1812, Bonaparte marched out of the remnants of Moscow to face his doom.

"God, my Creator, You have heard our prayers at last!" exclaimed Kutuzov. "From this moment, Russia is saved!"

Winter, the greatest weapon in Russia's arsenal, was on its way. And the wrath of an outraged populace would aid its lethal scourge. For the once-grande Armée, Russia became, in the words of one, "this enormous tomb." In all, 400,000 soldiers died; 100,000 more were taken prisoner. Some of those who managed to survive recounted the horror of that unforgiving retreat: tales of frozen bodies, half eaten by wolves, of menacing peasants quick to torture, of starvation so severe that dung became nourishment.

"We continued to advance without knowing where our

steps were taking us," one French soldier wrote. "A raging storm drove in our faces the snow that was falling out of the sky in large flakes, together with that which it swept up from the ground, and seemed to desire with all its might to oppose our progress. The horses could no longer move forward over the frozen ground and collapsed; the convoys and, for the first time, the cannon remained behind for lack of teams to draw them. The route over which the Grande Armée was hurrying to Smolensk was strewn with frozen corpses. But the snow had soon covered them like an immense shroud, and little mounds, like the tombs of the ancients, showed us only faint traces of our buried comrades in arms."

Even after Napoleon recrossed the Nieman, the conflict between emperors was still not over. Alexander had sworn that only one of them would end up with a crown. And so it came to be: The Russian tsar was hailed in Paris as Europe's liberator, while the Corsican ogre he pursued to the last ended up a permanent resident of Elba.

Chapter 10

___

Nicholas I (1825–1855):

"A Condescending Jupiter"

The emperor of Russia is a military commander,
and each of his days is a day of battle.

—Grand Duke Constantine, brother of Nicholas I

The childless Alexander I was succeeded not by the legal heir, his brother Constantine, who rejected the crown, but by his next younger brother, Nicholas. The new emperor was an impressive sight indeed. "Colossal in stature," as one American observer described him; "with a face such as one finds on a Greek coin . . . he bore himself like a god." But behind this "regular Jupiter . . . every inch a king," as another called him, lurked a trembling despot, terrified of losing control. His was a look of "worried severity," the Frenchman Astolphe de Custine wrote. And it was those two essential qualities—fear and ferocity—that defined the sovereign who would rule Russia for three decades with the absolute repression he believed was essential to his survival. "If the Emperor has no more of mercy in his heart than he reveals in his policies, then I pity Russia," Custine wrote; "if, on the other hand, his true sentiments are really superior to his acts, then I pity the Emperor."

Crime and Punishment had yet to be written; the same was true of The Brothers Karamazov. And on a bitter cold December day in 1849, it appeared they never would. For it was then that the author of these future literary classics happened to be facing a firing squad. Fyodor Dostoevsky had taken a grave risk in meeting regularly with a group of fellow artists and intellectuals who freely expressed their thoughts on a variety of subjects, including the abject condition of the Russian serf. Such indulgences were downright dangerous during the repressive regime of Tsar Nicholas I, when strict adherence to the official doctrine of "Orthodoxy, Autocracy, Nationality" was required of all the emperor's subjects.

Having dared stray beyond this narrowly proscribed creed with their political discussions, the members of Dostoevsky's circle were denounced as subversives and duly arrested. Then, after enduring eight months of harsh imprisonment and interrogation at the Peter and Paul Fortress, the novelist and twenty other freethinkers in his circle were sentenced to death.

On the appointed day, the condemned were taken to the place of execution at Semenovsky Square, where three stakes had been erected for the occasion. "The horrible, immeasurably horrible minutes of awaiting death began," Dostoevsky wrote. "It was cold, so terribly cold. They removed not only our coats, but our jackets. And it was minus twenty degrees."

As Dostoevsky and the others stood shivering upon a black-draped scaffold awaiting their fate, the condemned men of the first group were tied to the stakes and hoods placed over their heads. "We were taken in threes," the writer recalled. "I was in the second group. I had no more than a minute left to live." Yet just as the firing squad raised their rifles and took aim, a sudden reprieve came from the emperor. Rather than a lethal lesson in the perils of independent thought, it was a cruel charade with the same message, orchestrated by Nicholas himself.

"I received the news of the termination of the execution dully," Dostoevsky remembered. "There was no joy at returning to the living. People around me were shouting and making noise. But I didn't care. I had already lived through the worst. Yes, the very worst. Wretched Grigoryev went mad.... How did the others survive? I don't know. We didn't even catch cold."

It was only after being returned to his prison cell that Dostoevsky came to fully embrace the joy of having his life restored—even though he now faced four years of hard labor in Siberia, followed by a forced induction into the army. He was alive. And Russian literature would be far richer for it. Others, however, were not so fortunate.

The nearly three-decade reign of Nicholas I was inaugurated in bloodshed when, in 1825, what became known as the Decembrist Rebellion was decisively crushed on the very first day of the new emperor's rule. Five of the rebel leaders were subsequently hanged, while numerous others—including members of Russia's most ancient noble families—were condemned to eke out whatever meager existence they could in the frozen Siberian wastelands. It was a fitting launch to the tsar's totalitarian regime, the likes of which would not be seen again until Stalin held sway less than a century later.

"Here everything is oppressed; cowering in fear," wrote Custine, the French observer of Nicholas's Russia; "everything is grim, silent, and blindly obedient to the invisible rod."

Every Russian was considered the emperor's slave—from the lowliest serf to the grandest nobleman—and with that came the requirement of total submission to the imperial will.

In the midst of a modernizing world, Nicholas I reinvigorated an autocracy reminiscent of Ivan the Terrible. He ruthlessly established himself as the sole font of authority, answerable to no one but God. "Everything must proceed from here," the emperor declared while pointing to his breast.

The Enlightenment that swept through the rest of Europe with its odious concepts concerning the rights of man would not infect Russia. Nicholas made certain of that. As Dostoevsky and countless others discovered, free expression was strictly forbidden and censorship elevated to an art. Indeed, the tsar himself spent endless hours poring over books, plays, and periodicals, searching for anything that might smell of subversion. And with the emperor's brutally efficient secret police force, complemented by a vast network of informers, ordinary Russians could never escape the feeling that invisible eyes and ears were everywhere. "They're in my soup!" one contemporary exclaimed.

With his imposing stature, refined classical profile, and a regal glare that one observer noted "had the quality of a rattlesnake to freeze the blood in your veins," Nicholas I looked every inch the autocrat. "Virgil's Neptune," Custine called him;[*] "one could not be more emperor than he." Yet beneath the godlike bearing that awed all who encountered him, Nicholas was a churning mass of anxiety and paranoia—the demons that drove him to rule with such unswerving ferocity.

---

[*] "He cannot smile at the same time with his eyes and his mouth," Custine also noted; "a disharmony which denotes perpetual constraint." The essayist Alexander Herzen was one of many others who commented on the emperor's eyes, which he described as "entirely without warmth, without a trace of mercy, wintry eyes."

"Nicholas I's insistence on firmness and stern action was based on fear, not confidence," wrote his biographer Nicholas Riasanovsky; "his determination concealed a state approaching panic, and his courage fed on something akin to despair."

The neuroses that plagued Nicholas may have had something to do with the fact that he was just four when his father, Emperor Paul, was murdered with the complicity of his older brother, Alexander, and he was left with an imperious mother who cared little for him.* The traumatized little boy was consigned to the care of his tutor, Count M. I. Lamsdorf, who was, as Nicholas later related, something less than nurturing:

"Count Lamsdorf instilled in us only the feeling of fear; such fear and certainty of his omnipotence, in fact, that our mother assumed only secondary importance in our understanding. This arrangement deprived us completely of any filial confidence in our mother, into whose presence we were rarely admitted alone and then, only as if some sort of sentence was being passed upon us. Incessant changes in the personnel of our entourage instilled in us from our earliest childhood the habit of searching for weakness in them in order to turn them to our advantage. . . . Fear, and efforts to escape punishments, occupied my mind more than anything else."

Fireworks, thunder, and cannons all frightened the emotionally deprived child, who often lashed out with an impotent rage at those around him. "Whatever happened to him,"

---

* Count Benckendorff, a close associate, wrote of Empress Maria: "Demanding of herself she was also demanding of her subordinates; always tireless, she did not favor them if they appeared tired; finally, loving sincerely and constantly those to whom she had deigned to give her friendship or whom she patronized because of the inclination of her heart or of her mind, she demanded from them complete reciprocity. The only failing of this extraordinary woman was her being excessively, one may say, exacting of her children and of the people dependent on her."

an observer reported, "whether he fell down, or hurt himself, or whether he believed that his wishes remained unfulfilled and that he was insulted, he would immediately use abusive words, hack with his little axe the drum and other toys, break them, and beat his playmates with a stick or with anything else at hand, even though he loved them very much, and had a particularly passionate attachment to his younger brother [Michael]."

The only comfort the young man seemed to find as he grew older was in rigid military discipline. Like his father (Paul) and grandfather (Peter III) before him, Nicholas delighted in constant drilling, designing uniforms, and inflicting punishment for the slightest infraction. A true martinet, he was thoroughly despised by the men serving under him. But for Nicholas, the military was a means of regimenting the chaos that would otherwise consume him.

"Here [in the army] there is order," he wrote, "there is a strict unconditional legality, no impertinent claims to know all the answers, no contradiction, all things flow logically one from the other; no one commands before he has himself learned to obey; no one steps in front of anybody else without lawful reason; everything is subordinated to one definite goal, everything has its purpose. That is why I shall always hold in honor the calling of a soldier. I consider the entire human life to be merely service, because everybody serves."

It was this concept of rigid harmony—of service and obedience, without question—that Nicholas I sought to impose on his subjects. "The emperor of Russia is a military commander," wrote his brother Constantine, "and each of his days is a day of battle."

Nicholas was never supposed to be emperor, at least according to the strict law of inheritance enacted by his father.[*] The childless Alexander I should have been succeeded by Nicholas's older brother Constantine, but the legal heir, then serving as the military governor of occupied Poland, had renounced his claim years before.[†] It was at that time Alexander named his second younger brother as his heir in a secret manifesto that he immediately had stashed away—perhaps with the intention of destroying the document should Constantine ever reconsider. Nicholas, who had never been prepared for the role of sovereign and was perfectly content imposing his will as a military commander, was horrified to learn that his future had now been inexorably altered. He later described his feelings:

"My wife and I remained in a position which I can liken only to that sensation that would strike a man if he were going calmly along a road sown with flowers and with marvelous scenery on all sides when, suddenly, an abyss yawns wide beneath his feet, and an irresistible force draws him into it, without allowing him to step back or turn aside."

The secrecy that had surrounded the altered succession proved to be most problematic when Alexander I died in 1825. Most Russians assumed that Constantine would be the next emperor. Further complicating matters, Nicholas himself swore fealty to his brother. He had been warned by the

[*] Peter the Great had once decreed that the sovereign could name an heir of his own choosing. A century later, Emperor Paul altered the law to limit the succession only to the monarch's oldest male son. Women were barred entirely from ever again inheriting the crown.

[†] In renouncing the crown, Constantine reportedly declared that he would be pleased to serve as the sovereign's "second valet; just not to be tsar on the throne."

military governor of St. Petersburg that a conspiracy to over-throw the government had been festering for some time among certain officers of the Guard, and that the hatred they felt for "martinet Nicholas" could very well precipitate a rebellion should he take the crown.

All too familiar with the fate of his forebears at the whim of the Guard—including the murder of both his father and grandfather—Nicholas was more than amenable to ceding the dangerous throne back to his older brother, the legal heir. Unfortunately, Constantine remained firm in his earlier renunciation. "My previous intention is immutable," he declared in a message from Warsaw. Now Nicholas was stuck. "Pray to God for me," he wrote to his sister. "Take pity on your wretched brother, victim of the Will of God and his two brothers."

The confusion surrounding the succession—when the oath of allegiance was sworn first to Constantine then almost immediately switched to Nicholas—afforded the rebel Guards officers and their followers an ideal opportunity to strike. And on December 26, 1825, the first day of Nicholas I's reign, they did. Fueled by fiery speeches and abundant amounts of vodka, they swept into the heart of St. Petersburg and amassed at Senate Square. The rebels were belligerent enough to call for the restoration of Constantine and the adoption of a constitution, but not yet cohesive enough to take definitive action. This gave the frightened new emperor valuable time to gather reinforcements and weigh his options from the nearby Winter Palace.

Hoping to distract a crowd that had gathered in front of the palace from joining the nascent rebellion at the square, Nicholas appeared before them and read aloud the late emperor's succession manifesto. It was then, in what the tsar later described as "the most terrible moment," that a mass of soldiers rushed toward his home to take it over, "and in case of resistance to destroy our entire family." The precarious situation was only defused when the sudden appearance of loyal Guards behind the emperor persuaded the menacing rebels to scurry back to their comrades.

In an effort to quell the mounting unrest, a succession of generals was sent to Senate Square to reason with the agitated men and persuade them to return to their barracks. Not one of them was successful. In fact, one general, a hero of the Napoleonic Wars, was slaughtered on the spot. The head of the Orthodox Church and the emperor's younger brother Michael also failed in their missions. Even a personal overture from the tsar himself was violently rejected. "They shot at me," Nicholas recalled; "the bullet flew over my head and fortunately no one was wounded. The laborers of St. Isaac's [a cathedral under construction nearby] began tossing lumber at us over the fencing."

At a time when the tsar was still considered God's representative on earth, taking shots at him in a public space was a sure sign that the rebels had abandoned all reason. The Russian author and historian Nicholas Karamzin was sickened by the events he witnessed that day, writing, "Is Peter's city really going to fall into the hands of three thousand half-drunken soldiers, mad officers, and the mob?"

By the time evening approached it was clear that some drastic action would have to be taken. "I had to make the decision to put a swift end to this," Nicholas wrote; "otherwise the mob might join the rebels and then the [loyal] troops surrounded by the mob would be in the most difficult circumstances." A bloody clash seemed inevitable.

"Your Majesty, there is nothing to be done," announced Adjutant General Vasilchikov. "We need grapeshot!"

"Do you want me to spill the blood of my subjects on the very first day of my reign?" said the emperor.

"In order to save your empire," replied Vasilchikov.

Nicholas's mother, Dowager Empress Maria, was appalled by the prospect. "Oh, my God!" she cried. "What will Europe say about us! My son is ascending the throne in blood!"

But for all that, Nicholas knew what he had to do. Even as a ten-year-old boy, he had written of King Louis XVI's stupidity in failing to crush his rebellious subjects while he still had the chance. And Louis ended up with his head sliced off. There would be no similar revolution in Russia—the force of cannon would ensure that. The end came that night as scores of Decembrists fell under fire and the rest fled. A massive roundup of the rebel leaders followed, with Nicholas himself conducting the interrogations. Then there were the reprisals. In a gleeful twist of the knife, the emperor left it to one of the leading liberals of his late brother's reign to pronounce the death sentences.

"Dear, dear Constantine," Nicholas wrote to his older brother. "Your will has been done: I am Emperor, but, my God, at what a price! At the price of my subjects' blood!"

The new emperor emerged from the Decembrist revolt like a frightened and angry bull after finally managing to gore its tormenting matador. And as he cast about his ferocious glare in search of any further challenges to his might, all of Russia trembled.

Like his revered predecessor Peter the Great, Nicholas I meant to transform Russia. Not with an eye toward the West, however, but far, far away from its pernicious influences—back to a time when the tsar ruled supreme over blindly obedient subjects with no concept of personal liberty. "Only autocracy corresponds to the spirit of the Russian people," he declared. And only Nicholas seemed to possess the qualities to impose it.

"No one was better created for the role of autocrat," wrote Anna Tyutcheva, one of the empress's ladies-in-waiting. "His impressive handsomeness, regal bearing, and severe Olympic profile—everything down to his smile of a condescending Jupiter, breathed earthly deity. There was something solemn and reverential in the palace air. People spoke in hushed tones and were slightly bowed . . . in order to appear more obliging . . . everything was imbued with the presence of the lord."

The emperor was a jealous god who insisted upon ruling alone. Gone were the days of powerful ministers and influential favorites that every monarch since Peter the Great kept close to them. "I don't need smart men; I need loyal ones," insisted Nicholas, who was equitable only in the sense that he believed *all* men were beneath him. The tsar personally controlled every aspect of government—from foreign policy to the fight against cholera—as he deemed himself the only one capable of doing so. "You should know that I have neither a mind nor a will," wrote one official. "I am merely a blind tool of the emperor's will."

Perhaps the only man who wielded any real influence in Nicholas's government was Sergei Uvarov, who formulated the official creed of "Orthodoxy, Autocracy, Nationality"—the holy trinity of despotic Russia. As minister of education, Uvarov was charged with a rather simple task: to keep the people stupid. "If I can extend Russia's childhood another fifty years I will consider my mission accomplished," he declared.

An ignorant population was a docile one, which is why the emperor was incensed to learn that in one instance a potential constitution, formulated during his brother's reign, had been printed in Poland. "The publication of this paper is most annoying," he wrote to Prince Paskevich in Warsaw. "Out of one hundred of our young officers [stationed in Poland] ninety will read it, will fail to understand it or will scorn it, but ten will retain it in their memory, will discuss it—and, the most important point, will not forget it. This worries me above everything else. This is why I wish so much that the guards be kept in Warsaw as briefly as possible. Order Count Witt to try to obtain as many copies of this booklet as he can and to destroy them, also to find the manuscript and send it to me."

The emperor made it his personal task to suppress any publication that might give his subjects the absurd idea that they were free to choose their own destinies. Literature and newspapers were thoroughly scrutinized, often by the tsar himself, and even ellipses used to replace censored text were forbidden lest the reader "fall into the temptation of thinking about the possible contents of the banned part." Writers suffered immeasurably under Nicholas, and any who dared stray from the official doctrine were usually branded as criminally insane. This designation, rather than imprisonment, was a means of silencing voices forever, as it was thought no one would listen to the ravings of a lunatic.

Alexander Nikitenko, a former serf elevated to the position of censor, was also a freethinker who sought, as he wrote, "to give secret aid to literature." "At first we feverishly wanted to be heard," Nikitenko recorded in his diary, a vivid account of that repressive era. "But when we saw that they were not fooling with us; that our talent and intelligence were doomed to grow torpid and rot at the bottom of our souls ... that any bright thought was a crime against the social order, when, in a word, we were told that educated people were pariahs in our society, and that ... a soldier's discipline was considered the only principle—then our entire young generation became morally depleted."

And that's just the way Nicholas liked it. "I've cut them once and for all from interfering in my work," he gloated. But it wasn't enough just to stifle writers and intellectuals. The emperor aimed to control all of his subjects. He managed this with the help of his secret police, or Third Department, along with an army of informants eager to curry favor. "With Germanic tenacity and precision," the essayist Alexander Herzen wrote, "Nicholas tightened the noose of the Third Department around the neck of Russia."

As with every other aspect of governing, however, the emperor was not content to leave all the surveillance to the Third Department. He made himself appear omnipresent by ceaselessly traveling all over Russia to observe things for himself. "Fifteen days have now passed since I left you," Nicholas wrote to his wife, Empress Alexandra, "but I have seen and done much. We are not wasting our time. This manner of traveling, when one can bear it, is really good, because one sees everything, and they never know when or where I am going to arrive. They expect me everywhere, and if anything is not well, they at least try to make it so."

The emperor's unannounced pop-ins often proved traumatizing to those unfortunate enough to receive them—like the administrators of one high school. Nicholas strode into a classroom and saw that one of the best and brightest students was leaning on his elbow as he listened to a history lecture. The instructor was instantly dismissed on the emperor's orders for allowing such a gross breach of discipline. Then, upon encountering another such egregious incident, Nicholas personally fired the school principal.

And still the tsar wasn't finished with the school. He returned unexpectedly on another occasion, and Alexander Nikitenko recorded what ensued: "The sovereign arrived angry, went everywhere, asked about everything, with the obvious intention of finding something wrong. He did not like the face of one of the pupils.—'What sort of an ugly . . . mug is this!' he exclaimed, looking at him with fury. In conclusion he told the director:

"'Yes, in appearance you have everything in order, but what mugs your pupils possess! The First High School must be first in everything: they have not that vivacity, that fullness, that nobility which distinguishes, for instance, the pupils of the Fourth High School!'"

Nicholas's wrath was not limited to people who displeased him, but inanimate objects as well. In 1829, the warship *Raphael* surrendered in a battle with the Turks. The emperor was incensed with the vessel and wrote to the admiral of the fleet: "Trusting in the help of the Almighty I persevere in the hope that the fearless Black Sea fleet, burning with the desire to wash off the shame of the frigate 'Raphael,' will not leave it in the hands of the enemy. But, when it is returned to our control, considering this frigate to be unworthy in the future to fly the flag of Russia and to serve together with the other vessels of our fleet, I order you to burn it."

There were times when the tsar's intrusive involvement in the affairs of his subjects actually transcended the absurd, as when he declared after the annulment of one woman's marriage, "The young lady shall be considered a virgin." Such was the state of absolute control in Russia that one observer wryly commented, "Fish swam in the water, birds sang in the forest because they were permitted to do so by the authorities."

Nicholas I found great relief from the burdens of micromanaging the Russian Empire in his family, to which he was entirely devoted. Still, the tsar demanded the same blind obedience from them as he did from any one of his other subjects. And woe to that unfortunate relative who defied or displeased him—like his son and heir, the future Alexander II. "Don't be a milksop!" was the emperor's usual admonition to the young man, but that was merely gentle chiding compared to those instances when the tsarevitch really made his father mad. "Begone!" Nicholas thundered after some misdeed. "You are not worthy of approaching me after such behavior; you have forgotten that obedience is a sacred duty. I can forgive anything except disobedience."

Tensions between father and son became particularly fraught when young Alexander refused to give up his Polish mistress, a woman Nicholas found entirely unsuitable for the heir to the Russian throne. To resolve the issue, the emperor was prepared to follow the example of the one Romanov predecessor he admired most. "But for me the State counts above everything else," he wrote to his wife in 1839; "and much as I love my children, I love my fatherland much more still. And, if this becomes necessary, there is the example of Peter the Great [see Chapter 2] to show my duty; and I shall not be too weak to fulfill it." Alexander obligingly gave up the girl.

Even the emperor's beloved wife, Alexandra, was not immune to her husband's bouts of fury. Nicholas had fallen in love with the Prussian princess, whom he endearingly called "Mouffy," when he visited her father's kingdom as a young man. And nineteen years after they married, he was still smitten.

"God has given you such a happy character that it is no merit to love you," Nicholas wrote to Alexandra in 1836. "I exist for you, yes, you are I—I do not know how to say it differently, but I am not your salvation, as you say. Our salvation is *over there* yonder, yonder where we shall all be admitted to rest from the tribulations of life. I mean, if we earn it down here by the fulfillment of our duties. Hard as they may be, one performs them with joy when one has a beloved being at home near whom one can breathe again and gain new strength. If I was now and then demanding, this happens because I look for everything in you. If I do not find it, I am distressed, I say to myself, no, she does not understand me, and these are unique, rare, but difficult moments. For the rest, happiness, joy, calm—that is what I seek and find in my old Mouffy. I wished, as much as this was in my power, to make you a hundred times happier, if I could have divined how this end could have been obtained."

In many ways Alexandra was the perfect mate for the temperamental emperor: sweet, submissive, and just flighty enough not to harbor any political opinions she might be tempted to express. "Her tender nature and shallow mind replaced principles with sensitivity," wrote the empress's lady-in-waiting Anna Tyutcheva. "Nicholas had a passionate adoration for this frail and exquisite creature of a strong nature for a weak thing, who obediently turned him into her sole ruler and legislator. . . . Nicholas placed her in a golden cage of palaces, brilliant balls, and handsome courtiers. . . . In her magical dungeon she did not once think of freedom. She did not allow herself to dream of any life beyond the golden cage."

The one occasion Alexandra did seek a respite from her gilded existence at court, Nicholas made her regret. The empress's health was always fragile—a constant source of irritation to her robust and restless husband—but in 1845 it grew markedly worse. Alexandra's physician recommended she avail herself of the healing sunshine of Sicily to restore her strength, and the empress agreed. But with an attachment to his wife that bordered on obsessive, Nicholas reacted as if the doctor had suggested she sleep with the Third Army Battalion.

Alexandra recorded in her diary that the emperor "appeared beside himself, that is, in his own way like no other man could be, not storming or angry, or crying, but icily cold and that towards me. He did not address to me two sentences in the course of an entire week. Those were such bad days, such a burden, such tugs at the heart that I had to become sick and nervous. But I shall write no more about this."

Rather than tormenting poor Mouffy as she tried to improve her health, the emperor might have taken comfort in the arms of one of his mistresses. There were plenty to choose from, after all. Indeed, like so many of his Romanov ancestors, Nicholas's libido knew few limits.

"He gave his attention . . . not only to all the young beauties in the court—the ladies-in-waiting—but also the young women he met during walks," reported Custine. "If someone caught his fancy on a walk or at the theater, he told his adjutant. She would then be checked. If there was nothing against her, the husband (if she was married) or her parents (if a maiden) were informed of the honor that had befallen them. . . . The tsar never met resistance to his lust. . . . In that strange country sleeping with the emperor was considered an honor . . . for the parents and even the husbands."

In the spring of 1844, Nicholas I made a state visit to Britain, after which Queen Victoria, then just a young woman of twenty-five, recorded her impressions of the all-powerful Russian sovereign who had dominated his realm for nearly two decades:

"He is certainly a *very striking* man; still very handsome; his profile is *beautiful,* and his manners *most* dignified and graceful; extremely civil—quite alarmingly so, as he is full of attentions and *politesses.* But the expression of the eyes is *formidable,* and unlike anything I ever saw before. He gives me and Albert [the queen's consort] the impression of a man who is *not* happy and on whom the weight of immense power and position weighs heavily and painfully; he seldom smiles, and when he does the expression is *not* a happy one. . . .

"He is stern and severe with fixed principles of *duty* which *nothing* on earth will make him change: *very clever* I do *not* think him, and his mind is an uncivilized one; his education has been neglected; politics and military concerns are the only things he takes great interest in; the arts and all softer occupations he is insensible to, but he is sincere, I am certain, *sincere* even in his most despotic acts, from a sense that it *is* the *only* way to govern."

What the queen saw as sincerity actually amounted "to a burning conviction, by normal human standards bordering on the insane, of the absolute rectitude, the divine virtue of his own views," wrote historian Edward Crankshaw. "And yet, with this conviction there went a profound, concealed uncertainty." It was, in fact, fear—the inner terror that had haunted the emperor since he was a boy and which he masked with unswerving despotism. The refuge of the frightened was, as it always had been, immobility; a desperate clinging to a fixed order, without growth, risk, or enlightenment. Thus, Crankshaw concluded, "The reign of Nicholas I was not a development; it was a prolonged situation."

In July 1849, the emperor wrote a rather self-pitying letter to his wife in which he expressed the concept of *duty* as the essence of his very being. But, if he replaced that word and idea with *fear*—raw, all-consuming terror—the emperor would have presented a near-perfect encapsulation of himself and his reign:

"How remarkable really is my fate. I am told that I am one of the mightiest rulers of the world, and one must say that everything, that is, everything that is permissible, should be within my reach, that, within the limits of discretion, I should be able to do what I please and where. But in fact just the opposite is the case as far as I am concerned. And if one asks about the basic cause of this anomaly, there is only one word: Duty! [*Fear!*] Yes, this is no empty word for those who have become accustomed from their youth to understand it as I have. This word has a sacred meaning which makes all personal considerations retreat, everything must keep silent in front of this one feeling, everything must step back, until one, together with this feeling, disappears into the grave. That is my key word. It is hard, I admit it, I suffer more from it than I can tell—but I have been created to suffer."

Decades of effort spent trying to sustain a stagnant empire in the face of an inevitably changing world began to take a physical and psychological toll on the emperor as early as 1846. "He has to make an effort to conquer fatigue, to do what seemed easy to him until now," the Austrian ambassador reported that year. "He has become silent. He avoids assemblies. He says that society, balls, and fetes have become a drudgery, and that he prefers to live like a bourgeois. . . . The conviction is gaining more and more ground that the Emperor, in spite of his constant work and energy, will not succeed in doing the good he wants to do, nor in destroying the evil he sees."

The decline of "Virgil's Neptune" had indeed commenced, and it would accelerate rapidly in the coming years as he witnessed the revolutions in central Europe he had worked so assiduously to prevent, the worsening health of his beloved Mouffy, and the continued strain of ruling Russia virtually alone. "Emperor Nicholas has aged ten years," reported the French diplomat Marquis de Castelbajac in 1854. "He is truly sick, physically and morally."

The crowning blow came with the devastating defeats the emperor's forces suffered in the Crimean War, a conflict Russia fought all alone against a coalition of European powers. Then, in February 1855, Nicholas, not yet fifty-nine, caught a slight cold but ignored it and continued his routine. After a review of his troops in subzero temperatures, pneumonia set in, and his condition quickly turned grave enough for his doctor to call in a priest.

"Then I am dying?" Nicholas asked calmly, his cold eyes boring into the doctor.

"Your Majesty," the physician replied, "you have only a few hours left."

The emperor, autocrat to the end, issued various orders in his final hours on March 2. Then, with his last breaths he addressed his son, soon to become Alexander II: "I wanted to take everything difficult, everything heavy upon myself and leave to you a peaceful, orderly, and happy realm. Providence determined otherwise. Now I shall ascend to pray for Russia and for you. After Russia, I loved you above everything else in the world. Serve Russia."

Now, all that was left was Nikitenko's terse assessment of the late emperor: "The main failing of the reign of Nicholas Pavlovich was that it was all a mistake."

Chapter 11

Alexander II (1855–1881):

"A Crowned Semi-Ruin"

Am I such a wild beast that they should hound me
to death?

—EMPEROR ALEXANDER II

*Alexander II was every bit the autocrat his father, Nicholas I, had
been; he just lacked the same ferocity. Even when he tried to adopt
the late emperor's icy glare, he came off looking more absurd than
scary. Still, the son surpassed his father in one significant way.
While Nicholas I had pronounced serfdom "an evil, palpable and
obvious to all," Alexander II actually did something about it. On
March 3, 1861—nearly two years before Abraham Lincoln issued
his Emancipation Proclamation—the emperor signed the order
freeing twenty million of his subjects from centuries of bondage to
masters who could beat, rape, and kill them with impunity. And
though the measure was more expedient than benevolent—"If we
don't give the peasants freedom from above, they will take it from
below," he had said—it nevertheless earned Alexander II the enduring sobriquet "Tsar-Liberator," and launched major reforms in
the courts and in the army, which had long forced serfs into its
ranks to be slaughtered on countless battlefields.*

*Yet ultimately the Tsar-Liberator's efforts failed. Rather than
quell dissention among his subjects as he intended, the reforms, and*

the easing of repression that accompanied them, left the people screaming for more. The most radical among them sought to destroy the monarchy itself. Alexander II became their target, terrorism their weapon. And for the next two decades they hunted him mercilessly. It would take at least seven attempts to kill the emperor—rendering him in the process what one contemporary called "a crowned semi-ruin"—before they finally succeeded in 1881.

It was April 4, 1866, and Alexander II had just concluded his usual walk through Peter the Great's Summer Garden. Just outside the park's ornate wrought-iron fence, a crowd of people had gathered as usual to catch a glimpse of their handsome, bewhiskered sovereign with the benevolent blue eyes as he concluded his stroll. Then, just as the emperor was about to enter his coach, a loud shot suddenly rang out and a young man was seen running from the crowd toward a nearby bridge. His name was Dmitri Karakozov, the son of a nobleman and a member of an underground dissident group. The would-be assassin—his shot apparently deflected by a man standing next to him by the name of Komissarov—was quickly apprehended and brought before the uninjured emperor, who proceeded to interrogate him. "Fellows, I did this for you!" Karakozov reportedly shouted to the bystanders as he was led away.

News of the tsar's deliverance from the assassin's bullet was greeted with patriotic acclaim across the capital, and Osip Komissarov, his savior, became an instant hero, feted as "the humble weapon of God's providence." The heir to the throne, the future Alexander III, recorded the celebratory mood of the city: "You can say without mistake that all of St. Petersburg came spilling out onto the street. Traffic, agitation was unimaginable. Running in all directions, primarily toward the Winter Palace, shouts, most of them with the words 'Karakozov!' 'Komissarov!,' threats and curses for the former, delighted exclamations for the latter. Groups of people, singing 'God Save the Tsar.' General delight and thunderous 'Hurrahs.' They brought in the man who saved him [Komissarov]. Papa kissed him and made him a nobleman.* Another terrific 'Hurrah.'"

On the day of the assassination attempt, the poet Apollon Maikov recalled fellow writer Fyodor Dostoevsky bursting into his apartment with the news. Maikov asked him if the tsar had been killed, and recorded the response: "No . . . saved him . . . he's fine . . . But they shot, they shot, they shot!" This, Maikov wrote, "Dostoevsky kept repeating in despair and shock."

"The writer understood that, despite the miss, the shot had in fact been a hit," explained Alexander II's biographer, Edvard Radzinsky. "Before, the tsars had been killed in the palace, secretly, and they were said to have died peacefully of hemorrhoidal colic or stroke or something. Now, someone had taken a shot at the tsar in public, shattering the inviolable aura of the sacred person that is the tsar. Alexander understood this, too."†

While the rest of Russia celebrated his deliverance, the emperor seethed. In the five years since he had liberated the serfs, youthful agitators had set fires in the streets, issued bloody proclamations, attacked his ministers, and now one of them had actually shot at him. So much for reform; the time

---

* The much-lauded Komissarov later died in obscurity of delirium tremens.

† It should be recalled that a shot also had been fired at Alexander's father, Nicholas I, during the Decembrist Revolt of 1825.

had come for reprisal. And while Alexander may have been incapable of approximating his father's fearsome glare, it appeared he was ready to adopt Nicholas I's harshest tendencies. Liberals in the government were swept from their ministries. "They are all cosmopolites, adherents of European ideas," declared General Michael Muravyev, known as "the Hangman" for his brutal suppression of rebellion in Poland. "Now real Russians must come to power!"

St. Petersburg shuddered when the Hangman was appointed to head the investigation into the attempted murder of the tsar, and a massive corralling of almost everyone suspected of leftist tendencies ensued. As for the assassin and one of his accomplices, both were sentenced to death. After unsuccessfully pleading to the emperor for his life, Karakozov was publicly executed on Semenovsky Square. He fainted on his approach to the gallows and had to be dragged to the noose. His accomplice was just about to suffer the same end when he learned at the last second that his sentence had been commuted to life with hard labor. It was an act reminiscent of Nicholas I's "benevolence" toward Dostoevsky on the same square almost sixteen years earlier.

The shock of near assassination was mitigated somewhat by the fact that the emperor was in love—not with the empress, long afflicted with lung disease, but with an enchanting young beauty nearly three decades his junior named Catherine Dolgorukaya, or Katya, as she was called. The besotted monarch, pushing fifty, was often seen squiring his teenage sweetheart on long walks through the park and kissing her under the trees. Eventually he appointed her to the household of the ailing Empress Maria, whose bed he had long abandoned. But unlike the endless parade of other ladies-in-waiting who had been installed just to service the emperor, Katya remained chaste.

The girl's steadfast virginity drove the lusty emperor to near madness until finally, in July 1866, two months after the assassin's bullet missed, she yielded at last. The forbidden fruit lost none of its flavor in the aftermath, as so often happens in such circumstances, and Alexander remained devoted. "When I saw you at a distance in the allée," he wrote to Katya that August, "my heart beat so hard that I trembled all over and my knees grew weak, and I kept wanting to squeal with joy." In another note several months later, the emperor further expressed his tender, adulterous sentiments: "Don't forget that you are my whole life, angel of my soul, and its only goal is to see you happy, as happy as one can only be in this world."

The emperor swore to his young love that one day he would make her his wife. In the meantime, though, Katya had to endure all the scrutiny and gossip that inevitably came with her position as royal mistress, but which she found unbearable. Taking pity, Alexander sent her on an extended visit to her brother in Naples. Court watchers immediately assumed the tsar had grown tired of his latest paramour and dismissed her as he had so many before. They were wrong. Alexander's ardor had only increased in Katya's absence, so much so that he arranged a secret assignation with her in Paris. It was there, in the midst of that joyful reunion, that the emperor would confront his second assassin.

The ostensible purpose of the imperial journey to Paris was to attend the opening of the World's Fair with Europe's other crowned heads and to lend Russia's tacit support to France in the face of increasing Prussian aggression. But on the night of his arrival, the tsar slipped away after midnight (much to the consternation of his worried retinue) and indulged in the *real* reason for his visit. The only time he spent away from Katya thereafter was to perform his official duties—one of which nearly proved lethal.

Alexander was traveling in an open carriage along the Bois de Boulogne, the French emperor Napoleon III seated beside him, when a man suddenly ran out from the crowd lining the route and fired twice at him. The shots were at dangerously close range, but the assassin had packed too much gunpowder into his pistol, which caused it to explode and misfire. The emperors' carriage raced off, and the would-be killer was immediately apprehended. It turned out that he was a young Polish émigré named Anton Berezovski, part of a disaffected generation whose homeland had long endured Russia's brutal occupation. Alexander expected he would be sentenced to death for the heinous crime of attempted regicide, but public opinion in France was firmly with the assassin. Berezovski was given a life sentence, which few doubted would eventually be commuted. Outraged by this insult from the ungrateful French, the Russian emperor immediately switched his allegiance back to Prussia, the armies of which eventually crushed Napoleon III.

It was while in Paris that Alexander II reportedly had his palm read by a fortune-teller who told him that seven attempts would be made on his life—and that the last one would be successful. If such a meeting did actually take place, the seer's forecast was certainly accurate. Two attempts had already been made, and there were five more to come.

A Russian sovereign had to always appear dignified in public to maintain the aura of semi-divinity and invincible majesty associated with the tsar. Yet on April 2, 1879, while fleeing from yet another potential killer, Alexander II appeared anything but regal. He was standing in the square outside the Winter Palace when a tall man approached. He was wearing a long black coat and a cap with a cockade similar to the ones worn by government officials. He saluted to the emperor, and then fired at him. The bullet whizzed just past the tsar, who began to run from his attacker. Another shot was fired by the pursuing assassin, after which Alexander pivoted and switched directions. Then three more shots came, with the proud Russian emperor zigzagging around the square after each one like a hare running for its life. Had it not been so perilous, the scene might actually have been comical. Alexander emerged from it humiliated but unharmed, and the next day celebrated his birthday. "A fine present that was," he harrumphed.

Terrorism was clearly taking a toll on the royal family. "I have seen their imperial majesties," Interior Minister Peter Valuev recorded in his diary two months after the latest assassination attempt. "Around them everything is as it was before, but they are not as they were before. Both left me with painful feelings. The Tsar has a tired look and himself spoke of nervous tension, which he is trying to conceal. A crowned semi-ruin. In an era when strength is needed in him, obviously it can't be counted on. . . . You can feel the ground tremble, the edifice about to tumble, but it is as if the residents don't notice this. The master and the mistress of the house vaguely sense evil but hide their inner terror."

Despite the emperor's efforts to maintain at least the appearance of normalcy, certain aspects of his life were inexorably altered. No longer was he able to roam freely in his own capital without an armed convoy to accompany him. "It's painful to see that," wrote Alexandra Bogdanovich, a St. Petersburg hostess. But for Empress Maria, the consequences were perhaps even more pronounced. Not only did she have to suffer a third attempt on her husband's life—after which she pitifully wailed, "There's no reason to live. . . . I can feel this killing me"—but she also had to accept the emperor's decision to move his mistress, as well as their three children, into the Winter Palace, where he felt they would be safer. It was as if the empress had been officially demoted, and all of St. Petersburg sympathized. As Radzinsky wrote of the reaction in the capital, "Instantly, the story became that Katya and the children were living directly above the empress, and the miserable, sick, and old empress had to listen to the patter of his illegitimate children's feet over her head."

Still, there was something far worse. The terrorists made it clear that their relentless hunt for the tsar would continue. Indeed, the day after the execution of their compatriot who had chased down the emperor in front of the Winter Palace, they issued the following proclamation: "We have picked up the glove thrown at us, we are not afraid of struggle and death, and in the end we will blow up the government, no matter how many may die on our side." And in pursuit of their sinister agenda, the killers now had a fearsome new weapon.

It was only a matter of time after Alfred Nobel invented dynamite in 1866 that Russian revolutionaries would adopt it for their own malevolent purposes. Now, instead of shooting the tsar, they would blow him up. The attack was planned for the fall of 1879, when Alexander was to return by train from his annual sojourn in the Crimea.

There was a routine in the way the emperor traveled by rail, and the terrorists learned just what it was: One train always carried the royal retinue, along with baggage and other supplies, and was followed at some distance by the imperial train—the fourth car of which Alexander always occupied. Armed with this information, along with their deadly new weapon, the assassins rented a home near the tracks in a small town just outside Moscow. From there, they dug a tunnel to a spot directly below the rail bed and planted the bomb.

On November 19, after the first train of the procession rumbled past, the mine was detonated just as the second passed over it. With that tremendous blast, the fourth car of the imperial train—the tsar's car—was tossed into the air and came crashing back to earth upside down. But Alexander wasn't in it.

"The imperial train usually travels a half hour behind the other one, usually called the retinue train," explained War Minister Dmitri Milyutin. "This time it went ahead of the retinue train. It was due to mechanical problems with the retinue train. The tsar did not want to wait while they changed the locomotive, and the imperial train went first."

The emperor had arrived safely at the Moscow station, where the reverberations from the distant explosion could be heard. "The fourth car of the retinue train had been turned into marmalade," he was later told. "There was nothing in it but fruit from the Crimea." Though Alexander had survived the most ferocious attempt on his life yet, there was little comfort to be had. "Am I such a wild beast that they should hound me to death?" he exclaimed in despair.

"The event of November 19 brought a grim color to our entire stay in Moscow," Milyutin reported. "We were still under that terrible impression during the trip [back] to St. Petersburg. All measures were taken to protect the imperial train from new dangers. We did not let them know in St.

Petersburg when the tsar would arrive. The troops of the imperial garrison, all the officers, officials, and even the imperial family waited for several hours in the streets and at the station, in extremely and unusually cold weather. All telegraph service was suspended. To make matters worse, there was a blizzard in the night. The emperor got to St. Petersburg only around three in the afternoon. He was sad and serious."

But there would be no safe haven in the capital—not even in Alexander's own home.

On the evening of February 5, 1880, a massive explosion rocked the Winter Palace just as the imperial family prepared to sit down to eat. The timing of the blast—detonated beneath the dining room by a terrorist who had infiltrated the palace posing as a resident carpenter—was synchronized to coincide precisely with the beginning of the dinner hour. Fortuitously enough, there was a slight delay in the usual schedule that evening due to the late arrival of several guests. Otherwise the entire room would have come crashing down around the family as they began to eat what might have been their last meal.

Instead, the emperor and the rest of the royal family were assembled in a gallery just outside the dining room when the explosion occurred. "The floor rose as if in an earthquake," recalled Empress Maria's brother, Prince Alexander of Hesse, who was one of the honored guests that night, "the gas lights in the gallery went out, there was total darkness, and the air was filled with the disgusting odor of gun powder or dynamite."

The dining room was almost entirely destroyed. A gaping hole in the wall attested to the power of the bomb; the windows were all blown out, and a thick layer of dust and debris covered everything. Grand Duchess Marie, the emperor's daughter-in-law (married to his son Vladimir and known to the family as "Miechen") recalled the horror after "the dining room vanished from our view, and we were plunged into impenetrable darkness."

"A poisonous gas filled the room, suffocating us, as well as adding to our horror," she told the painter Henry James Thaddeus. "How can I possibly describe the agony of mind we suffered, expecting as we did, at any moment, another explosion beneath us! It is impossible—impossible for me to tell or for you to conceive.

"The impending fear almost made our hearts stop beating as, silent and motionless, we awaited our doom. When the echoes of the explosion died away, a dead silence succeeded, which, united with the darkness prevailing, so dense as almost to be felt, conducted to render our helpless position still more painful and unendurable."

The family was frozen in fear, the grand duchess continued in her vivid account. "We dared not to move. There was no escape from the peril which surrounded us." It was then, she recalled, that "out of the darkness came the clear, calm voice of the Tsar," who suggested a prayer. Alexander's voice of authority "relieved the awful strain on our nerves, and brought comfort to our hearts." Weeping, they fell to their knees in supplication. "How long we remained so, I really don't know. It seemed an eternity of anguish before the guards appeared with candles little expecting to find us alive.

"Some of us were nearly demented when the welcome relief arrived, and our feelings were not calmed as we contemplated the awful nature of the destruction we had escaped. A few feet in front of the Tsar was a black chasm, where so short a time before had been the brilliantly lit dining-room filled with servants. Not a trace of it or them remained! It really seemed as if the hand of Providence had delayed the Tsar's arrival; otherwise we should have shared the same fate. The dim lights of the candles intensified the terrifying aspect of the scene before us, and we hastened to leave it for the comparative safety of our own apartments.

"The dread of further explosions haunted us like a hideous nightmare during that long and dreary night, whilst the fear of danger to the children nearly distracted me. Never, I pray, may I have to undergo such agony again."

While Alexander II and his family were fortunate enough to escape the explosion unscathed, at least physically, there were others who suffered hideously. The amount of dynamite smuggled gradually into the palace by the resident assassin turned out to be insufficient to blow the royals to pieces but more than enough to decimate a large group of guards gathered in their quarters directly beneath the dining room. Hearing agonized screams, the emperor's sons rushed to the source.

"When we ran in, we found a terrible scene," recalled the future Alexander III: "the entire large guards room where people lived was blown up and everything had collapsed more than six feet deep, and in that pile of brick, plaster, slabs and huge mounds of vaults and walls lay more than fifty soldiers covered with a layer of dust and blood. It was a heartbreaking picture, and I will never forget that horror in my life!"

Meanwhile, the emperor had an urgent concern of his own: his mistress Katya, who for obvious reasons had not been invited to the dinner honoring her rival's brother. After stumbling through the dark and smoky palace to her apartments on the third floor, he was relieved to find his beloved waiting for him in the doorway with a candle. As for the ailing Empress Maria, she appeared to be less of a worry. Heavily sedated in her sickroom, she slept right through the explosion. Four months later she was dead.

As St. Petersburg reeled from this most audacious terrorist strike, the emperor managed to remain stoic in the face of yet another attempt on his life. "The tsar called me to his study [the day after the palace explosion]," the war minister, Milyutin, recorded in his journal. "As in the previous similar incidents, he maintained total presence of mind, seeing in this case a new manifestation of God's finger saving him for the fifth time from villainous attack."

Yet while Alexander II firmly believed that his life had been preserved through divine intervention, he nevertheless recognized that the extremists were gaining strength from their constant assaults. And in order to maintain something of the autocratic order in Russia, he concluded that he would have to cede a measure of his God-given power to the people who demanded it. Death intervened, however, before he could execute his plan.

Perhaps it was the emperor's sense of his own mortality that prompted his hasty marriage to Katya just over a month after the death of his wife. It was an unseemly breach of mourning etiquette, but Alexander seemed not to care. He was determined to lap up whatever happiness he could in the time he had left. Much to the disgust of his family, who revered the late empress and considered Katya to be nothing but a scheming gold digger, he installed his new bride in his dead wife's apartments, gave her the title of princess, and legitimized their three children with imperial titles as well. It was all too galling for the rest of the Romanovs.

"This marriage of the Tsar's six weeks after the death of our dear Tsarina, is hard enough to bear in itself," Grand Duchess

Marie, Miechen, vented in a letter to the late empress's brother. "But that this woman, who for fourteen years has occupied such a very invidious position, should be introduced to us as a member of the family surrounded by her three children is more painful than I can find words to express."

As his family continued to grumble, the emperor demanded that they put an end to their snubs and honor Katya properly. Some even believed he eventually planned to make her empress. Certainly he was smitten enough. Miechen, who longed for the day when "the Tsar's eyes must at length be opened to the worthlessness of the creature who seems to have him bound as in a spell," nevertheless noted ruefully, "Up to the present he is utterly and blissfully happy, looks very well, and years younger."

Alas, the newlyweds had very little time left together before the assassins struck again.

Rather than placating the terrorists, word of the tsar's planned concessions to the people only intensified their zeal. They were convinced that such limited measures would only diminish whatever revolutionary momentum existed in Russia. Thus, before he could ruin their movement with his reforms, a new way was quickly devised to kill Alexander II. The date for the deed was set for March 13, 1881, a Sunday, when the emperor made his usual weekly visit to the Mikhailovsky Manege to review the troops.

Alexander was known to take one of two routes on the way back from the review to the Winter Palace: either through Malaya Sadovaya Street or along the Catherine Canal. The assassins were prepared either way. They had rented a shop on Malaya Sadovaya, from the basement of which they burrowed a tunnel and deposited a bomb directly below the street. If the tsar came that way, they would detonate the explosive just as his carriage passed over it. To ensure success in the event that the bomb failed or the explosion was ill-timed, three conspirators, each armed with dynamite, were positioned along the street to complete the job. If, alternatively, Alexander traveled along the Catherine Canal, the same men would have time to scurry over to that route and hurl their explosives there.

"Alexander II must die," one of the assassins wrote in his last will and testament on the eve of the murder. "His days are numbered. He will die and we, his enemies, his killers, will die with him. . . . History will show that the luxuriant tree of freedom demands human sacrifices. . . . [F]ate has doomed me to an early death, and I will not see victory, I will not live a single day, a single hour in the radiant time of triumph. . . . But I believe that with my death I will have done everything I had to do, and no one in the entire world can demand more of me."

Katya was filled with foreboding on Sunday morning as her husband of six months prepared to leave for the troop review. She tearfully begged Alexander not to go, but he didn't heed her warning. Instead, he gave Katya what turned out to be quite the farewell. "Before leaving for the guards parade on March 1[3], the tsar toppled the princess onto the table and took her," the journalist Alexis Suvorin recorded in his diary after a conversation with the imperial physician, Dr. Eugene Botkin. "She told this to Botkin herself."

Meanwhile, the terrorists were making their final preparations, and by the time Alexander embarked on his return journey from the military review they were ready. The sudden withdrawal of the sentries posted along Malaya Sadovaya

Street indicated that the emperor had opted for the Catherine Canal route instead. Along the way, he popped into the Mikhailovsky Palace to visit his cousin, Catherine, reportedly in a vain attempt to persuade her to accept his new wife. This gave the bomb throwers more than enough time to take their places along the alternative route.

After about half an hour, the tsar left the palace and reentered his carriage, which immediately sped away. That's when the first assassin approached with his weapon wrapped in a handkerchief. "After a moment's hesitation, I threw the bomb," the killer later testified. "I sent it under the horses' hooves in the supposition that it would blow up under the carriage. . . . The explosion knocked me into the fence."

It also killed or maimed a number of bystanders, but the emperor survived—dazed, but unharmed. The bomb had exploded just as the carriage passed over it, and as a result, only the back of the vehicle was damaged. Alexander emerged, shaking. "The tsar crossed himself," recalled Colonel Adrian Dvorzhitsky; "he was a bit unsteady and understandably upset. When I asked him about his health, he replied, 'Thank God, I am not wounded.'"

The would-be assassin was quickly apprehended and disarmed of a pistol and dagger. But Dvorzhitsky heard him shout to one of his accomplices and realized the tsar was still in grave danger. He urged Alexander to leave the scene at once, but the emperor disregarded him as he walked toward the man who had just tried to murder him. Someone asked how he fared, to which Alexander responded, "Thank God, I'm fine." Then, pointing to the mass of dead and wounded, he said, "but look . . ." At this the assassin sneered, "Is it thanks to God?"

After confronting the bomb thrower, the emperor started

back to his ruined carriage. Again Dvorzhitsky pleaded with him to leave. Alexander stopped for a moment, then replied, "All right, but first show me the site of the explosion." It was then that the second killer emerged and hurled his bomb at the emperor.

"I was deafened by the new explosion," Dvorzhitsky recounted, "burned, wounded, and thrown to the ground. Suddenly, amid the smoke and snowy fog, I heard His Majesty's weak voice: 'Help!' Gathering what strength I had, I jumped up and rushed to the tsar. His Majesty was half-lying, half-sitting, leaning on his right arm. Thinking that he was merely wounded heavily, I tried to lift him, but the tsar's legs were shattered, and the blood poured out of them.

"Twenty people, with wounds of varying degree, lay by the sidewalk and on the street. Some managed to stand, others crawled, still others tried to get out from beneath bodies that had fallen on them. Through the snow, debris, and blood you could see fragments of clothing, epaulets, sabers, and bloody chunks of human flesh."

In the midst of this nightmarish scene, Alexander was heard to mutter several times, "Cold, I'm cold." Then, when his brother Michael arrived, the tsar said, "Take me home quickly!" With his life slowly draining away as the blood continued to pulse out of his ruined legs, he was placed on a sled and rushed to the Winter Palace. One of the men who helped move him was the third assassin, his unexploded bomb still on hand.

The emperor's nephew, Grand Duke Alexander ("Sandro" to the family), hurried to the palace when he heard what had happened. "The big spots of black blood on the marble steps and then along the corridor showed us the way to the tsar's study," he recalled. "Father [Grand Duke Michael, the emperor's brother at the scene of his assassination] stood in the doorway, giving orders to the servants. . . . Emperor Alexander II lay on a couch by the desk. He was unconscious. . . . He looked horrible. . . . One eye was shut, the other stared ahead without expression. . . . Members of the Imperial Family came in one after the other. The room was overflowing. . . . The heir [soon to be Alexander III] came in and wept, saying, 'This is what we have come to,' and embraced the grand dukes, his brother, Vladimir Alexandrovich, and his uncle, Mikhail Nikolayevich.

"Princess Yuryevskaya [Katya], half-dressed, ran in. They said that some overzealous guard tried to stop her from entering. She fell on top of the tsar's body, covering his hands with kisses and shouting, 'Sasha! Sasha!' It was unbearable."

One witness to the bloody horror at the palace that Sunday was a young boy of thirteen, the future Nicholas II, Russia's last tsar—destined to die less than three decades later under similarly gruesome circumstances. Before that would happen, though, it was the boy's father who emerged as the new emperor after Alexander II—hounded to the end—finally found peace.

Chapter 12

Alexander III (1881–1894): A Colossus of Unwavering Autocracy

The Guardian of Russia

—ALEXANDER III ON HIS WIFE, EMPRESS MARIE

FEODOROVNA

His father called him "the bullock," an apt description for the lumbering, hardheaded behemoth who succeeded Alexander II in 1881 and immediately set about dismantling the liberalizing policies he believed contributed directly to his father's murder. "Constitution?" Alexander III snorted. "They want the emperor of all of Russia to swear to cattle?" A profoundly biased nationalist, religious fanatic, and ferocious anti-Semite, the uncouth autocrat hardly presented the picture of an enlightened modern monarch. "I have such a dislike to the fat Czar," Britain's Queen Victoria sniffed. "I think him a violent . . . Asiatic full of hate, passion & tyranny." But Alexander III had one redemptive quality that softened him and brought out the best in his humanity: his wife, Empress Marie. Theirs was an unlikely love story—born out of tragedy and altered destinies—but it was genuine, enduring, and, most unusual in a Russian royal marriage, faithful until death.

The Romanovs were gathered in grief in the spring of 1865 as twenty-one-year-old Grand Duke Nicholas—their beloved

"Nixa"—lay dying of tuberculosis before them. It was simply incomprehensible that Alexander II's bright, handsome, and vibrant heir—"the crown of perfection," as his uncle Constantine called him—would soon be gone. And with him, all the best hopes for the glorious future of the imperial dynasty.

Among the distraught family members surrounding the tsarevitch in those final hours was his petite, seventeen-year-old fiancée, Princess Dagmar of Denmark, known to the family as "Minnie." Her dark eyes, Nixa had once rhapsodized, "speak for her: they are so kind, intelligent, animated." Also present was Nixa's adoring brother, Alexander, or "Sasha," as he was called (like his father). To the distress of all, this hulking, somewhat dim-witted ox of a man—whose only demonstrable skill seemed to be bending metal to his will with his bare hands—was about to replace his far more promising sibling in the line of succession.

Nixa commended both his fiancée and his brother to his father. "She is so sweet, isn't she?" he said of Minnie, after which he implored the grief-stricken emperor, "Papa, take care of Sasha; he is such an honest and good person." Then, before taking his final breaths, the young man silently took the hands of Dagmar and Alexander and joined them together. As one witness noted, "It seemed like the Tsarevitch was handing his fiancée over to his beloved brother, to whom he was also leaving his place on earth."

The sad circumstances that resulted in Minnie and Sasha's eventual engagement did not bode well for a happy future together. Nor did the fact that each of their hearts lay elsewhere: Minnie's with the memory of her dead fiancée; Sasha's with his mistress, Princess Maria Mescherskaya, one of his mother's maids of honor. Although the new heir recognized that the velvety-eyed Maria could never be his consort, he was still most reluctant to abandon her in favor of Minnie.

"I want to refuse to marry Dagmar, whom I cannot love and don't want," Alexander lamented in his diary. "Perhaps it would be better if I relinquished my right to the throne. I feel incapable of ruling. I have too little respect for people and get fed up with everything that concerns my position."

Disgusted by his son's pining intransigence, Alexander II sent Maria away and sharply reminded the new heir of his duty. With that imperial command, Sasha had little choice but to travel to Copenhagen and ask for Minnie's hand—an odious task that became surprisingly pleasant when Alexander arrived and found himself attracted to the young princess who should have been his sister-in-law. When at last he mustered the courage to propose, Sasha found Minnie more than receptive. She kissed him passionately and assured him that she could love no other. "We both burst into tears," Alexander recalled, "then I told her that my dear Nixa helped us much in this situation and that now of course he prays about our happiness."

On September 1, 1866, Princess Dagmar left her relatively humble life in Denmark—where she and her sister Alexandra (the future queen of England) once shared a bedroom and sewed their own clothes—for the staggering opulence of the Russian court. The famed author Hans Christian Andersen, who had known Minnie since she was a little girl, was there to see her off. "Yesterday, at the quay, while passing me by, she stopped and took me by the hand," he wrote. "My eyes were full of tears. What a poor child! Oh Lord, be kind and merciful to her! They say that there is a brilliant court in Saint Petersburg and the tsar's family is nice; still, she heads for an unfamiliar country, where people are different and religion is different and where she will have none of her former acquaintances by her side."

Minnie arrived in St. Petersburg to a rapturous welcome and instantly enchanted her future subjects with her effortless grace and vivacity. "Dagmar's popularity was growing," observed Alexander's friend S. D. Sheremetyev. "She was seen as a key to prosperity, all the hopes were laid on her and she would light the hearts with her eyes, her simplicity and charm promised happiness and peace."

The only one who seemed less than enthralled with Dagmar's arrival was Alexander, who, socially awkward as he was, thoroughly hated all the public ceremonies associated with the event. "In general, the tsarevitch was impossible in the role of fiancé," wrote Sheremetyev. "He showed himself in public only because it was his duty, he felt revulsion for illuminations and fireworks. Everyone pitied the bride, deprived of the graceful and gifted bridegroom [Nixa] and forced to join another without love, a crude, unpolished man with bad French. That was the reigning assessment in court circles."

Yet despite the vast differences in temperament between the extroverted Minnie and the sullen Sasha, this odd couple managed to endear themselves to each other. They were married on November 9, 1866, in a lavish ceremony at the Winter Palace chapel, followed by a honeymoon neither would ever forget. While Minnie giggled uncontrollably when Sasha appeared before her in the traditional wedding night attire—a heavy silver gown, with matching slippers curled at the toes, and a silver turban topped by cupid figures—her new husband recorded his own impressions of the evening:

"I locked the door behind me. All the lights were turned off in her room. . . . I walked into the dressing room, locked the door and reached for the handle on the bedroom door. It felt as if my heart was trying to escape from my body. Afterwards I closed both doors to the dressing room and walked over to Minny [*sic*]. She was already lying on the bed. It is impossible to describe the feelings that overwhelmed me as I pulled her towards me and embraced her. We embraced and kissed each other for a very long time. I then said my prayers, locked the door to the study, blew out the candles and lay down on the bed. I took off my slippers and my silver dressing gown and felt my darling's body against my own. . . .

"How I felt thereafter I don't wish to describe here. . . .

"Afterwards we talked a lot. Both of us had many questions and many answers. Thus we spent our first night together— and we never slept!"

Alexander's contentment with his new bride, who was given the name Marie Feodorovna upon her conversion to Orthodoxy, extended well beyond the honeymoon suite. Minnie became his constant companion and encouraged him as he began training to become Russia's next tsar. It was a daunting task, given Sasha's total lack of preparation prior to Nixa's death and his grievous deficiency in inherent ability. (His tutor lamented that Alexander "had been so badly misused by Nature, who sent him into the world with the shabbiest of intellectual gifts.") Yet with his cheerful bride by his side, Sasha persisted. Minnie somehow managed to make everything better.

"All the reports . . . of [Alexander's] being so unhappy with Minny—and she having married him to please her mother— are not true," the Crown Princess of Prussia reported to her mother, Queen Victoria. "I think they are very domestic and attracted to each other and he makes a very good husband."

Alexander himself affirmed his feelings in a diary entry

several weeks after his wedding: "God grant ... that I may love my darling wife more and more, she who loves me with all her heart, a love for which I am so grateful, and for the sacrifice that she made by leaving her parents and her fatherland for my sake. I often feel that I am not worthy of her, but even if this were true, I will do my best to be."

Though their private intimacy was apparent, what the public saw of the couple left the impression that there was very little to recommend them to each other. Minnie was sparkling and vivacious, with a joie de vivre that enchanted all who met her. "No wonder the emperor [Alexander II] likes her, and no wonder the Russians like her," wrote an American observer, Thomas W. Knox. "I like her, and I am neither emperor nor any other Russian, and never exchanged a thousand words with her in my life."

The young empress-to-be loved nothing more than a party, where she invariably dazzled. At one ball not long after her marriage, an observer noted that she was "indefatigable" and "in high spirits . . . with her cheeks flushed by dancing, she had a freshness of look very rare in Russia." The tsarevitch, on the other hand, much preferred solitary pursuits like hunting and fishing. "He looked like a big Russian *muzhik* [peasant]," Alexander's future finance minister, Sergei Witte, wrote; "in manner he was more or less bear-like." When he was dragged to obligatory social events, much against his will, Sasha was indeed as awkward and ungainly as a dancing Russian bear. Once, after a partner thanked him for a dance, Alexander replied bluntly: "Why can't you be honest? It was just a duty neither of us could have relished. I have ruined your slippers and you have made me nearly sick with the scent you use."

Yet beneath this boorish exterior, Sasha had a "wonderful

heart, good humor, and fairness," as Witte observed. "I like him very much," the Crown Princess of Prussia ("Vicky") wrote in the report to her mother, Queen Victoria. "He is awkward, shy and uncouth, from being so very big, but he is simple and unpretending not proud and capricious as most Russians are, and has something straightforward and good-natured about him which I like and I think you would also." Furthermore, Vicky noted of Minnie, "She seems quite happy and contented with her fat, good-natured husband who seems far more attentive and kind to her than one would have thought."*

So it was that the ursine tsarevitch and his petite bride settled into harmonious domesticity at the Anichkov Palace and began to raise a family. Their firstborn was the doomed future emperor Nicholas II, whose arrival in 1868 thrilled his father: "God has sent us a son. . . . What a joy it was—it is impossible to imagine. I rushed to embrace my darling wife; who at once grew merry and was awfully happy." Young Nicholas was followed by five siblings: Alexander (who died of meningitis before his first birthday), George, Xenia, Michael, and Olga. At their father's insistence, the royal children were reared under relatively Spartan conditions amid the opulence of the palace. They slept on cots and were served only the simplest of meals. But they had parents who adored them.

A contented Sasha wrote to his wife after nearly twelve

---

* In the same correspondence with the queen, Vicky also wrote of Minnie: "I was pleased to see that she has not become grand—and does not give herself airs as all the Russian Grand Duchesses do. She has remained simple and unaffected; she has only been a short while in Russia since her marriage—but it does not seem as if the splendors of the Russian Court would dazzle her, and turn her head nor the servile flattery, which is the tone there, could spoil her. She seems so little occupied with herself."

years of marriage: "My dear love Minny ... I would to embrace you in my thoughts and with my whole heart wish us both our old, sweet, dear happiness; we do not need a new one, and preserve, O Lord, that happiness which we, thanks to his grace, have enjoyed for more than 11 years."

Alas, the family's tranquil existence at the Anichkov Palace was shattered in 1881, when Emperor Alexander II was finally killed after six previous assassination attempts. "Oh, what sorrow and despair, that our beloved Emperor should be torn away from us and even in this *dreadful* way!" Minnie wrote to her mother, Queen Louise of Denmark. "No, anyone who has not seen the appalling sight himself can never imagine anything like it! The poor, innocent Emperor—to see him in that terrible condition was truly heartrending! His face and head and upper body were untouched but his legs were completely crushed and torn up to the knees, so that at first I did not understand what I was actually looking at, a bleeding mass with half a boot on the right foot; all that was left was the sole of his foot! Never in my life have I seen anything like it; no, it was horrible."

Sasha was as devastated as his wife by the sight of his father's shattered body. He wept bitterly. Now "the bullock" who had once exclaimed in despair "I was not raised to be Emperor" assumed the role he had long dreaded. "A strange change came over him in that instant," Grand Duke Alexander (Sandro) wrote of the new sovereign. "This was not the same tsarevitch Alexander Alexandrovich, who liked to amuse the small friends of his son, Nicky, by tearing a deck of cards in half or bending an iron rod into a knot. In the course of five minutes he was completely transformed. Something incomparably greater than the simple consciousness of the duties of the monarch illuminated his heavy figure. A fire burned in his tranquil eyes."

Indeed, Emperor Alexander III emerged from his father's murder to become, in the words of one, "a colossus of unwavering autocracy."[*]

With St. Petersburg "reeking of dynamite—a nest of invisible assassins," as a visiting Englishman described it at the time, Alexander III launched his campaign to crush dissent and subdue the liberalizing elements in government he had long believed encouraged the violence and rebellion of his father's reign. As the emperor's nephew, Grand Duke Alexander, later wrote, "the future of the empire, possibly of the entire world, depended upon the issue of the coming contest between the new Czar of Russia and the fast increasing forces of destruction."

Alexander's tutor and advisor, the ultraconservative Constantine Pobedonostsev, had long despaired of imparting the nuances of rule to his intellectually limited student. But the future tsar had no problem absorbing the simple creed that defined the reign of his grandfather, Nicholas I: "Orthodoxy, Autocracy, Nationality." In fact, these united entwined precepts spoke to the very soul of the emperor, whose entire education consisted of what one courtier described as an "unshakable belief in the omnipotence of the tsars of Russia."

Now that Alexander ruled, Pobedonostsev warned him: "If siren songs are sung to you about the necessity of pacification,

[*] So described by author Edvard Radzinsky in *Alexander II: The Last Great Tsar* (see Bibliography).

of continuation of the liberal regime, and yielding to so-called public opinion, oh, please God, do not . . . hearken to them. This will mean ruin, the ruin of Russia and of you." The emperor hardly needed to be reminded. Within two months of his accession he issued the Manifesto of Unshakable Autocracy, in which he declared that he would "take up vigorously the task of governing . . . with faith in the strength and truth of the autocratic power that we have been called upon to affirm and safeguard for the popular good from any infringement."

The war against subversion was on, beginning with the hanging deaths of Alexander II's assassins, while the Okhrana, or secret police, was established to ferret out other dangerous elements for the gallows. But the enemy wasn't so easily cowed. Because of the lurking menace, Alexander and his family were forced to live under the tightest security at Emperor Paul's fortress palace of Gatchina—the so-called citadel of autocracy—where they were essentially prisoners for their own protection.

The threat of terrorism was in fact so insidious that it entirely pervaded the emperor and empress's coronation in Moscow, which took place in May 1883, two years after Alexander III's accession. Mary King Waddington, wife of a French diplomat, noted the "highly charged atmosphere" surrounding the event, while Mrs. Frederic Chenevix Trench, wife of the military attaché to the British embassy, observed of the "stringent" security measures that "no amount of precaution seems too minute to counteract and prevent possible machinations of the Nihilists."

Mrs. Trench reported that on the morning Alexander and Marie were set to make their ceremonial entry into the Kremlin, "several anonymous letters had been received by both the Emperor and the Empress telling them to prepare for the worst if they persisted in the intention of going in state to the Kremlin. . . . Yet, there sat the Empress with a smile on her face, not knowing at what moment there might be a desperate attempt upon her own or upon the Emperor's life. Not only did the imperial couple receive such letters of warnings, but many of the attendants who were to form part of the pageant, and the littlest pages and postilions who accompanied the Empress's chariot, each received separate letters telling them that they would not reach the Kremlin alive."

Despite the ominous warnings, the coronation in the Kremlin's Cathedral of the Assumption was a splendid display of sacred imperial tradition. Alexander first crowned himself, then his wife as she knelt before him. After that, Marie unexpectedly rose and warmly embraced the emperor. "I cannot describe, cannot express how touching and tender it was to see these embraces of husband and wife and kisses under the imperial crown," recalled Alexander's cousin Constantine (K.R. to the family)—"this ordinary human love in the glitter and radiance of imperial majesty."

When it was all over, Marie, who some reported as having looked "very much agitated" and "very pale" during the ceremony, recounted the day in a letter to her mother. "I felt myself literally as a sacrificial lamb," she wrote. "I wore a silver train and was bare-headed having only a small pearl necklace on my neck. . . . We had a truly blissful feeling on return to our rooms when everything ended! I had the same feeling as right after I had given birth to a baby."

By nearly every account, Marie made a splendid empress— "the idol of the Russian people," as Princess Catherine Radziwill called her. Whether working on one of her numerous charitable endeavors or greeting guests at a glittering ball, the empress consistently maintained the same graciousness and regal effervescence that left those who met her in awe. "She was very short, but her bearing, her distinguished and forceful personality, and the intelligence which shone in her face, made her the perfect figure of a queen," wrote Crown Princess Cecilie, daughter-in-law of the German kaiser. "Wherever she went, her winning smile conquered the hearts of people. The way in which she bowed when passing in her carriage was charming in its gracefulness. She was extraordinarily well loved in Russia, and everyone had confidence in her . . . and [she was] a real mother to her people."

Certainly Marie dressed the part of empress, always resplendent in jewels and the most flattering fashions. "Her Majesty the Empress of the Russias, she gives me the inspiration sublime, divine," declared the renowned Parisian couturier Charles Frederick Worth of his imperial client. "And when she carries my work she so improves it. I do with difficulty recognize it. Bring to me any woman in Europe—queen, *artiste,* or *bourgeois*—who can inspire me as does Madame Her Majesty, and I will make her confections while I live and charge her nothing." Still, behind the baubles and expensive French gowns was a woman entirely unique in her appeal. Writing of Marie, the American observer Knox noted that there was "no lack of diamonds" on her person, "but sparkle bright as they may, they cannot surpass the beauty of her keen, clear, and flashing eyes."

Although the emperor was personally frugal—"Neither in the Imperial family nor any of the nobility was there anyone who better appreciated the value of a ruble or a kopeck than Emperor Alexander III," Witte wrote—he never begrudged his wife her extravagances. As one German reporter observed, "Because the Emperor is unsociable, he is glad that his wife finds inexhaustible joy in dancing and amusements, even though she runs up bills to the goddess of fashion, which are not seldom as long as those of Josephine, the first wife of Napoleon, who spent half her life in the dressing room."

But there was another, more compelling reason for the emperor's indulgence: Sasha simply loved his Minnie. She was "the only person on the face of the earth in whom the Autocrat of all the Russias puts any real trust," *The London Reader* reported in 1888. "In his gentle consort he has unlimited confidence." Indeed, Alexander called his wife "the Guardian of Russia."

Yet while the emperor lovingly doted on his adored empress, he remained to the rest of the world the same gruff Russian bear he had always been. "He glowered rather than looked," one junior officer recalled, "and had the habit of thrusting his head forward in the most menacing way, when anything displeased him." During dinner one night, the Austrian ambassador spoke of the growing unrest in the Balkans and hinted that his nation might mobilize two or three army corps. In response, the emperor picked up a fork, twisted it in a knot, and tossed it contemptuously onto the ambassador's plate. "That," he announced, "is what I am going to do to your two or three army corps."

Alexander III was a fierce nationalist, and though his genetic descent was almost entirely German, he considered himself a true Russian—and looked it, too, right down to his traditional costume of baggy trousers, colored shirts, and high boots. The emperor's motto was "All for Russia," and an intense program of "Russification" accompanied it. All the diverse regions and ethnicities throughout the empire were now to speak the same national language and observe the same religion and customs.

And, of course, the preservation of the ancient order always remained the paramount objective of Alexander III's reign. "Everything about him suggested strength, solidity, and unshakeable resolve," wrote historian W. Bruce Lincoln. "He suffered no self-doubts or even questioned that his major purpose was to preserve the Romanovs' autocracy undiluted by concessions to public opinion."

But the reactionary Goliath needed to relax once in a while. Perhaps nowhere did Alexander III feel more cozy and at home than during the imperial family's retreats out of Russia to visit Fredensborg, the country estate of the empress's parents in Denmark, where royal relations from across Europe converged each year to spend time together. "We are an immense family gathering," wrote the tsar's brother-in-law, Britain's future King Edward VII—"quite a Babel, seven different languages spoken, never sitting down to dinner less than fifty or sixty."

All cares of state and security were abandoned during these Danish sojourns, and as the emperor's daughter Olga later wrote, "No member of the Okhrana was there to guard us from dangers which did not exist." Amid the estate's lush lawns, the mighty Alexander III was simply good old Uncle Sasha, who never failed to entertain the scads of royal children who adored him. "[He was] an unending delight," recalled the emperor's nephew, Prince George of Greece; "when he was with us he was just a schoolboy up to all kinds of pranks."

The only difficult part of visiting Fredensborg was leaving it, "that awful moment of tearing ourselves away from one another, not knowing where and how our next meeting may be," as the empress's sister Alexandra described it. "Poor little [Minnie]," she continued. "I can see her now, standing at the top of the steps in utter despair, her eyes streaming over with tears, and trying to hold me as long as she could. Poor Sacha [*sic*] too felt the parting very much and cried dreadfully."

It was during one such farewell that Emperor Alexander stooped down to kiss the children of the Prince and Princess of Wales. "Good-bye, my dears," he said. "You are going back to your lovely English home, and I to my Russian prison."

It was true that the imperial family continued to live in fortresslike conditions. While Alexander III's efforts to stamp out subversion had been largely effective—reducing the revolutionary movement to what one socialist bitterly called "a cottage industry"—terrorist threats nevertheless persisted. And so did the security measures that confined them. "A lane of troops [were used] to protect him from the bombs, and mines, and other machinations of his own subjects," wrote biographer Charles Lowe. "Every bridge, every culvert, every level-crossing of the railway lines by which he journeyed was guarded by well-trained sentries, and the whole route patrolled by soldiers . . . and his Majesty's destination was never known until he reached it."

In 1887, Alexander III was spared the fate of his father when a band of revolutionaries was discovered with a cache of bombs hidden in books. Among those hanged for the thwarted crime was Alexander Ulianov, older brother of the ferocious socialist who would later emerge as Lenin. The following year, in what may have been a terrorist attack (though never proven), the train carrying the imperial family violently derailed and nearly crushed them all to death. It was only by means of the emperor's brute strength that he shouldered the wreckage long enough for his family to escape. "The bullock," it seemed, had triumphed.

"Tsar Alexander III, only forty-nine years old, was still approaching the peak of his reign [in 1894]," wrote Robert K. Massie. "The early years had been devoted to reestablishing the autocracy in effective form. Now, with the empire safe and the dynasty secure, he expected to use the great power he had gathered to put a distinctive stamp on Russia. Already there were those who, gazing confidently into the future, had begun to compare Alexander III to Peter the Great."*

But the Russian bear was vulnerable after all; his kidneys were failing. Some attributed the tsar's physical decline to the train accident six years before, when he saved his family but perhaps depleted whatever vigor he had remaining. In September 1894, he traveled to Livadia, the imperial retreat in the Crimea, where it was hoped the temperate climate might help restore his health. But Alexander continued to fail.

"To see that great man, always so respected, so dignified and yet so full of fun, tormented morally and physically by his cruel disease, was sad indeed," wrote Prince Nicholas of Greece. "It was like seeing a magnificent building crumbling."

Still, the emperor struggled to perform one last duty. His son Nicholas's fiancée, Princess Alix of Hesse-Darmstadt was due to arrive at Livadia, and he insisted upon getting dressed to greet her properly. That done, Alexander retired back to bed and prepared for the end. A priest came to help ease his passage—"an *exceedingly gripping* moment," Empress Marie

---

* Minister of War Peter Vannovsky was one such enthusiast. "He is like Peter the Great with his knout," the minister exclaimed. Foreign Minister Nicholas de Giers was of a decidedly different opinion, however. "No," he responded sorrowfully, "it's just the knout without Peter the Great."

wrote, "in which my angelic Sacha's whole wonderful, devout soul was revealed."

Finally, on November 1, Emperor Alexander III sensed his final moments. "I feel the end approaching," he whispered. "Be calm. I am calm." He died with his head resting on the shoulder of his beloved Minnie.

Chapter 13

Nicholas II (1894–1917):
"An Absolute Child"

Show your mind and don't let others forget who you are.

—EMPRESS ALEXANDRA TO NICHOLAS II

Having squashed most dissent with his meaty fist, Alexander III left his son a relatively safe and secure throne. But Nicholas II lacked his father's muscle. The new emperor was essentially a gentle, passive soul, but fatally weak. And though he adored his domineering wife, Empress Alexandra, the rest of Russia thoroughly despised her. It was a toxic pairing that would end with Nicholas and Alexandra, along with the Romanov dynasty, hurtled into a bloody abyss.

The jeweled egg created by Fabergé for Tsar Nicholas II in 1913 was exquisite—just as would be expected from the master craftsman who had spent years making such whimsical objets d'art for the imperial family. The theme reflected the three hundredth anniversary of Romanov rule in Russia being celebrated that year, and featured on the surface eighteen miniature portraits of the dynasty's sovereigns—each painted on ivory, set in diamonds, and connected by gold emblems of royal power. Inside the delicate masterpiece was a rotating globe with two golden insets indicating Michael Romanov's domains in 1613 and those vastly expanded ones ruled by his descendant Nicholas three centuries later. The emperor presented Fabergé's latest imperial egg to his wife, Alexandra, that Easter, no doubt unaware of the poignant irony that his gift—an homage to Russia's monarchy—would within just four years become a splendid artifact of a bygone era.

The tercentenary celebrations of 1913 came on the eve of war and revolution that would ultimately sweep away Michael Romanov's dynasty forever. That such a cataclysm could occur would have seemed almost absurd two decades before, when Nicholas II inherited a throne left strong and secure by his father Alexander III in 1894. Yet that's precisely when the seeds of destruction were sown.

Nicholas dreaded the prospect of becoming sovereign, and indeed it was a role for which the slight, unassuming young man was entirely unsuited. "What am I going to do," he sobbed at his father's deathbed. "I am not prepared to be a Tsar. I never wanted to become one. I know nothing of the business of ruling." Raised in the shadow of the mighty Alexander III, Nicholas had been left with little to do but play. "He's an absolute child," the emperor said of the twenty-five-year-old tsarevitch just a year before his untimely death. "His opinions are utterly childish." The vacuous entries in Nicholas's diary seem to confirm his father's low opinion of his capacities.

"It is the diary—one is tempted to say the unamusing diary—of a nobody, of a man transparently immature and of patently insignificant interests," wrote historian Richard Charques. "Two lines on this official audience, three lines on that, the bare mention of a shattering disaster . . . triviality piled on triviality. The entries stretch out into a succession of daily observations of the weather, linked by a record of outdoor occupations, from taking the dogs for a walk or gathering mushrooms to shooting, cycling, skating or rowing, and the smallest incidents of domestic life. Resounding events on the dominant issues of the day are noted with bored unconcern or are not noted at all."

Some illustrative excerpts from the diary of a young man soon set to rule as an autocrat over a vast empire:

—"As always after a ball, I don't feel well. I have a weakness in the legs. . . . I got up at 10:30. I am persuaded that I have some kind of sleeping sickness because there is no way to get up."

—"Skating with Xenia [his sister] and Aunt Ella. We amused ourselves and ran like fools. Put on skates and played ball with all my strength."

—"We danced to exhaustion . . . afterwards supper . . . to bed at 3:30 a.m."

—"All day I found myself in a state of gaiety which has little in common with the period of Lent."

While in pursuit of all the banalities that came with living the life of a playboy prince—the endless balls and late-night carousing—Nicholas did have one overwhelming preoccupation: his enduring love for a beautiful, golden-haired German princess, Alix of Hesse-Darmstadt. "My dream is one day to marry Alix H.," he recorded in his diary late in 1890. "Have loved her for a long time, but even more deeply and strongly since 1889, when she spent 6 weeks of the winter in Petersburg. Have fought my feeling for a long time, trying to deceive myself with the impossibility of my cherished dream coming true. . . . The only obstacle or gap between her and me is the matter of religion. Other than that barrier there is no other, am nearly convinced that our feelings are mutual. All is up to God's will, and am putting my trust in his mercy, calmly and meekly, looking to the future."

Although Nicholas did marry Alix—just weeks after his father's death, the haste due to his refusal to face the daunting prospect of ruling Russia without her by his side—it was not simply a matter of overcoming the barrier of religion that the future tsar described in his diary. In fact, the subdued wedding ceremony at the Winter Palace, conducted amid the gloom of a court still in deep mourning for Alexander III, was the culmination of a long courtship that had triumphed over quite a few seemingly insurmountable obstacles.

Both of Nicholas's parents had been vigorously opposed to Princess Alix as a potential bride for the heir. Emperor Alexander rejected her because she was from an insignificant German duchy that offered Russia little in the way of a strategic alliance. The tsar preferred to strengthen ties with France by wedding his son to Princess Helena, a member of the deposed Bourbon dynasty. Empress Marie agreed, and with the all-pervasive influence his mother wielded over him, Nicholas was, as he wrote, "in an awkward position. . . . I am at the crossing of two paths; I myself want to go in the other direction, while Mama obviously wants me to take this one! What will happen?"

Marie had another reason for rejecting Alix. The German princess was undoubtedly lovely. ("Tall she was," as one contemporary glowingly described her, "and delicately, beautifully shaped, with white neck and shoulders. Her complexion was clear and rosy as a little child's. [She] had large eyes, deep and grey and very lustrous.") But Alix was also painfully, almost neurotically shy and socially awkward, lacking that unique grace and appeal that Marie possessed in such abundance and which she believed was absolutely essential in a future empress.

Britain's Queen Victoria, Alix's maternal grandmother, was another formidable opponent to a match with the Russian tsarevitch. The queen had always been protective of the princess, whom she had essentially adopted as a surrogate daughter after the death of Alix's mother, Alice, in 1878. The very idea of her precious "Alicky" being sacrificed to what Victoria viewed as the barbaric vagaries of Russia made the queen frantic with worry.

"The state of Russia is *so bad,* so rotten, that at any moment something dreadful might happen," Victoria wrote to Alix's sister (quite presciently, as it turned out); "the wife of the Heir to the Throne is in a most difficult and precarious position. . . . [The marriage] would have the very worst effect here and in Germany (where Russia's not liked) and would produce a great separation between our families."*

Alexander III hoped to distract his son from his obsession with Alix by sending him away on a tour of the East (during which Nicholas survived an assassination attempt in Japan after a crazed man struck him in the head with a sword). The emperor also thought a little romance with a buxom ballerina by the name of Mathilde Kschessinska might be just the tonic his son needed to overcome his infatuation with the unsuit-

---

* Actually, it was World War I that would ensure the "great separation" of families Victoria feared. A number of the queen's descendants—including her grandsons George V of Britain and Kaiser Wilhelm II of Germany—would face one another as mortal enemies.

able German princess. The emperor arranged the tryst, and was proven right—at least to some degree.

"I note a very odd phenomenon in myself," Nicholas recorded in his diary early in 1892: "never thought that two identical sentiments, two loves, could cohabit the soul simultaneously. Now it's over three years I have loved Alix H., and I constantly cherish the thought that God might let me marry her one day. . . . But ever since camp in 1890 I have loved little K. passionately. An amazing thing, our heart. At the same time do not cease to think of Alix, although it is true, one might conclude from this I am very amorous. To a certain extent, yes!"

In the end, though, Mathilde Kschessinska proved to be merely a temporary diversion for Nicholas, albeit a heated one. (As a consolation prize for her loss, the ballerina with imperial ambitions took up with Nicholas's first cousin, Grand Duke Andrei.) And, as Alexander III began to ail from kidney disease, parental opposition to the tsarevitch wedding the bride of his choice began to dissipate as well. The only obstacle that now remained was Alix herself. Although Nicholas repeatedly declared his love for her, and she reciprocated it, the princess was a confirmed Lutheran, unwilling to cast off her faith to become Orthodox, as would be required of Russia's next empress. "I live and die a Lutheran," she once declared. "Religion isn't a pair of gloves to pull on and off."

But desire competed fiercely with spiritual conviction, and, in the spring of 1894, the heart prevailed—with a little push from Alix's odious cousin Kaiser Wilhelm II of Germany,*

---

* The bombastic and ultramilitarist German emperor, loathed by most of his royal relations in Britain, was related to Alix through their mothers, both of whom were daughters of Queen Victoria.

who was then seeking closer ties with Russia (although the two nations would eventually be engaged in the monstrous world war that would see both Nicholas and Wilhelm knocked off their thrones), and reassurances from her sister Elizabeth ("Ella"), who had earlier married Nicholas's uncle Serge and recently converted to Orthodoxy. The differences in doctrine were negligible, Ella maintained, while assuring her sister that there was great spiritual comfort to be found in the Russian church's ancient rituals and traditions.

For the tsarevitch, a cherished dream had finally been fulfilled. "God Almighty only knows what that did to me," Nicholas wrote to his mother. "I was crying like a baby, as was she. No, dear Mama, I cannot express how happy I am. The whole world changed for me in an instant: nature, mankind—they all seem so good, and dear, and happy. I cannot even write, my hands are trembling so. . . . She [Alix] has completely changed—She is gay, amusing, and talkative."

Queen Victoria seemed to be the only one less than thrilled by the engagement, pronouncing herself "quite thunderstruck" by the unwelcome news. Yet though the queen had long (and correctly) foreseen nothing but danger for her granddaughter in Russia, she had no choice but to accept the situation. "Alicky had tears in her eyes," Victoria recorded in her diary after meeting with the couple, "but she looked very bright and I kissed them both."

Nicholas II ascended the Russian throne with the bold pronouncement that he would "safeguard the principles of autocracy as firmly and unswervingly as did my late, unforgettable father." But the reserved, gentle young emperor—just twenty-six when he succeeded—was hardly the Goliath Alexander

III had been. Alix saw this vulnerability in her new husband and was determined to stand firmly by his side—not only as a loving spouse, but as a twin pillar of imperial might. Yet before she could exercise the disastrous influence she eventually wielded over her husband, the new empress (called Alexandra after her conversion to Orthodoxy) first had to contend with the old one: Nicholas's "dear, darling mother," Marie.

Far from retiring after the death of her husband, Marie (now dowager empress) emerged from her grief as dazzling as ever. And she held absolute sway over her son. "Ask my mother," Nicholas would often respond to questions about important government matters, or, "I shall ask my mother." Having successfully served as Russia's empress for thirteen years, Marie felt herself uniquely qualified to guide and counsel her often hapless son. As Maria von Bock (daughter of Prime Minister Peter Stolypin) wrote of her: "How could anyone of such small stature exude such imperial stateliness? Kind, amiable, simple in her discourse, she was an Empress from head to toe, combining an inborn majesty with such goodness that she was idolized by all who knew her."

Alexandra, by contrast, was deeply introverted and nervous—new to Russia and entirely unfamiliar with the language and customs of that often bewildering country. "She was not born to be Empress of one of the largest countries on the face of the earth," Maria von Bock noted. It was natural, then, that the far more experienced dowager empress would assume such a position of authority. But the fact that she dominated Nicholas, and unwittingly reduced him to apparent insignificance, inevitably caused deep resentment.

Even before she married Nicholas, Alix tried unsuccessfully to loosen Marie's firm grip on affairs. It was during the waning days of Alexander III, when the bride-to-be arrived at the imperial retreat at Livadia in the Crimea, only to find her fiancé, the future tsar, being completely overlooked as the emperor lay dying. All reports of Alexander's condition were delivered to Marie, and all important decisions left to her. Nicholas merely stood by, impotent. Alix was appalled.

"Sweet child," she wrote in Nicholas's diary, "pray to God. He will comfort you. Don't feel too low. Your Sunny is praying for you and the beloved patient. . . . Be firm and make the doctors come to you every day and tell you how they find him . . . so that you are always the first to know. Don't let others be put first and you left out. You are father's dear son and must be told all and asked everything. Show your mind and don't let others forget who you are."

Nicholas, however, seemed unable, or unwilling, to heed his Sunny's advice. As the horror of his encroaching succession overwhelmed him, it was "Mother dear" to whom he turned. This recipe for discord was only exacerbated when Nicholas and Alexandra moved into Marie's home at the Anichkov Palace after Alexander III died. Though they were now Russia's new emperor and empress, it was Mama who still ruled. As if to punctuate Marie's dominance, royal tradition held that a dowager empress took precedence over a reigning one. So, at all ceremonials, it was Marie who stood beside her son, while Alexandra was left behind them on the arm of some random grand duke. And, as if this wasn't symbolic enough of the state of affairs, Marie refused at first to relinquish the imperial jewels that came to her daughter-in-law by right.

Essentially, though, the mounting tension between the two empresses came down to personalities. "They tried to understand each other and failed," wrote Nicholas's sister, Olga.

"They were utterly different in character, habits, and outlook."

With the emperor busy ruling Russia—and his mother ruling him—Alexandra was left with little to do but fret. "I feel myself completely alone," she confided to a friend in Germany. "I weep and worry all day because I feel that my husband is so young and so inexperienced. . . . I am alone most of the time. My husband is occupied all day and spends his evenings with his mother."

Tensions between the empress and her mother-in-law extended to other members of the Romanov family as well—particularly with the Grand Duchess Marie Pavlovna ("Miechen" to the family), wife of Nicholas's uncle, Vladimir. (See family tree.) Miechen took an almost instant dislike to Alix and, according to Countess Kleinmichel, a leading hostess, "consistently used her powerful influence in Petersburg society to promote anything that could harm the Empress. She incited ladies holding high positions to give [bad] advice to the Tsarina, applauded their courage when they criticized her adversely, and made public the contents of their letters or the gist of their conversations."

Yet while Miechen's campaign against Alexandra was as ruthless as it was relentless (and would later intensify dangerously), the empress inadvertently assisted it with her own, often misunderstood, behavior. Socially she was a disaster. At court ceremonials and entertainments, where she was expected to shine, Alexandra instead became flushed with discomfort and embarrassment. She "felt absolutely lost," recalled Baroness Sophie Buxhoeveden, and yearned "to disappear under the ground." This extreme reticence was cruelly misconstrued. "Society did not know her," concluded Baroness

Buxhoeveden, "and her timidity was ascribed to haughtiness, and her reserve to pride."

The withering criticism, which served to make the empress all the more insecure and to retreat further into herself, soon spread far beyond the gossipy parlors of St. Petersburg when a horrific tragedy took place in May 1896, just after Nicholas and Alexandra were formally crowned in Moscow.

Although the emperor and empress had been given a rather cool reception by the crowds as they entered the Kremlin on the eve of the coronation (in contrast to the "almost deafening" greeting given Dowager Empress Marie upon her arrival), the ceremony itself was splendid. It took place on a glorious day in May, at the ancient seat of Russia's sovereigns, with all the dazzle and pageantry long associated with the sacred anointment of God's representative on earth. Shortly after, though, disaster struck.

Ordinary Russians had been invited to celebrate the coronation in an open field outside Moscow, where soldiers usually practiced military maneuvers. Free beer and souvenir mugs were to be distributed, and the newly crowned imperial couple was scheduled to make an appearance. The crowds began gathering before dawn for the festivities, but as their numbers grew ever larger, a rumor swept through the masses that the supply of beer and mugs was limited and would be distributed on a first come, first served basis. A mad rush ensued and, in the midst of it, thousands were trampled and crushed. When it was all over, the expanse where the soldiers practiced resembled an actual battleground, with scores of dead and injured littered across it.

"The *dreadful* accident . . . was appalling beyond all description," Dowager Empress Marie wrote to her mother in Denmark, "and has . . . draped a *black veil* over all the splendor and glory! Just imagine *how many* poor unfortunate people were *crushed* and fatally injured."

Nicholas and Alexandra were horrified by what had happened. They visited the injured in hospitals and paid the burial expenses for the dead. Alexandra wept bitterly. But on the night of the terrible event a coronation ball hosted by the French ambassador was planned. Much expense had been lavished on the affair, with silver and rare tapestries imported from Paris and Versailles, as well as one hundred thousand roses from the south of France. The emperor's influential uncles insisted that he attend the affair lest offense be given to one of Russia's few allies. Alas, Nicholas reluctantly agreed.

"We expected that the party would be called off," said Sergei Witte, minister of finance. "[Instead] it took place as if nothing had happened and the ball was opened by Their Majesties dancing a quadrille." For many, an indelible image was formed of a callous young tsar, with "the German woman" by his side, dancing on the fresh corpses of his trampled subjects.

After a period of time spent living under the dowager empress's roof after their marriage, Nicholas and Alexandra finally moved out of Mama's palace and settled into a place of their own. The empress eschewed the sprawling Winter Palace—traditional home of the tsars—in favor of the relatively modest Alexander Palace at Tsarskoe Selo (the Tsar's Village), an imperial retreat outside St. Petersburg. Here, in what Nicholas described as "that charming, dear precious place," the couple would reside, largely isolated from the rest of Russia, until revolution finally forced their permanent relocation in 1917.

"Tsarskoe Selo was a world apart, an enchanted fairyland to which only a small number of people had the right of entry," wrote Gleb Botkin, son of Nicholas II's court physician. "It became a legendary place. To the loyal monarchists, it was sort of a terrestrial paradise, the abode of earthly gods. To the revolutionaries, it was a sinister place where blood-thirsty tyrants were hatching their terrible plots against an innocent population."

To Nicholas and Alexandra, though, Tsarskoe Selo was simply home. While she cocooned herself from society in her mauve-colored boudoir, he went about "the awful job I have feared all my life": ruling Russia. The empress would have far preferred to have her husband beside her at all times—confined, as author Edward Crankshaw wrote, "to a sort of ever-lasting cozy tea-party." In fact, she wanted to dominate him. But that role was still reserved for the tsar's mother, as well as his formidable uncles: the brothers of Alexander III.

"Nicholas II spent the first ten years of his reign sitting behind a massive desk in the palace and listening with near-awe to the well-rehearsed bellowing of his towering uncles," wrote Grand Duke Alexander ("Sandro"), the tsar's cousin. "He dreaded to be left alone with them. In the presence of witnesses his opinions were accepted as orders, but the instant the door of his study closed on the outside—down to the table would go with a bang the weighty first of Uncle Alexis . . . two hundred and fifty pounds . . . packed in the resplendent uniform of Grand Admiral of the Fleet. . . . Uncle Serge and Uncle Vladimir developed equally efficient methods of intimidation. . . . They all had their favorite generals and admirals . . . their ballerinas [who served as their mistresses] desirous of organizing a 'Russian season' in Paris;

their wonderful preachers anxious to redeem the Emperor's soul . . . their clairvoyant peasants with a divine message."

Another pernicious influence on the young emperor was Kaiser Wilhelm II of Germany—the same cousin "Willy" who had earlier helped orchestrate Alexandra's acceptance of Nicholas's marriage proposal. For years Russia had pursued an expansionist policy in Asia—occupying Manchuria, for example, and making aggressive forays into the Korean peninsula. The pinnacle of this Asian adventurism was the seizure from Japan of the Chinese fortress city of Port Arthur in 1898, giving Russia its only warm-water access to the Pacific. It was the bellicose German kaiser who encouraged this aggressive policy, flattering and cajoling the impressionable "Nicky," confirming upon him the meaningless title "Admiral of the Pacific." Willy's motive was simple self-interest: He wanted the tsar distracted in the east, which would allow him to pursue his own agenda in Europe without Russian interference. Unfortunately, Nicky found Willy's siren call irresistible.

The emperor was thoroughly convinced of Russia's superiority over the "little short-tailed monkeys," as he derisively referred to the Japanese. Nevertheless, when diplomatic relations with them finally broke down over Russia's continued excursions into Korea, Nicholas wavered over the idea of actually going to war. There were hawks, like Minister of the Interior Vyacheslav Plehve, who advocated "a short, victorious war" to help distract the people from a rapidly reemerging revolutionary movement wrought by vast and insidious social injustices. But Sergei Witte, among others, was vehemently opposed to any such engagement. "An armed struggle with Japan . . . would be a great disaster," he warned the emperor;

far from stifling revolt, it would certainly transform "the latent dissatisfaction of our domestic life" into overt political violence.

The gentle, retiring Russian sovereign was a man who relied as much on fate as upon the advice of others—or his own judgment—to resolve an issue. And so it was with the Japan crisis. "War is war," he said, "and peace is peace. But this business of not knowing either way is agonizing." It was only with Japan's surprise attack on Port Arthur in February 1904 that Nicholas's decision was made for him. "Is this undeclared war?" he exclaimed upon receiving the news. "Then may God help us!"

The attack on Port Arthur resulted in a brief surge in Russian nationalism. "Everyone was mixed together," one newspaper reported. "Generals and tramps marched side-by-side, students with banners, and ladies, their arms filled with shopping. Everyone was united in one general feeling." But what was supposed to be "a short, victorious war" turned out to be a protracted catastrophe. Japan had emerged as an industrial and military giant over the last generation, capable of easily replenishing their troops, while Russian forces had to travel vast distances to the front on the still-incomplete Trans-Siberian Railroad. The losses were staggering, and as they mounted patriotism rapidly devolved into widespread discontent—just as Witte had predicted.

"You have no idea the intensity of feeling aroused in Russia during the last few months," Countess Kleinmichel wrote at the end of 1904. "Our *mujiks* [peasants] are now objecting to being killed for what they call *a bit of territory we've never heard of.* . . . Not a week passes without a mutiny in the barracks, or riots along the line when reservists leave for the front. . . . In the universities it's even worse; revolutionary demonstrations, provoked by the slightest incident, are every-day occurrences. You can be sure that the peasants will come on the scene before long. That will mean the end of Tsarism and Russia!"

Yet bleak as the situation had become in 1904, it served merely as a preview for the momentous year that followed—what Dowager Empress Marie called "the year of nightmares."

The new year, 1905, opened with a debilitating setback for Russia, news of which the French ambassador recorded in his diary: "Port Arthur, the Gibraltar of the Far East, the great fortress, symbolizing Russian domination in the China Seas . . . surrendered this morning." Not only did the fall of this strategic gem have the effect of "piling national humiliation on national anger," as Crankshaw wrote; it also unleashed widespread strikes by workers long disgruntled with the abysmal living and working conditions to which they were subjected as Russia rapidly industrialized. What resulted was, at least to that point, the nadir of Nicholas II's reign.

A youthful priest by the name of George Gapon was able to marshal the workers' simmering discontent into a mass march on the Winter Palace, where he planned to present their grievances directly to the tsar. On Sunday, January 22, the rally began. Enormous crowds began to peacefully march to the palace from all directions. Jubilant in their expectations, they carried crosses, icons, and portraits of Nicholas, while singing the imperial anthem, "God Save the Tsar."

Although the converging processions to the center of the city were celebratory, the sheer mass of people proved overwhelming to the soldiers charged with maintaining order. A number of them opened fire, and men, women and children fell by the hundreds. "The day, which became known as 'Bloody Sunday,' was a turning point in Russian history," wrote biographer Robert K. Massie. "It shattered the ancient, legendary belief that tsar and the people were one. As bullets riddled their icons, their banners and their portraits of Nicholas, the people shrieked, 'The Tsar will not help us!' It would not be long before they added the grim corollary, 'And so we have no Tsar.'"

Nicholas, who was actually at Tsarskoe Selo when the slaughter took place, recorded the tragedy in his journal that night: "A painful day! Serious disorders took place in Petersburg when the workers tried to come to the Winter Palace. The troops have been forced to fire in several parts of the city and there are many killed and wounded. Lord, how painful and sad this is!"

Other members of the imperial family reacted with revulsion as well. "We're lost, aren't we?" cried the tsar's uncle, Grand Duke Paul; "within and without, everything's crumbling!" Similarly, Paul's wife, Olga, declared, "What a horrible day! Now we shall have revolution—it's the end! . . . Today's disaster is irreparable!"

The response to Bloody Sunday was a call for revolt and terrorism rarely seen in Russia since the days of Alexander II. "The Revolution has come," declared the Marxist Leon Trotsky. From his hiding place, Father Gapon wrote a public denunciation of "Nicholas Romanov, formerly Tsar and at present soul-murderer of the Russian empire," while the Russian Social Democratic Party issued a violent manifesto: "Yesterday you saw the savagery of the monarchy. You saw the blood running in the streets. . . . Who directed the soldiers' rifles and shot against the breasts of the workers? It was the Tsar! The Grand Dukes, the ministers, the generals, the scum of the Court . . . may they meet death!"

Three weeks later, the tsar's uncle (and Alexandra's brother-in-law), Grand Duke Serge, did indeed meet death—in an assassination even more ghastly than that of his father Alexander II (see Chapter 11). He was blown to smithereens after a bomb was tossed into his carriage. "The unfortunate grand duke was reduced to pieces and we literally found nothing of his head, which must have been shattered into tiny pieces," recounted the tsar's cousin, Grand Duke Nicholas. "Parts of his body, such as two fingers, were found on the roof of the Palace of Justice, and those which were laying on the snow, were fragments full of blood and frightful limbs, etc."*

Such was the specter of violence in the capital that the emperor and empress were unable to attend Serge's funeral, as it was deemed far too dangerous. However, the murdered grand duke's brother Paul, who had been exiled for having married a commoner without the tsar's consent, was allowed back home to attend. And what he found after meeting with his nephew Nicholas II was troubling. According to Paul, the tsar seemed oblivious—both to the perils of the continuing war with Japan, with the massive losses that accompanied it, and to the rising revolutionary fervor that resulted.

The emperor "discussed the war with *alarming complacency*," as the French diplomat (and future ambassador) Maurice Paléologue reported Paul saying in a conversation he had

---

* After the assassination of her husband, Alexandra's sister Ella founded a convent in Moscow and became a nun. Her life of charitable work came to a ghastly end under the Bolsheviks in 1918, when she was tossed, still alive, down a mine pit and left to die with several others.

with the grand duke. "The revolutionary outbreaks hardly worry him at all; he claims that the masses are not in the least interested in them; he believes he is one with the people."

The tsar's mother was far more realistic about the situation than her son, and offered Paul a bleak outlook: "We've lost our last chance of winning in the Far East; we're beaten already; we ought to make peace at once; otherwise there'll be a revolution." When the grand duke asked his sister-in-law if she had been so candid with her son, the dowager empress replied, "I tell him so every day, but he won't listen to me; he doesn't realize our military situation any better than the position at home. He can't see that he's leading Russia into disaster."

Marie's dire assessment proved all too accurate as "the year of nightmares" progressed. On May 27, the Russian Baltic Fleet, after sailing halfway around the globe over seven months, was ambushed by the Japanese as it made its way up the Tsushima Strait. More than four thousand Russians were killed in the epic naval battle that ensued—the largest since Trafalgar a century before—and six thousand more were captured. In all, twenty warships were lost, forcing Russia's surrender the next day. After receiving the report, Nicholas II "turned ashen pale," according to his sister Olga; "he trembled, and clutched at a chair for support. Alicky broke down and sobbed. The whole palace was plunged into mourning that day."

After this ignominious surrender, there was no choice now but to end the entire war. Sergei Witte deftly negotiated rather favorable peace terms for Russia,* but as author W.

---

* The peace conference was held in Portsmouth, New Hampshire, and mediated by President Theodore Roosevelt, who won the Nobel Peace Prize for his efforts. The real winner was Witte, however, who managed

Bruce Lincoln noted, "even [he] could not shield Nicholas from being the first ruler in Europe to admit defeat at the hands of Asians."

Meanwhile, violence and disturbances were erupting across Russia at an alarming rate, which, Lincoln wrote, made it evident that Bloody Sunday had been but "the first bloodletting of the year." "What's happening to Russia?" exclaimed Grand Duke Constantine (known as K.R.). "What disorganization, what disintegration, just like a piece of clothing that is beginning to rip and tear along the seams, and fall open."

Even Nicholas now seemed at last to grasp the seriousness of the situation. "It makes me sick to read the news," he wrote; "strikes in schools and factories, murdered policemen, Cossacks, riots. But the ministers, instead of acting with quick decision, only assemble in council like a lot of frightened hens and cackle about providing united ministerial action." Yet despite the tsar's lament, the ultimate authority and responsibility rested, as it always had in autocratic Russia, with the sovereign. And he was helpless.

"My poor Nicky!" his mother wrote. "May God give you *the strength and wisdom* in these terribly difficult times to take the right measures and so overcome this evil. . . . May God help you, that is my constant prayer." Mother also had a bit of advice left for the emperor who had begun listening to her less and less. "I am sure that the only man who can help you now and be useful is [Serge] Witte . . . he certainly is a man of genius, *energetic* and clear sighted."

By mid-October, in what Lincoln called "a storm unlike

---

to obtain favorable concessions for Russia and was awarded the title of count by the tsar. "He went quite stiff with emotion," recounted Nicholas, "and then tried three times to kiss my hand." The warm feelings were not to last. (See footnote on page 258.)

any Russia had ever seen," the entire country was paralyzed by strikes. Workers from virtually every sector walked off their jobs in the cities, while peasants rampaged through the countryside, burning and pillaging. "The revolution was at hand," wrote Massie; "it needed only a spark."

"So the ominous quiet days began," Nicholas wrote to his mother. "Complete order in the streets, but at the same time everybody knew that something was going to happen. The troops were waiting for the signal but the other side would not begin. One had the same feeling as before a thunder storm in the summer. Everybody was on edge and extremely nervous. . . . Through all these horrible days I constantly met with Witte. We very often met in the early morning to part only in the evening when night fell. There were only two ways open: to find an energetic soldier to crush the rebellion by sheer force. There would be time to breathe then but as likely as not, one would have to use force again in a few months, and that would mean rivers of blood and in the end we should be where we started."

One of the few men thought capable of crushing dissent and establishing what would in effect be a military dictatorship was the tsar's imposing cousin, Grand Duke Nicholas ("Nikolasha," to the family), commander of the St. Petersburg Military District. But the grand duke made quite clear his opposition to any such plan by brandishing a gun and declaring that if the emperor "wants to force me to become a dictator, I shall kill myself in his presence with this revolver."

That left the only other option Witte outlined for the emperor, which Nicholas described to his mother: "The other way out would be to give the people their civil rights, freedom of speech and press, also to have all laws confirmed by a State Duma—that of course would be a constitution. Witte defends this energetically. He says that, while it is not without risk, it is the only way out at the present moment."

After much debate, Nicholas II—"invoking God's help," as he wrote—signed what became known as the October Manifesto, granting the people liberties previously unimaginable. In that moment Russia became a semiconstitutional monarchy. And while the emperor retained certain prerogatives, such as conducting foreign affairs and the appointment of ministers, the age-old autocracy was no more.

"My dear Mama, you can't imagine what I went through before that moment," Nicholas wrote to Marie. "There was no other way out than to cross oneself and give what everyone was asking for. My only consolation is that such is the will of God, and this grave decision will lead my dear Russia out of the intolerable chaos she has seen for nearly a year."

The rest of the imperial family reacted with horror to what the tsar had done. In a stroke, he had hobbled the very institution he had sworn to uphold at his coronation. "That was the end," wrote Nicholas's cousin and brother-in-law, Grand Duke Alexander ("Sandro"—married to the tsar's sister Xenia). "The end of the dynasty and the end of the empire. A brave jump from the precipice would have spared us the agony of the remaining twelve years."

Nicholas himself was tormented by his decision. "I am too depressed," he tearfully confided to Prince Vladimir Orlov. "I feel that in signing this act I have lost the crown. Now all is finished."

All the more distressing was the fact that the October Manifesto did little to quell the violent upheavals. "For the most part the peasant disturbances are still going on," Nicholas reported to his mother. "They are difficult to put down because there are not enough troops or Cossacks to go round.

But the worst thing is another mutiny of the naval establishments in Sebastopol and part of the garrison there. How it hurts, and how ashamed one is of it all."

That December, a massive revolt in Moscow resulted in the deaths of five thousand people, with fourteen thousand more wounded. "The driving force behind both the troops and the rebels is no longer that of enthusiasm or any human impulse," a correspondent for *The New York Times* reported. "It is the force of superhuman hate, and hence the deeds reported are not acts of patriots, soldiers, or otherwise, but the enormities of madmen."*

So 1905 came to a close. And out of the chaos and destruction of the "year of nightmares" emerged one of the darkest, most mysterious figures in Russian history—the "Holy Devil" who would lead the Romanov dynasty to its ultimate destruction twelve years later: Rasputin.

---

* Nicholas bitterly turned on Count Witte as the experiment in constitutional government he had advocated seemed to fail. "As for Witte," the tsar wrote to his mother, "since the happenings in Moscow he has radically changed his views; now he wants to hang and shoot everybody. I have never seen such a chameleon of a man. That, naturally, is the reason why no one believes him any more."

Chapter 14

Nicholas II (1894–1917):

Gliding Down a Precipice

Hearken unto Our Friend [Rasputin]. Believe him. He has your interest and Russia's at heart. It is not for nothing God sent him to us, only we must pay more attention to what He says.

—EMPRESS ALEXANDRA TO NICHOLAS II

The tragedies and mishaps of Nicholas II's first decade of rule were punctuated in 1904 by the cruel discovery that the tsar's long-awaited heir, Tsarevitch Alexis, was suffering from the debilitating and incurable disease of hemophilia. The apparently miraculous ability of a peasant mystic by the name of Grigori Rasputin to control the suffering child's symptoms led Empress Alexandra to the disastrous belief that he had been sent by God. Together, Alexandra and her unkempt guru would control the fate of Russia— through war and revolution—and further propel the Romanovs to their ultimate doom.

"We made the acquaintance of a man of God," Nicholas II recorded in his diary at the end of 1905—"Gregori [Rasputin], from the Tobolsk region."

The tsar's reference to this first meeting with the strange Siberian peasant with apparently mystical powers was merely a passing one, a seemingly insignificant addition to his daily log. For though Rasputin would eventually come to dominate Nicholas's reign—and fatally undermine it in the process—he was, at the time, just one more in a parade of dubious holy men, false prophets, and charlatans who managed to infiltrate the inner sanctum of the Alexander Palace.

The reclusive empress had been desperate enough to be drawn in by these frauds because of her continued inability to bear a son to inherit the throne. After ten years of marriage, she had only given birth to a succession of girls—four in all: Olga, Tatiana, Marie, and the child destined to become perhaps the most famous Romanov of all, Anastasia. Each of these grand duchesses was healthy and vibrant, but because of a law enacted by the mad emperor Paul that (out of hatred for his mother Catherine the Great) debarred women from ruling Russia, the imperial crown was in danger of passing out of Nicholas's immediate family.

In her frantic efforts to conceive a son, Alexandra subjected herself to all manner of hokum. She bathed in waters believed to be beneficial for sex selection, for example, and admitted into her presence an assortment of malformed and deranged mystics, one of whose epileptic seizures were taken to be signs of divine intercession. A French quack named Philippe, with his self-proclaimed power to control gender, was imported to Russia and, at the tsar's command, given a medical degree to enhance his respectability. In another instance, Alexandra was advised that a long-dead holy man by the name of Seraphim would intercede on her behalf, but only if he was canonized. Accordingly, Tsar Nicholas had Seraphim declared a saint— notwithstanding the fact that one of the most important indications of saintliness in the Orthodox Church, an uncorrupted corpse, was found to be lacking when Seraphim's rotting body was exhumed.

Then, in August 1904, a miracle happened: Alexandra delivered a beautiful baby boy. He was named Alexis, after the second Romanov tsar. "Oh, it cannot be true!" the empress cried. "It cannot be true! Is it really a boy?" To his overjoyed mother, Alexis instantly became "my sunbeam."

"I could see she was transformed by the delicious joy of a mother who had at last seen her dearest wish fulfilled," recalled Pierre Gilliard, who tutored Nicholas and Alexandra's daughters, and eventually Alexis as well. "She was proud and happy in the beauty of her child."

Nicholas, too, was ecstatic over the arrival of his long-awaited heir. Alexander Mossolov, head of the Court Chancellery, recalled being taken by the happy emperor to see Alexis in his nursery. "I don't think that you have yet met my dear little Tsarevitch," Nicholas said. "Come along and I will show him to you."

"We went in," Mossolov continued. "The baby was being given his daily bath. He was lustily kicking out in the water.... The Tsar took the child out of his bath towels and put his little feet in the hollow of his hand, supporting him with the other arm. There he was, naked, chubby, rosy—a wonderful boy."

"Don't you think he's a beauty?" asked the beaming father.

The boy was indeed angelic, "with long fair curls, great grey-blue eyes under the fringe of long, curling lashes and the fresh pink color of a healthy child," as Gilliard described him. But Nicholas and Alexandra soon made a devastating discovery about the health of their precious son, for beneath that rosy skin ran blood that wouldn't clot. It was the hallmark of a hideous, incurable disease called hemophilia, the first sign of which appeared when the tsarevitch was just six weeks old. "Alix and I are very disturbed at the constant bleeding in little Alexis," Nicholas recorded in his diary. "It continued from his navel until evening."

Before long, indications of the dread malady became unmistakable. Every bump or minor trauma, harmless for most children, became a life-or-death ordeal for Alexis. It was as if seemingly ordinary childhood accidents set off subdural explosions in the boy. Blood flowed unceasingly from broken vessels, pooling in great swelling masses that corroded the surrounding tissue and cartilage before finally being reabsorbed into the body. In the process, the normally happy and carefree child would be left immobilized for weeks, tortured with excruciating pain, and never far from death.

Empress Alexandra "hardly knew a day of happiness after she knew her boy's fate," remembered her friend Anna Vyrubova. "Her health and spirits declined, and she developed chronic heart trouble. . . . Although the boy's affliction was in no conceivable way her fault, she dwelt morbidly on the fact that the disease is transmitted through the mother and that it was common in her family."*

Indeed the empress's entire world collapsed. Her answered prayers for a son were now accompanied by a never-ending nightmare. Anxiety plagued her, since she knew that with the smallest accident she could lose her sunbeam in an instant. Exhaustion depleted her as she kept vigil by Alexis's bedside for days at a time, barely sleeping, while trying to nurse him back to health. And perhaps worst of all, despair overcame

---

* Alexandra's grandmother Queen Victoria carried the hemophilic gene, which was then passed down matrilineally to many of her numerous descendants—Tsarevitch Alexis being one.

her as her beloved child pitifully wailed for the comfort and relief she was helpless to provide. "No tragedy affected Alexandra as deeply as her son's hemophilia," wrote her biographer Greg King. "It was not, for her, merely an illness; it became an active force working within her son."

Nicholas was as shattered as his wife by the cruel fate to which his son had been consigned. "The emperor aged ten years overnight," noted one of Nicholas's cousins. "He could not bear to think that the doctors had sentenced his son to death or life as an invalid. . . . For [Alexis's] imperial parents, life lost all sense." Yet no matter how deeply Nicholas grieved, he still had an empire to manage. And with Alexandra fully immersed in the welfare of the tsarevitch, which drained her entirely, the emperor was left without the comfort of his consort.

"She keeps to her bed most of the day, does not receive anyone, does not come out to lunches and remains on the balcony day after day," Nicholas confided to his mother. "[Eugene] Botkin [the court physician] has persuaded her to go to Nauheim [a German spa] for a cure in the early autumn. It is very important for her to get better, for her own sake, and the children's and me. I am completely run down mentally by worrying over her health."

Other than the fact that he was heir to an empire, upon whom all hopes for the dynastic future rested, the little boy at the center of the Romanov family tragedy was in many ways just a typical youngest child—a charmer, doted on by his parents, adored by his four older sisters, and, as Gilliard noted, "endowed with a naturally happy disposition. . . . When he was well the palace was, as it were, transformed. Every one and every thing seemed bathed in sunshine."

But keeping the tsarevitch well was a constant struggle. To

prevent injury, which might prove lethal, the child's activities were severely curbed. There was to be no climbing trees or riding bikes. Running free was absolutely forbidden. Two sailors, Andrei Derevenko and Klementy Nagorny, were assigned to become the boy's constant companions—male nannies of sorts—and to protect him at all costs from hurting himself.* "Luckily his sisters liked playing with him," Gilliard wrote. "They brought into his life an element of youthful merriment that otherwise would have been sorely missed."

Yet despite enthusiastic siblings, a mountain of elaborate toys, and a menagerie of pets, Alexis nevertheless lacked something essential: the opportunity just to be a rough-and-tumble boy. "Why can other boys have everything and I nothing," he once blurted in frustration.

It was Pierre Gilliard who recognized the damaging effect Alexis's insulated, overprotected existence would have on the formation of his character. And the tutor was determined to do something about it. Shockingly, the emperor and empress allowed him to cut away the strict constraints on Alexis's every movement. All went well, until the boy fell off a chair upon which he was standing and endured a hideously painful brush with death.

"I was thunderstruck," Gilliard wrote. "Yet neither the Tsar nor the Tsaritsa blamed me in the slightest. So far from it, they seemed intent on preventing me from despairing. . . . The Tsaritsa was at her son's bedside from the first onset of

---

* "Derevenko was so patient and so resourceful, that he often did wonders in alleviating the pain," recalled Anna Vyrubova. "I can still hear the plaintive voice of Alexei begging the big sailor, 'Lift my arm,' 'Put up my leg,' 'Warm my hands,' and I can see the patient, calm-eyed man working for hours to give comfort to the little pain-wracked limbs." The sailor, however, would soon reveal another, darker side (see following chapter).

the attack. She watched over him, surrounding him with her tender love and care and trying a thousand attentions to alleviate his sufferings. . . . Think of the torture of that mother, an impotent witness to her son's martyrdom in those hours of anguish—a mother who knew that she herself was the cause of those sufferings, that she had transmitted the terrible disease against which human science was powerless. Now I understand the secret tragedy of her life. How easy it was to reconstruct the stages of that long Calvary."

It is uncertain when exactly Rasputin reappeared at Tsarskoe Selo after first being introduced to the emperor and empress late in 1905. But the self-proclaimed holy man (often referred to as "the *staretz*")* came highly recommended by some of the church's top clergy, as well as several members of the tsar's extended family—and the immediate effect he had on Alexis seemed nothing short of miraculous.

"He was taken to the bedside of the tsarevitch," reported one palace insider. "The child looked at him and began to bubble with laughter. Rasputin laughed too. He laid his hand on the boy's leg and the bleeding stopped at once. 'There's a good boy,' said Rasputin. 'You'll be alright. But only God can tell what will happen tomorrow.'"

In an instant, the grubby, unschooled peasant had accomplished what the tsarevitch's doctors had long since deemed impossible. And for the empress, he quickly came to represent a deliverance from darkness—the divine instrument of her son's salvation. "Rasputin was the intermediary between

---

* By strict definition, a *staretz* was an *aesthetic* holy man, something Rasputin most certainly was not. But he was often referred to as such by his contemporaries and so will be here as well.

her and God," Gilliard wrote. "Her own prayers went unanswered but his seemed to be." Soon, others began to believe in the healing powers of the *staretz* as well.

"There is no doubt about that," wrote Nicholas's sister Olga. "I saw those miraculous effects with my own eyes and that more than once."* Indeed, even the imperial surgeon, Professor S. P. Federov, was impressed by what he witnessed: "And look, Rasputin would come in, walk up to the patient, look at him and spit. The bleeding would stop in no time. . . . How could the empress not trust Rasputin after that?"

Historians have long been baffled by the peasant's mysterious healing effect on Alexis and his apparent ability to control the vicious disease that plagued the boy. Some dubious theories have been proposed to explain it. One such supposition was that the so-called *staretz* had been in league with someone inside the palace who kept him updated on the tsarevitch's condition. This allowed the "healer" to appear just as the boy's symptoms were starting to subside naturally.

Others have been more circumspect in their analysis, noting, for example, that some of the personal qualities possessed by Rasputin lent themselves well to calming the suffering child—a process modern medicine now regards as critical to a hemophiliac's recovery after an injury. Certainly many of Rasputin's contemporaries remarked upon his uncanny ability to soothe and comfort—"the gift of bringing calm and serenity to the soul," as one described it. There was also the self-

---

* "The poor child lay in pain, dark patches under his eyes and his little body all distorted and the leg terribly swollen," Olga recalled of one occasion. "The doctors were just useless . . . more frightened than any of us . . . whispering among themselves." The next morning, after a visit from Rasputin, Olga observed, "The little boy was not just alive—but well. He was sitting up in bed, the fever gone, the eyes clear and bright, not a sign of any swelling in the leg."

possession and supreme authority in his voice, as well as his penetrating eyes, which though they both attracted and repelled those upon whom he fixated them, were almost universally described as hypnotic.

"Our eyes met and I was instantly struck by his uncanny appearance," recalled Lili Dehn, one of the empress's ladies-in-waiting and a constant companion. "At first he appeared to be a typical peasant from the frozen north, but his eyes held mine, those shining steel-like eyes which seemed to read one's inmost thoughts." Maurice Paléologue, the French ambassador, recorded a similar impression: "The whole expression on the face was concentrated in the eyes—light-blue eyes [others describe them as green] with a curious sparkle, depth and fascination. His gaze was at once penetrating and caressing, naïve and cunning, direct and yet remote. When he was excited, it seemed as if his pupils became magnetic."*

Whatever the source of Rasputin's apparent mastery over the tsarevitch's disease—and it may very well simply have been a gift for healing—Empress Alexandra sincerely believed this plainspoken peasant was, quite literally, Heaven sent. And with these divinely ordained credentials, Rasputin became one of the few true intimates of the royal family. To their new "Friend," the emperor and empress were not Their Majesties, but "Papa" and "Mama"—his welcoming hosts.

"They would kiss three times in the Russian fashion, and

---

* Prime Minister Peter Stolypin also described Rasputin's hypnotic glare, though in a less than glowing account: "He ran his pale eyes over me, mumbled mysterious and inarticulate words from Scriptures, made strange movements with his hands, and I began to feel an indescribable loathing for this vermin sitting opposite of me. Still, I did realize that the man possessed great hypnotic power, which was beginning to produce a fairly strong moral impression on me, though certainly one of revulsion. I pulled myself together."

then start to talk," reported General A. I. Spiridovich, chief of the tsar's personal security service. "He would speak to them of Siberia, of the needs of peasants, of his pilgrimages. Their Majesties would always discuss the health of the tsarevitch or their current worries about him. When he withdrew after an hour's conversation with the Imperial Family he always left Their Majesties cheerful, their souls filled with joyous hope. They believed in the power of his prayers to the very end. . . . No one could shake their faith in him."

It was a strange tableau: the loftiest personages in Russia intimately conversing in their imperial sanctum with one of the many millions of peasants over whom they ruled but rarely ever saw or noticed. Rasputin delighted in this unique access, but refused to modify his essential earthiness to blend in better with his opulent surroundings (even if the material of his traditional attire did become richer over time). He ate with his hands and wiped his mouth with his beard. His language was blunt, even at times to the point of rudeness, but the royals didn't mind: This is what made him a man of the people.

"All the children seemed to like him," wrote their aunt Olga. "They were completely at ease with him. I still remember little Alexis, deciding he was a rabbit, jumped up and down the room. And then, quite suddenly, Rasputin caught the child's hand and led him to the bedroom. . . . There was something like a hush as though we found ourselves in church. In Alexis's bedroom, no lamps were lit; the only light came from the candles burning in front of some beautiful icons. The child stood very still by the side of the giant, whose head was bowed. I knew he was praying. It was all most impressive. I also knew that my little nephew had joined him in prayer. I really cannot describe it—but I was then conscious of the man's sincerity."

Until Rasputin hit on her.

So there it was: Behind the façade of piety the *staretz* presented to Nicholas and Alexandra lurked an unapologetic lecher; a Siberian satyr who blithely bedded all classes of women with the frequency and relish of a jackrabbit. "He has enough for all," his oft-betrayed (and apparently resigned) wife once said.

"He would be surrounded by his admirers, with whom he also slept," Rasputin's secretary reported. "He would do his thing with them quite openly and without shame. He would caress them . . . and when he or they felt like it he would simply take them to his study and do his business. . . . I often heard his views, a mixture of religion and debauchery. He would sit there and give his instructions to his female admirers.

"'Do you think that I degrade you? I don't degrade you, I purify you.'

"That was his basic idea. He also used the word 'grace,' meaning that by sleeping with him a woman came into the grace of God."

Rasputin's remarkable success with women—"He had too many offers," reported his secretary—may be attributed, at least in part, to the pseudoreligious concept he espoused in which it was held that in order to be truly forgiven, one had to gravely sin first. This gave his female followers just the excuse they needed to leap into bed with the magnetic mystic (whose frequent visits to public bathhouses, where his female disciples were granted the privilege of washing his genitals, belies his lingering reputation for being dirty and foul-smelling).

"Women," wrote Rasputin's biographer René Fülöp-Miller, "found in Gregori Elfimovich [his patronymic] the fulfillment of two desires which had hitherto seemed irreconcilable, religious salvation and the satisfaction of carnal appetites. . . . As in the eyes of his disciples, Rasputin was a reincarnation of the Lord, intercourse with him, in particular, could not possibly be a sin; and those women found for the first time in their lives a pure happiness, untroubled by the gnawings of conscience."

While Rasputin was very careful to conceal his lecherous side from his imperial patrons, he certainly seemed to suffer no inner turmoil over the apparent dichotomy of his nature. "Contradictions," he declared, "what of them, for you they are contradictions, but I am me, Gregori Rasputin, and that's what matters; look at me, see what I have become!"

It was true that the rough Siberian peasant, who had spent many years roaming Russia, living hand to mouth while preaching his un-Orthodox brand of religion, had now reached the very apex of society. And to these who had witnessed the "Holy Devil's" unlikely rise, it was appalling. "In the salons of St. Petersburg, which I frequented fairly regularly, Rasputin was the sole topic of conversation," reported the Russian minister to Bulgaria. With time, the talk became increasingly salacious.

Much of the gossip revolved around the empress's relationship with the *staretz*, and came as a direct consequence of Nicholas and Alexandra's decision to keep their son's incurable disease a palace secret. Lacking awareness of Alexis's condition, and Rasputin's apparently efficacious treatment of it, society became convinced something unsavory was happening between the already unpopular, semireclusive empress and the crude, hypersexual peasant whose gross promiscuity was now public knowledge.

The chatter became louder and more ferocious when a series of purloined letters from members of the imperial family to Rasputin were published in 1911. One of the most damning was from the empress, whose normally florid style of writing—exercised in this case by a devoted disciple addressing her spiritual master—could be easily misinterpreted as a steamy love letter:

My Beloved, unforgettable teacher, redeemer and mentor:

How tiresome it is without you. My soul is quiet and I relax only when you, my teacher, are sitting beside me. I kiss your hands and lean on your blessed shoulders. Oh, how light do I feel then! I only wish one thing: to fall asleep, forever on your shoulders and in your arms. What happiness to feel your presence near me. Where are you? Where have you gone? Oh, I am so sad and my heart is longing. . . . Will you soon again be close to me? Come quickly, I am waiting for you and I am tormenting myself for you. I am asking for your Holy Blessing, and I am kissing your blessed hands. I love you forever.

Yours,

Mama

Rasputin did little to dispel the rumors—quite the contrary, in fact. The *staretz* basked in the prestige his access afforded him. "He began to feel he had a politico-historical mission," wrote his biographer Alex de Jonge, "professing to have become convinced that somehow his destiny was linked to the destiny of the nation and the ruling house."

Rasputin bragged about his influence with the emperor and empress with all the subtlety with which he used to seduce gullible sex partners. "The tsar thinks I'm Christ incarnate," he crowed. "The tsar and the tsarina bow down to me, kneel to me, kiss my hands. The tsarina has sworn that if all turn their backs on Grisha [his nickname] she will not waver and still always consider him her friend."

There was more than an element of truth to Rasputin's grandiose pronouncement, for though Russia's sovereign may not have exactly groveled at the peasant's feet, Alexandra was indeed his fierce and uncompromising defender. "Saints are always culminated," the empress said to Dr. Botkin in reaction to the public outrage over Rasputin. "He is hated because we love him," she told her friend Anna Vyrubova. "They accuse Rasputin of kissing women, etc. Read the Apostles, they kissed everybody as a form of greeting."

Anyone who dared impugn her "mentor," the man she considered the salvation of her son, and of Russia, earned the empress's unswerving enmity. Prime Minister Peter Stolypin—widely regarded as Russia's ablest politician, and the best hope to lead the nation into its semiconstitutional future—despised Rasputin[*] and was thus, in turn, hated by Alexandra. Even Stolypin's assassination in 1911 did little to temper her wrath. "Those who have offended God in the person of our Friend may no longer count on divine protection," the vengeful empress proclaimed. Similarly, Stolypin's successor, Vladimir Kokovtsov, also faced Alexandra's antipathy over Rasputin and eventually found himself out of a job.

Dowager Empress Marie was mortified to read the lurid accounts of Rasputin's debauchery, and more aghast still that Alexandra continued to receive him anyway. "My poor daughter-in-law does not perceive that she is ruining both the dynasty and herself," Marie confided to Prime Minister Kokovtsov in February 1912. "She sincerely believes in the

[*] See footnote on page 267.

holiness of an adventurer, and we are powerless to ward off the misfortune which is sure to come."

In an effort to persuade Nicholas and Alexandra of the looming danger Rasputin represented, the dowager empress had what was described to the Bulgarian minister as a "heart-to-heart talk" with them. Addressing the empress, according to this account, Marie stated bluntly, "It is no question of you, or your affections, your convictions or rather your religious manias. It is a question of the Emperor, of the Dynasty, of Russia! If you go on this way, you will be the undoing of us all!"

Alas, if Marie expected any support from her son in her attempt to break Rasputin's spell, she was gravely disappointed. Nicholas proved every bit as unyielding as his wife on the subject—domestic harmony absolutely depended upon it. "Better one Rasputin than ten fits of hysterics a day," the tsar once remarked in an unguarded moment.

Besides, to Nicholas II, Rasputin "was just a good, religious, simple-minded Russian," as he told his security chief. "When in trouble or assailed with doubts, I like to have a talk with him, and invariably feel at peace with myself afterwards."

The emperor, who described himself as "suffocating in this atmosphere of gossip, lies, and malice," was, like Alexandra, particularly sensitive to challenges against the *staretz* in the Duma and in the press. As far as he was concerned, it was no one's business whom they invited to their home—a stance Rasputin, protecting his own position, actively encouraged. "What are these questions about Gregori?" he said to the emperor. "It is the devil's doing. No questions should be asked."

Basil Shulgin, a monarchist member of the Duma, wrote about the two sides of Rasputin, whom he called "a Janus," and the ocean of misunderstanding between the emperor and his subjects that resulted:

"To the imperial family he [Rasputin] had turned his face as a humble *staretz* and, looking at it, the Empress cannot but be convinced that the spirit of God rests upon this man. And to the country he has turned the beastly, drunken, unclean face of a bald satyr from Tobolsk. . . . And because of the man's fateful duality . . . neither side can understand the other. So the Tsar and his people, however apart, are leading each other to the edge of the abyss."

A leap further toward that chasm came in the fall of 1912, when Rasputin solidified his power after he at least appeared to have rescued Tsarevitch Alexis from what was by far the most frightening trauma the boy had yet suffered.

The imperial family had retreated to their vast hunting estate in Poland when, in the midst of their relaxed vacation, eight-year-old Alexis took a terrible tumble jumping into a boat. At first it appeared the fall had caused minimal internal damage—just some swelling and bruising below the groin. But then, after the family moved on to their smaller estate at Spala, the empress took her son on a fateful carriage ride through the surrounding forest paths. Before long, Alexis began to wince in pain and cry out every time the carriage jolted. Duly alarmed, Alexandra ordered the driver to return to the lodge as quickly as possible.

"The return drive stands out in my mind as an experience in horror," recalled Anna Vyrubova, who had accompanied mother and son on the ride. "Every movement of the carriage, every rough place in the road, caused the child the most exquisite torture and by the time we reached home, the boy was almost unconscious with pain."

The doctors were, as usual, helpless as the blood from broken vessels flowed unceasingly, filling a large area around the original injury and creating a massive hematoma. Pain-relieving drugs were never administered to Alexis for fear of their addictive qualities, so the boy lay in agony as his life slowly ebbed away.

"The days between the 6th and the 10th [of October] were the worst," the emperor reported to his mother. "The poor darling suffered intensely, the pains came in spasms and recurred every quarter of an hour. His high temperature made him delirious night and day, and he would sit up in bed and every movement brought the pain on again. He hardly slept at all, had not even the strength to cry, and kept repeating, 'Oh Lord, have mercy upon me.'"

So intense and unrelenting was the pain that the normally exuberant young boy began to see death as a welcome relief. "When I am dead, it will not hurt anymore, will it?" he whispered at one point. And at another, the child solemnly instructed his parents to "build me a little monument of stones in the woods." Nicholas and Alexandra both believed that time was rapidly drawing near.

As her dying child struggled desperately, the empress remained where she always did—by his side, providing whatever poor comfort she could. "During the entire time," recounted Anna Vyrubova, "the Empress never undressed, never went to bed, rarely even laid down for an hour's rest. Hour after hour she sat beside the bed where the half-conscious child lay huddled on one side, his left leg drawn up. . . . His face was absolutely bloodless, drawn and seamed with suffering, while his almost expressionless eyes rolled back in his head. Once, when the Emperor came into the room, seeing the boy in this agony, and hearing the faint screams of pain, the poor father's courage completely gave way and he rushed, weeping bitterly, to his study."

So there she was, the empress left all alone, her husband too consumed by his own grief, while the doctors shook their heads in despair. Not even Rasputin was present, but far, far away, on a visit to his homeland. Yet despite the vast distance, Alexandra cabled him anyway, begging for the holy man's intercession. Hours later—as the public announcement of the tsarevitch's death was being drafted and his funeral planned—a response arrived from Siberia: "The Little One will not die. Do not allow the doctors to bother him too much." Alexis began to improve almost immediately, and with that Rasputin became invincible.

On June 28, 1914, Archduke Franz Ferdinand, heir to the Austro-Hungarian throne, was assassinated along with his wife in Sarajevo, precipitating the international crisis that ultimately led to World War I. That very same day, while visiting his home village in Siberia, Rasputin was stabbed in the stomach by a fanatic disciple of the monk Iliodor, his sworn enemy. "I have killed the Anti-Christ," the crazed assassin screamed. As it turned out, she had only wounded him, albeit grievously. The attack was severe enough to have nearly gutted the *staretz* and left him powerless to prevent the looming disaster of war. Had he been able to see the tsar in person, Rasputin later said, peace would surely have been maintained.

While no one expected war in the immediate aftermath of Franz Ferdinand's murder, it became increasingly likely as ultimatums were issued and alliances called upon. Russia began to mobilize to defend Serbia against possible attack by

Austria-Hungary and Germany, which prompted Rasputin to send Nicholas II a stern warning from his sickbed. "Let papa not plan war," he insisted; "it will be the end of Russia and all of us, we shall lose to the last man." The emperor angrily tore up the telegram.

Despite Rasputin's dire prediction, there was no stopping Nicholas, and on August 2, 1914, he issued a declaration of war against Germany and Austria-Hungary. The emperor's bellicose stance had a profound effect on his people. All strife seemed to vanish as the country came together in a surge of nationalism not seen in more than a century (and certainly greater than that which briefly accompanied the onset of Russia's war with Japan a decade earlier). "Here was a Russia which I had never known," wrote the British diplomat Robert Bruce Lockhart—"a Russia inspired by a patriotism which seemed to have its roots deep down in the soil."

A massive, exuberant crowd gathered in front of the Winter Palace—the very place where so many had been slaughtered during Bloody Sunday years before. When the emperor and empress appeared on the balcony above, the people immediately prostrated themselves. "To those thousands on their knees," wrote Paléologue, "at that moment the Tsar was really the Autocrat, the military, political and religious director of his people, the absolute master of their bodies and souls."

It was a demonstration of loyalty of which the emperor had long been deprived. "Never in all Nicky's twenty years of luckless reign had he heard so many spontaneous hurrahs," wrote one of his cousins. Indeed, as one contemporary noted, he had never been "so beloved, so respected, so popular in the eyes of his subjects at that moment. . . . Portraits of the monarch were in all the principal shop windows, and the veneration was so deep that men lifted their hats and women—even well-dressed, elegant ladies—made the sign of the cross [as they passed]."

Even the much-derided empress enjoyed a brief respite from her subjects' contempt. Princess Julia Cantacuzene, a granddaughter of President Ulysses S. Grant who married the emperor's chief of staff, recounted a touching scene inside the Winter Palace when, as Nicholas and Alexandra made their way through a crowd after a prayer service, many of those gathered surged forward for closer contact with their sovereign:

"Our beautiful Empress, looking like a Madonna of Sorrows, with tears on her cheeks, stretched her hand in passing to this or that person, now and then bending gracefully to embrace some woman who was kissing her hand. Her Majesty that day seemed to symbolize all the tragedy and suffering that had come upon us; and, feeling it deeply, to give thanks to this group for the devotion their attitude implied. Her expression was of extraordinary sweetness and distress, and possessed beauty of a quality I had never seen before in the proud, classic face. Everyone was moved by Her Majesty's manner in a moment when she must be tortured by thoughts of her old home."

And so it was in the summer of 1914: a nation united behind its sovereign; revolutionaries dispersed, disheartened, and in hiding; and, as the empress called it, "a 'healthy war' in the moral sense," to be waged against a malevolent enemy. "God is with us!" the emperor confidently declared (as did Kaiser Wilhelm).

"One breathes very easily in this pure atmosphere," one member of the Duma wrote, "which has become almost unknown among us." But that was before the monstrous realities of war—all the misery, bloodshed, and despair—revealed themselves and soon drove Mother Russia to her knees. From the outset, Russian losses were staggering. In fact, just five months after the conflict started, one million soldiers had been killed, wounded, or captured. Within a year, the war effort was on the verge of collapse. It certainly wasn't due to a lack of fighting men; more than fifteen million eventually marched off as part of what the British press called "the Russian steamroller." Nor was there any absence of valor. As early as October, the emperor was pleading with his troops to preserve themselves.

"I have not the slightest doubt about your courage and bravery," he told a group of graduating cadets, "but I need your lives, because useless losses in the officer corps may lead to serious consequences. I am sure that every one of you will give his life willingly, when it becomes necessary, but do it only in cases of exceptional emergency. In other words, I am asking you to care for yourselves."

The essential problem was Russia itself. As Massie wrote, "behind the massive façade of an enormous empire, the apparatus of government, the structure of society and economy were too primitive, too inflexible, and too brittle to withstand the enormous strains of a great four-year war."

Russia's railway system was entirely inadequate to efficiently transport men and supplies to the front: "The Supreme Command ordered, but the railroads decided," as General Albert Knox, a British military attaché, put it. Furthermore, there were not enough factories to produce vital war materials, or, because of blockades, the ability to import them. Thus, without adequate arms or ammunition, "the

Russian steamroller," was left helpless in the face of the enemy's awesome weaponry. And in this vulnerable state, Knox
wrote, brave men were "churned into gruel."

"In recent battles, a third of the men had no rifles," reported one general. "These poor devils had to wait patiently
until their comrades fell before their eyes and they could pick
up weapons. The army is drowning in its own blood." In one
instance, a private was bold enough to approach a general visiting the front. "You know, Sir, we have no weapons except
the soldier's breast," he said. "This is not war, Sir, this is
slaughter." But it was an enemy general, Paul von Hinden-
burg, who perhaps best articulated the overwhelming extent
of Russia's human sacrifice:

"In the ledger of the Great War the page upon which the
Russian losses were written has been torn out. No one knows
the figures. Five or eight million? We, too, have no idea. All
we know is that sometimes in our battles with the Russians
we had to remove the mounds of enemy corpses from before
our trenches in order to get a clear field of fire against fresh
assaulting waves. Imagination may try to reconstruct the figure of their losses, but an accurate calculation will remain forever a vain thing."

In the fury of war, and the crushing number of casualties
that came with it, anti-German sentiment in Russia grew
fierce. Bach, Brahms, and Beethoven were banished from or-
chestral programs, while rampaging mobs looted and burned
stores owned by Germans. Even Christmas trees were legally
banned. "I am going to find out about it and then make a
row," the empress announced in response to this assault on
tradition. "It's no concern of theirs nor the church's and why
take away a pleasure from the wounded men and children

because it originally came from Germany—the narrow-mindedness is too colossal."

The most ferocious attacks were aimed not at Christmas trees, but rather at the German-born empress herself. Never popular to begin with, the war brought out the most latent hatred of her subjects, who falsely accused her of being an operative for her homeland and the worst kind of traitor. In one particularly vicious story that made the rounds, a general was supposedly walking through the palace when he encountered Tsarevitch Alexis weeping. "What is wrong, my little man," the general reportedly asked, to which the boy was said to answer: "When the Russians are beaten, Papa cries. When the Germans are beaten, Mama cries. When am I to cry?"

Although Empress Alexandra was a thoroughly flawed individual, whose foolish decisions during the war would ultimately prove fatal, she was nevertheless a sincere patriot. "Twenty years I have spent in Russia," she once declared, "half my life—and the fullest, happiest part of it. It is the country of my husband and son. I have lived the life of a happy wife and mother in Russia. All my heart is bound in this country I love."

After years spent malingering in her mauve boudoir, Alexandra plunged herself into the war effort with uncharacteristic vigor and sense of purpose. She and her older daughters enrolled in a Red Cross training program for nurses, and soon enough she arranged to have the empty Catherine Palace at Tsarskoe Selo transformed into a makeshift hospital.

"I have seen the Empress of Russia in the operating room," wrote Anna Vyrubova, "holding ether cones, handling sterilized instruments, assisting in the most difficult operations, taking from the busy surgeons amputated legs and arms, removing bloody and even vermin-infested dressing, enduring all the sights and smells and agonies of that most dreadful of all places, a military hospital in the midst of war."

For Alexandra, working in the hospital in some ways had the immediacy of the front lines. "How near death always is!" she wrote to her husband. And in her chosen role, the empress served with distinction. Unfortunately, though, nursing wasn't her only wartime occupation. Had it remained so, and Alexandra let affairs of state alone, perhaps a Romanov might still be sitting on the Russian throne. Instead, in her grab for power, she led the dynasty to total ruin—with Rasputin right by her side.

Historians have long been inconsistent about the nature of the relationship between the empress and the mystic peasant during the war years. Some have asserted that it was Alexandra who set the agenda, and that she used her guru merely to endorse with his blessing what she had already decided. Others maintain that Rasputin was in control, and that given his success in healing her son, the empress concluded that he could run the empire just as well. Perhaps the truth existed somewhere in between—that the ambitions of both merged harmoniously. Yet whatever the precise formula, it proved deadly.

Certainly the two shared a common enemies list of those who they believed threatened them. And topping the roster in 1915 was General Vladimir Dzhunkovsky, commander of all the police in the empire, who made the fatal error of informing the emperor of all Rasputin's sexual shenanigans when he ripped off his mask of holiness outside the palace. It was quite a colorful indictment.

The *staretz* had gained so much influence because of his royal connections that people from all segments of society flocked to his St. Petersburg apartment seeking favors. "Three to four hundred people would call on Rasputin daily," one witness reported; "one day it was seven hundred. . . . I saw uniformed guards, students, school girls asking for financial support. There were officers' wives asking for favors for their husbands, parents asking for military exemption for their sons."

The price was often monstrously steep for women seeking the holy man's services, but there was no cash involved. In one instance, a woman sought Rasputin's help in having her husband returned from administrative exile in Siberia. According to a police report, she paid dearly. "Neither her tears, her entreaties, her talk of her children had any effect," the report read, "and taking advantage of her distraught condition and regardless of the fact that there were people in the next room, he took her by force, and then visited her several times in her hotel, constantly promising that he would arrange matters, and take a petition to the tsar from her. . . . She was eventually persuaded to return home. Rasputin did nothing about the petition because, as he put it, 'she was insolent.'"

Because the *staretz* was under constant police surveillance, a dossier grew fat with such tales, all of which were widely disseminated to people who lapped up every salacious detail. "Rasputin's apartments are the scene of the wildest orgies," wrote the American ambassador George Marye. "They beggar all description and, from the current accounts of them, which pass freely from mouth to mouth, the storied infamies of the Emperor Tiberius on the Isle of Capri are made to seem modest and tame."

Perhaps the most infamous of all Rasputin's exploits (and

the one that led to Dzhunkovsky's downfall) occurred in the spring of 1915, when the *staretz* traveled to Moscow, ostensibly to pray at the tombs of the patriarchs in the Kremlin. But there was much more fun to be had than that. "I was at Yar, the most luxurious night haunt of Moscow, with some English visitors," reported Robert Bruce Lockhart. "As we watched the musical performance in the main hall, there was a violent fracas in one of the private rooms. Wild shrieks of a woman, a man's curses, broken glass and the banging of doors. Headwaiters rushed upstairs. The manager sent for the police. . . . But the row and roaring continued. . . . The cause of the disturbance was Rasputin—drunk and lecherous, and neither police nor management dared evict him."

Outrageous as the story was, Lockhart only told half of it. When the police arrived, Rasputin dropped his trousers and began waving his genitals in the faces of other diners. And that, he declared, was just how he behaved in front of the tsar. As for Alexandra, he bragged that he could do anything he liked with "the old girl." Finally the drunken *staretz* was dragged away, "snarling and vowing vengeance."

Needless to say, Nicholas was not pleased when he read Dzhunkovsky's report of the incident, and angrily confronted Rasputin. The wily peasant meekly admitted to some details, like his drunkenness, claiming he had been led astray. As for the other, far more serious charges, he simply denied them. Still, the emperor ordered him back to Siberia for a spell. Alexandra, too, was furious about the report, but not because of her mentor's behavior, which she either did not believe or conveniently chose to ignore. Rather, she was incensed that Dzhunkovsky had shared the devastating information—not only with Nicholas, but others as well.

"My enemy Dzhunkovsky . . . has shown that vile, filthy

paper to [Grand Duke] Dmitri," the empress wrote to her husband. "If we let Our Friend be persecuted we and our country shall suffer for it. . . . I am so weary, such heartaches and pain from all this—the idea of dirt being spread about one we venerate is more than terrible. Ah, my love, when at *last* will you thump your hand upon the table and scream at Dzhunkovsky and others when they act wrongly—one does not fear you—and one *must*—they must be frightened of you, otherwise all sit upon us."

Rasputin eventually got his revenge on the police chief who reported him. "Your Dzhunkovsky's finished," he taunted the officers outside his apartment. And so he was, for within several months Dzhunkovsky lost his post.

Coinciding with Dzhunkovsky's downfall was that of the tsar's cousin, Grand Duke Nicholas Nikolavich ("Nikolasha," to the family), commander in chief of the Russian forces. "He was the most admired man in the army, not only an old-fashioned soldier, but deeply Slav," wrote Paléologue. "His whole being exuded a fierce energy. His incisive measured speech, flashing eyes and quick, nervous movements, hard, steel-trap mouth and gigantic stature [he stood six feet six inches tall] personify imperious and impetuous audacity." Alexandra and Rasputin hated him.

The empress's animosity stretched back at least as far as the horrible year of 1905, when Nikolasha threatened to shoot himself in front of the tsar if Nicholas did not accede to the formation of the Duma—the representative body whose very existence Alexandra viewed as an affront to the autocracy. Then there was the fact that Nikolasha was an ardent opponent of "Our Friend" Rasputin. According to one story, the *staretz* wanted to visit army headquarters and received the following reply from Nikolasha: "Yes, do come—I'll hang you." Thus was launched a vigorous campaign against the commander in chief, the man revered in the army as what Knox called "a sort of legendary champion of Holy Russia."

"I have absolutely no faith in N[ikolasha]," Alexandra wrote to Nicholas in one of a barrage of letters on the subject—"know him to be far from clever and having gone against a Man of God, his work can't be blessed or his advice good. . . . Russia will not be blessed if her sovereign lets a Man of God sent to help him be persecuted. I am sure. . . . You know N.'s hatred for Gregory is intense."

Alexandra's assault on Nikolasha included not-so-subtle digs at the passive emperor, whom she encouraged to be more like the man people perceived the commander in chief to be. "Forgive me, precious One, but you know you are too kind and gentle," she wrote in the spring of 1915—"sometimes a good loud voice can do wonders, and a severe look—do my love, be more decided and sure of yourself. . . . You think me a meddlesome bore, but a woman feels and sees things some-times clearer than my too humble sweetheart . . . a Sovereign needs to show his will more often."

The empress also urged Nicholas to remember that Raspu-tin's was the only voice (besides hers) of any value to him. And if the *staretz* believed Nikolasha should be removed, well then, there was no other choice but to trust him. "Hearken unto Our Friend," she wrote. "Believe him. He has your inter-est and Russia's at heart. It is not for nothing God sent him to us, only we must pay more attention to what He says. His words are not lightly spoken and the importance of having not only his prayers but his advice is great. . . . I am haunted by Our Friend's wish and know it will be fatal for us and for the country if not fulfilled. He means what he says when he speaks so seriously."

Alexandra's anti-Nikolasha campaign was ultimately abetted by the war itself. Warsaw fell in August 1915, and with the army in full retreat, so was its commander in chief. Nikolasha's fall did not cause much consternation, given the circumstances. But news of his replacement certainly did.

"There is a far more horrible event which threatens Russia," Minister of War Alexis Polivanov reported to the Council of Ministers on August 6. "I feel obliged to inform the government that this morning, during my report, His Majesty told me of his decision to remove the Grand Duke and to personally assume the supreme command of the army."

The ministers' response was swift and unequivocal. "The execution of the Emperor's decision is absolutely impossible, and one must resist him with all means," declared Minister of the Interior Prince Shcherbatov. Equally adamant was Minister of Foreign Affairs Serge Sazonov, who said that "in general, all this is so terrible that my mind is in chaos. Into what an abyss Russia is being pushed." Ten of the horrified ministers sent the emperor a collective letter, begging him to reconsider his decision, which, they wrote, "threatens Russia, You, and Your dynasty with the direst consequences." Nicholas ignored their plea. And when eight ministers then tendered their resignations in protest, he simply refused to accept them.

The council's negative reaction was not due to Nikolasha's removal, which was expected, but to the very idea that the weak and vacillating tsar, with no demonstrated talent for strategy, would be taking his place. "Most of all, they feared the influence Aleksandra [cited author's spelling] and, through her, Rasputin exercised upon the Emperor," wrote W. Bruce Lincoln. "A neurotic Empress suffering from delusions of persecution and a crafty, nearly illiterate peasant would be the two closest advisers of the Commander in Chief of Russia's armies."

Members of the imperial family shared the ministers' dismay. Bertie Stopford, attached to the British embassy, recalled Grand Duchess Marie (Miechen) blurting out at dinner one night, "It is quite disastrous," after which, Stopford wrote, "We both cried in our soup. . . . Everybody during dinner was much depressed by this news." Dowager Empress Marie was particularly distressed by her son's decision. "There is no room in my brain for all this," she cried.

Even in the face of all this opposition, Alexandra could not have been more pleased. Immediately after his departure for army headquarters to assume command, the empress wrote Nicholas a long letter—tinged with the triumph of a wife who had just obtained from her husband exactly what she wanted.

"I cannot find words to express all I want to," she wrote. "My heart is far too full. I only long to hold you tight in my arms and whisper words of intense love, courage, strength and endless blessing. . . . You have fought this great fight for your country and throne, alone with bravery and decision. Never have they seen such firmness in you and it cannot remain without fruit. . . . Your faith has been tried—your trust—and you remained firm as a rock, for that you will be blessed. God anointed you at your coronation, He placed you where you stand and you have done your duty, be sure, quite sure of this and He forsaketh not His Anointed. Our Friend's [Rasputin's] prayers arise day and night for you to Heaven and God will hear them."

Having sent the emperor off to run the war—armed with a magic comb blessed by Rasputin and accompanied by the instructions "Remember to comb your hair before all difficult

tasks and decisions, the little comb will bring its help"—
Alexandra began to consolidate her power at home. "I long to
poke my nose into everything," the empress wrote in one letter shortly after the tsar's arrival at headquarters. In another,
she asserted herself more: "Lovey, I am here, don't laugh at
silly old wify, but she has 'trousers' on unseen. . . . I long to
show my *immortal* trousers to those poltroons." Sure enough,
"silly old wify" was soon wearing the pants.

"Alexandra was intoxicated by power," wrote Greg King.
"Her marriage to a man regarded as semidivine exposed Alexandra to the ultimately fatal idea that unquestionable, absolute authority was invested in certain persons, endowing them
with the ability to make judgments with a certainty provided
by God. Over the years, she saw her husband falter in his role.
With each perceived mistake Nicholas made, Alexandra drew
herself toward the centers of power. If Nicholas could not
stand firm, Alexandra would. She clearly felt herself stronger
and more capable than her husband. Nicholas might hold the
power in the government, but Alexandra claimed and exercised it. For her, there were no moments of self-doubt, no
second thoughts. Her convictions were firm, and she would
not allow the weak character of her husband to stand in the
way of what she saw as his duty."

During his first months away, Alexandra bombarded
Nicholas with a mixture of feverish love letters, admonitions,
and outright commands:

"Quickly shut [dissolve] the Duma," she wrote just days
after the emperor's departure. "The Duma, I hope, will at
once be closed," she reiterated the following day.

"Shcherbatov is impossible to keep [as minister of internal
affairs]. . . . Better quick to change him."

"Samarin [director-general of the Holy Synod] goes on

speaking against me. Hope to get you a list of names and trust we can find a suitable successor before he can do any more harm."

Far from being offended by his wife's presumption, Nicholas seemed to relish it. "Think, my wify, will you not come to the assistance of your hubby now that he is absent," he wrote. "What a pity that you have not been fulfilling this duty long ago or at least during the war! I know of no more pleased feeling than to be proud of you, as I have been all these past months, when you urged me on with untiring importunity, exhorting me to be firm and stick to my own opinions."

With power now firmly in her grasp, Alexandra accelerated her campaign to rid the government of ministers and other officials she perceived to be her personal enemies, Rasputin's, or both. In what historian Michael T. Florinsky described as "an amazing, extravagant, and pitiful spectacle . . . without parallel in the history of civilized nations," men rose and fell with astonishing frequency. During a sixteen-month period, Russia had four different prime ministers, five ministers of the interior, four ministers of agriculture, and three ministers of war. The rapid rate of turnover was such that Prince Vladimir Volkonsky suggested a sign be placed on the government ministry building: "Piccadilly—the show changes every Saturday."

As good men continued to be driven out, Alexandra wrote gleefully to the emperor, "I am no longer in the slightest bit shy or afraid of ministers and speak like a waterfall in Russian." Nicholas was delighted with her efforts. "It rests with you to keep peace and harmony among the Ministers," he wrote in September 1916; "thereby you do a great service to me and to our country. . . . Oh, my precious Sunny, I am so happy to think that you have found at last a worthy occupation! Now I shall naturally be calm, and at least need not worry over internal affairs."

In fact, Nicholas all but abdicated sovereignty of his own realm, ceding it to his wife and thus, by association, to Rasputin as well. "As a consequence of Aleksandra's meddling and Nicholas's grateful acceptance of her advice in all except the rarest instances, Russia's government was deprived of every reasonable statesman," Lincoln wrote. "By the fall of 1916, Aleksandra's performance of her 'worthy occupation' had left her country with a motley assortment of rogues, incompetents, non-entities, and madmen at the head of her government."

Two of the most egregious appointments in Alexandra's game of "ministerial leapfrog" (as one called it at the time) were Boris Stürmer, described by a colleague as "false and double-faced," and Alexander Protopopov, dismissed by British ambassador George Buchanan as "mentally deranged." Rasputin adored them both.

After leaving "a bad memory wherever he occupied an administrative post," as Foreign Minister Serge Sazonov put it, Stürmer emerged from total bureaucratic obscurity to become Russia's new prime minister in February 1916. His one qualification from Alexandra's perspective: "He very much values Gregory [Rasputin], which is a great thing." However, French ambassador Paléologue probed a little deeper in his assessment of the new head of government: "He . . . is worse than a mediocrity—third-rate intellect, mean spirit, low character, doubtful honesty, no experience and no idea of State business. The most that can be said for him is that he has a rather pretty talent for cunning and flattery. . . . His appointment becomes intelligible on the supposition that he has been selected solely as a tool, in other words, actually on account of his insignificance and servility. . . . [He] has been . . . warmly recommended to the Emperor by Rasputin."

And if Stürmer was the ideal man to serve as prime minister, then it stood to reason that he would make a fine foreign minister as well. So, after removing Sazonov, described by Alexandra as "such a pancake," she and Rasputin arranged for their man Stürmer to hold a second key position in the government. The diplomatic corps was stunned. "I can never hope to have confidential relations with a man on whose word no reliance can be placed," concluded the British ambassador, while Paléologue continued his withering critique of the new foreign *and* prime minister: "His look, sharp and honeyed, furtive and blinking, is the very expression of hypocrisy . . . he emits an intolerable odor of falseness. In his bonhomie and affected politeness one feels that he is low, intriguing, and treacherous."

Yet Stürmer came off as a seasoned elder statesman compared to Alexander Protopopov, the "lunatic," as Mossolov called him, whom Alexandra and Rasputin championed as minister of the interior—perhaps the most sensitive and critical post of all. "Under this office came the police, the secret police, informers and counterespionage," wrote Massie—"all the devices which, as a regime grows more unpopular, become all the more necessary to its preservation." With Protopopov at the helm, the tsarist regime in Russia would collapse within a year.

Nicholas II, though always acquiescent to his wife's wishes, hesitated when it came to appointing Protopopov—even with the empress's essential endorsement of "He likes Our Friend for at least four years, and that says much for a man." From headquarters the emperor wrote, "I must consider this question as it has taken me completely by surprise. Our Friend's opinions of people are sometimes very strange, especially with appointments to high office." Of course Alexandra eventually got her way. "It shall be done," Nicholas telegraphed her. Then, in a separate letter, he wrote, "God grant that Protopopov may turn out to be the man of whom we are now in need." The empress soothingly reassured her husband that indeed he was. "God bless your new choice of Protopopov," she wrote. "Our Friend says you have done a very wise act in naming him."

No sooner had he assumed his post than Protopopov began demonstrating unsettling signs of insanity. Perhaps that had something to do with the scorching case of advanced syphilis from which he suffered. As vice president of the Duma, the new interior minister retained his seat there and spoke lovingly of the icon he kept at his desk. "He helps me do everything," Protopopov said of the inanimate object; "everything I do is by His advice." Michael Rodzianko, president of the Duma, reported more odd behavior: "He rolled his eyes repeatedly, in a kind of unnatural ecstasy. 'I feel that I shall save Russia. I feel that I alone can save her.'"

Apparently Alexandra and Rasputin felt the same way. So, with the organization of food supplies being one of the most pressing problems facing the country, they decided to have this critical responsibility transferred from the Ministry of Agriculture to a madman. The empress issued the order without informing the tsar.

"Forgive me for what I have done," she wrote to Nicholas— "but I had to—Our Friend said it was absolutely necessary. . . . I had to take this step upon myself as Gregory says Protopopov will have all in his hands . . . and by that will save Russia. . . . Forgive me, but I had to take this responsibility for your sweet sake."

By the fall of 1916, with Alexandra's appointees firmly in place, Russia was in complete chaos. Millions of men had been killed or wounded in a senseless war, food supplies were scarce, the economy was broken, and revolution was once again in ferment. "We live in abnormal times and are gliding down a precipice," one official observed.

"There is no firewood in Petersburg, and not much to eat," wrote the poet Zinaida Gippius. "The streets are filled with rubbish. The most frightening and crude rumors are disturbing the masses. It is a charged neurotic atmosphere. You can almost hear the laments of the refugees in the air. Each day is drenched in catastrophes. What's going to happen? It is intolerable. 'Things cannot go on like this,' an old cab-driver says."

But the sorry state of Russia did go on, and the monarchy was held directly responsible. "Everywhere one hears the same indignant outcry," a countess wrote after returning from Moscow. "If the Emperor appeared on the Red Square to-day he would be booed. The empress would be torn to pieces." Nicholas's cousin, Grand Duchess Marie (daughter of his exiled uncle Paul—see family tree), also observed the roiling discontent with the imperial regime during that perilous autumn of 1916.

"It was about this time I first heard people speaking of the emperor and empress with open animosity," Marie recounted. "The word 'revolution' was uttered more openly and more often; soon it would be heard everywhere. The war seemed to recede to the background. All attention was riveted on interior events, Rasputin, Rasputin, Rasputin, it was like a refrain: his mistakes, his shocking personal conduct, his mysterious power. This power was tremendous; it was like dusk enveloping all our world, eclipsing the sun. How could so pitiful a wretch throw so vast a shadow? It was inexplicable, maddening, almost incredible."

While Grand Duchess Marie lamented "Rasputin, Rasputin, Rasputin," it was her brother Dmitri who would actually do something about the hated *staretz* (see next chapter). Meanwhile, the rest of the imperial family was in a frenzy. "We're heading straight for a revolution!" cried Marie and Dmitri's father, Grand Duke Paul. "The first step has been taken! . . . If revolution breaks out, its barbarity will exceed anything ever known. . . . It will be hellish. . . . Russia won't survive it!"

Despite all the family warnings, Empress Alexandra still ruled Russia while her passive husband's realm rapidly disintegrated. Finally, in utter desperation, Grand Duke Nicholas Mikhailovich, a respected historian, first cousin of Alexander III, and future victim of the Bolshevik Revolution, outlined his grave concerns in a letter sent to the emperor.

"You often told me you trusted no one and were constantly being betrayed," the grand duke wrote. "If this is true the remark should apply above all to your wife, who, though she loves you, is constantly leading you in error, surrounded as she is by people in the grip of the spirit of evil. . . . Believe me, if I stress my desire that you should cast off the chains that imprison you, it is not for personal motives . . . but only with the hope of saving you and your throne and our dear country from the terrible and irreparable catastrophe that lies ahead."

Nicholas never bothered to read the letter. Instead, he passed it to the empress, whose reaction to it was sadly predictable. "I am utterly disgusted," she fumed; "it becomes next to high treason. . . . You, my love, far too good and kind and soft—such a man [Grand Duke Nicholas Mikhailovich] needs to be held in awe of you. . . . Wife is your staunch One and stands as a rock behind you."

Visiting Tsarskoe Selo in December 1916, Alexandra's sister Ella, widow of the assassinated Grand Duke Serge and now a nun[*], discovered just how immobile and unfeeling a rock the empress could be when it came to any suggestion that she curb her political activities. "She dismissed me like a dog," wrote Ella, who would never see her sister again. "Poor Nicky, poor Russia."

No matter how vehemently anyone else objected to it, in the empress's own estimation her interference in government was entirely justifiable. "I am but a woman fighting for her Master and Child," she wrote to Nicholas, "her two dearest ones on earth—and God help me being your guardian angel."

Nicholas II was fully aware that his empire was crumbling around him, yet he seemed incapable of taking any action to reverse the fatal course. "Why?" the French ambassador asked the emperor's aunt Miechen. "Because he's weak," the grand duchess replied. "He hasn't the energy to face the Empress's brow-beating, much less the scenes she makes! And there's another reason which is far more serious: he's a fatalist. When things are going badly he tells himself it's God's will and he must bow to it! I've seen him in this state before, after the disasters in Manchuria and during the 1905 troubles."

"But is he in that frame of mind at the present moment?" asked Paléologue.

"I'm afraid he's not far from it," Miechen replied. "I know he's dejected, and worried to find the war going on so long without any results."

The emperor was in fact utterly depleted by care. "I was

---

[*] See footnote on page 253.

shocked to see Nicky so pale, thin and tired," his sister Olga recalled of the tsar's visit to Kiev in November 1916. "My mother was worried about his excessive quiet."* Pierre Gilliard also noted the emperor's abject state during the visit. "He had never seemed to me so worried before," the tsarevitch's tutor wrote. "He was usually very self-controlled, but on this occasion he showed himself nervous and irritable, and once or twice he spoke roughly to Alexis."†

While in Kiev, the emperor's mother strongly advised him to rid himself of the incompetent Stürmer in his dual roles as prime minister and foreign minister. With the Duma now in open revolt, Nicholas had little choice but to do just that. And though Alexandra grudgingly accepted the decision, she balked at the one condition Stürmer's successor, Alexander Trepov, insisted upon to accept the post: the removal of Rasputin's syphilitic protégé, Protopopov.

---

* Dowager Empress Marie had moved to Kiev in the midst of the government turmoil with the declaration that she "would not remain a witness of the shame any longer." It was a move her daughter-in-law, the empress, eagerly welcomed: "It's better Motherdear stays on at Kiev where the climate is milder and she can live more as she wishes and hears less gossip."

† Despite the obvious dangers to his health, the tsarevitch often accompanied his father during the war, and stayed with him at headquarters. "It is very cosy to sleep by his side," Nicholas wrote to Alexandra of one father-son sojourn in October 1915. "I say prayers with him every night since the time we were on the train; he says his prayers too fast, and it is difficult to stop him. He was tremendously pleased with the review; he followed me, and stood the whole time while the troops were marching past, which was splendid. Before the evening we go out in a car . . . either into the wood or on the bank of a river, where we light a fire and I walk about nearby. He sleeps well, as I do, in spite of the bright light of his [icon lamp]. He wakes up early in the mornings between 7–8, sits up in bed and begins to talk quietly to me. I answer him drowsily, he settles down and is quiet until I am called."

The emperor tried to explain to his wife the necessity of Protopopov's dismissal, and even begged her, "Do not drag Our Friend into this. The responsibility is with me, and therefore I wish to be free in my choice." Of course there was virtually no chance of Alexandra letting *that* happen. "Change nobody now," she wrote stridently; "otherwise the Duma will think it's their doing and that they have succeeded in clearing everybody out. . . . Darling, remember that it does not lie in the man Protopopov or x.y.z. but it's the question of monarchy and your prestige now, which must not be shattered in the time of the Duma. Don't think they will stop at him, but will make all others leave who are devoted to you one by one— and then ourselves. Remember . . . the Tsar rules and not the Duma."

A furious row apparently ensued after Alexandra arrived at headquarters to meet with her husband—a scrap from which she, not surprisingly, emerged victorious. "Yes," wrote the emperor in what Massie noted is the only evidence of tension between the couple in all their voluminous correspondence, "those days spent together were difficult, but only thanks to you have I spent them more or less calmly. You were so strong and steadfast—I admire you more than I can say. Forgive me if I was moody or unrestrained—sometimes one's temper must come out!. . . Now I firmly believe that the most painful is behind us and that it will not be as bad as it was before. And henceforth I intend to become sharp and bitter [toward his wife's opponents]. . . . Sleep sweetly and calmly."

Thus the unbalanced Protopopov endured to drive Russia deeper into ruin. And there was nothing the new prime minister could do about it. "Alexander Fedorovich," the tsar wrote sternly to Trepov after he tried to resign. "I order you to carry out your duties with the colleagues I have thought fit to give you." In desperation, the hapless Trepov attempted to give the all-powerful Rasputin a hefty bribe to stay clear of the government. But the Holy Devil just laughed at him.

Alexandra was jubilant over her latest success. "I am fully convinced that great and beneficial times are coming for your reign and Russia," she wrote after the Protopopov clash. "Be firm . . . one wants to feel your hand—how long, years, people have told me the same 'Russia loves to feel the whip'—it's their nature—tender love and then the iron hand to punish and guide. How I wish I could pour my will into your veins. . . . Be Peter the Great, Ivan the Terrible, Emperor Paul—crush them all under you—now don't you laugh, naughty one."

All Nicholas could do was respond meekly, with just a whisper of resentment: "My dear, Tender thanks for the severe scolding. I read it with a smile, because you speak to me as though I was a child. . . . Your 'poor little weak-willed' hubby, Nicky."

The inescapable fact was that no matter how much Alexandra encouraged, cajoled, and even bullied, Nicholas II would never be the iron-willed emperor she wanted him to be. In fact, Rasputin had it right about the tsar when he observed, "He is a simple soul. He was not cut out to be a sovereign; he is made for family life, to admire nature and flowers, but not to reign. That's beyond his strength. So, with God's blessing we come to his rescue."

That Nicholas remained essentially the same kind, decent gentleman he always had been was made touchingly evident during his trip to Kiev, where he visited a military hospital. "We had a young, wounded deserter, court-martialed and condemned to death," recounted the emperor's sister Olga. "Two soldiers were guarding him. All of us felt very troubled about him—he looked such a decent boy. The doctor spoke of him to Nicky who at once made for that corner of the ward. I followed him, and I could see the young man was petrified with fear. Nicky put his hand on the boy's shoulder and asked very quietly why he had deserted. The young man stammered that, having run out of ammunition, he had got frightened, turned and ran. We all waited, our breath held, and Nicky told him that he was free. The next moment the lad scrambled out of bed, fell on the floor, his arms around Nicky's knees, and sobbed like a child. I believe all of us were in tears.

"I have cherished the memory all down the years. I never saw Nicky again."

Chapter 15

Nicholas II (1894–1917):

A Bloody End

When I perish they will perish.

—RASPUTIN

By the end of 1916, Russia was seething with discontent. Bread lines were long, supplies scarce. The government was run by a band of rogues and incompetents, all personally selected at the whim of Empress Alexandra and her peasant cohort. Calls for violence were increasing. "To prevent a catastrophe, the Tsar himself must be removed, by terrorist methods if there is no other way," shouted the socialist Alexander Kerensky. Indeed, Nicholas II would lose his throne in the throes of revolution, and, along with his family, face imprisonment, degradation, and eventually slaughter. But first there was the matter of Rasputin, the so-called Holy Devil, to be resolved.

On December 2, 1916, an archconservative monarchist by the name of Vladimir Purishkevich rose to speak before his colleagues in the Duma. The subject was Rasputin, and in the rousing oratory for which he was renowned, Purishkevich denounced "the evil genius of Russia"—the very devil threatening to destroy both the tsar and the nation. "It requires only the recommendation of Rasputin to raise the most abject citizen to high office," he thundered. "The Tsar's ministers . . . have been turned into marionettes, marionettes whose threads have been taken firmly in hand by Rasputin and the Empress Alexandra Feodorovna." Then, in a concluding flourish greeted with wild applause, he challenged his peers:

"If you are truly loyal, if the glory of Russia, her mighty future which is closely bound up with the brightness of the name of Tsar mean anything to you, then on your feet, you Ministers. Be off to Headquarters and throw yourselves at the feet of the Tsar and beg permission to open his eyes to the dreadful reality, beg him to deliver Russia from Rasputin and the Rasputinites big and small. Have the courage to tell him that the multitude is threatening in its wrath. Revolution threatens and an obscure *moujik* [peasant] shall govern Russia no longer."

While the rest of the audience stood and roared its approval, one man in the observation gallery remained seated, "pale and trembling," as one witness noted, seething with inspired indignation. His name was Prince Felix Yussoupov, scion of one of Russia's wealthiest families, a cross-dressing playboy,* and a relative of the Romanovs through marriage to the emperor's only niece, Irina (daughter of Nicholas's sister Xenia). The day after Purishkevich's speech, an excited Yussoupov met with him privately to discuss the Rasputin problem.

"What can be done?" Purishkevich asked, recounting the conversation in his diary.

"Eliminate Rasputin," Yussoupov replied with "an enigmatic smile" and unblinking, intensely focused eyes.

---

* Yussoupov reportedly bragged that once, when dressed as a woman, Britain's King Edward VII tried to seduce him.

"That's easy to say," countered the Duma member. "But who will carry out such a deed when there are no decisive or resolute men left in Russia?"

"One cannot count upon the government," Yussoupov answered. "But it is possible to find such people in Russia nevertheless."

"You think so?

"I am confident of it," was the reply, delivered with an icy calm, "and one of them stands before you."

Soon enough, the two men made a murderous pact. To help carry out the deed, Yussoupov recruited his friend (and reputed lover) Grand Duke Dmitri, who after the exile of his father Paul* had been semi-adopted by his older cousin, the emperor. A young officer named Ivan Sukhotin and an army doctor, Stanislav Lazovert, completed the assassins circle. The plot was simple—though in execution it turned out to be anything but. The victim would be lured to one of Yussoupov's palaces with the promise of meeting his beautiful wife, Irina, who was actually visiting the Crimea, and there the hated *staretz* would be slain.

Rasputin long had intimations of his own violent demise, which were often accompanied by warnings to the imperial family that if anything happened to him they would share his fate. "When I perish they will perish," he once predicted. Shortly before his death he wrote to the tsar, "I shall be killed. I am no longer among the living. Pray, pray, be strong, think of your blessed family."

Despite this gloomy forecast, Rasputin happily went off to his assassin's palace on the night of December 29,

---

* Grand Duke Paul, uncle of Nicholas II, had been exiled because he married a commoner without the emperor's approval.

1916—freshly bathed and dressed in his finest attire to meet the lovely Irina. A lethal reception awaited him, though certainly not the one his killers planned.

Yussoupov had spent weeks cultivating his victim. "My intimacy with Rasputin—so indispensable to our plan—increased each day," he later wrote. And by the time of the murder the two appeared to be old pals. Rasputin was delighted, in fact, to add to his list of prominent acquaintances a man of such position and wealth, a powerful friend who was even willing to personally pick him up and drive him to his fateful date.

Killer and prey arrived shortly before midnight to a cellar room in the palace specially prepared for the murder. There was a cozy fire already burning in the hearth, and a tray full of Rasputin's favorite cakes—each previously laced by Lazovert with what he assured the conspirators was enough cyanide to kill several men. Just in case, though, the wine was spiked as well. Irina was giving a party, Yussoupov told Rasputin, and she would meet them just as soon as she saw off the last of her guests. Meanwhile, the other assassins were waiting upstairs, playing "Yankee-Doodle" on the phonograph to provide a soundtrack for the grand duchess's imaginary soirée.

Alone with the target, Yussoupov nervously offered him some of the cakes, which Rasputin proceeded to gobble down with slurping gulps of tainted wine. Instead of dropping dead, though, the *staretz* became mirthful and, spotting a guitar in the corner of the room, asked the prince to play some of the Gypsy music he favored so much. While Yussoupov all but sputtered out one song after another, Rasputin merrily tapped along, showing no ill effects from the poison whatsoever. After two and a half hours of this, Yussoupov wrote, "my head swam."

In desperation, he excused himself under the pretext of

checking on Irina and ran upstairs to consult with the other killers. Lazovert was useless, having already fainted twice from the tension, while Grand Duke Dmitri suggested they give up and go home. Purishkevich objected, however. They couldn't just let Rasputin leave with all that cyanide surging in his system. What if he inconveniently expired somewhere else? "You wouldn't have any objections if I just shot him, would you?" the agitated Yussoupov finally asked the group. "It would be quicker and simpler."

With Purishkevich's revolver hidden behind his back, Yussoupov went back downstairs to find Rasputin clearly intoxicated from the poisoned wine—but most assuredly not dead. He suggested a visit to the Gypsies: "With God in thought, but mankind in the flesh," the lecherous mystic said with a wink. The prince replied that it was too late to go out for such a romp and instead directed Rasputin's attention to a crystal and silver crucifix standing in a richly ornate cabinet. The holy man declared that he actually preferred the cabinet to the cross, to which Yussoupov answered, "Gregory Efimovich, you'd far better look at the crucifix and say a prayer." With that, the assassin fired at Rasputin's chest; he dropped "like a broken marionette" on the white bearskin rug. The deed was done, or so it seemed.

Hearing the shot, the others rushed downstairs. Lazovert felt for a pulse and found none. Rasputin was then lifted off the carpet to avoid staining it with his blood, after which the other conspirators left the room to make preparations for the disposal of the body. Yussoupov was alone with what he thought was the corpse when one of Rasputin's eyes flickered open, quickly followed by the second. "I saw both eyes," recounted the prince—"the green eyes of a viper—staring at me with an expression of diabolical hatred."

As Yussoupov stood there in frozen terror, Rasputin suddenly bolted up and seized his would-be murderer by the throat, tearing at his clothes. Horrified, the prince broke away and fled up the stairs, the *staretz* in pursuit like an enraged wounded beast. Purishkevich recalled hearing a "savage, inhuman, cry," followed by his accomplice's frightened command, "Purishkevich, fire, fire! He's alive! He's getting away!" Then, near the stairway, he saw Yussoupov, his eyes "bulging out of their sockets," as he "hurled himself towards the door . . . [and into] his parents' apartment."

Now it was left to Purishkevich to finish the assassination that had descended into something of a farce. The *staretz* had staggered outside. "What I saw would have been a dream if it hadn't been a terrible reality," Purishkevich wrote. "Rasputin, who half an hour before lay dying in the cellar, was running quickly across the snow-covered courtyard towards the iron gate which led to the street. . . . I couldn't believe my eyes. But a harsh cry, which broke the silence of the night persuaded me. 'Felix! Felix! I will tell everything to the Empress!' It was him, all right, Rasputin. In a few seconds, he would reach the iron gate. . . . I fired. The night echoed with the shot. I missed. I fired again. Again I missed. I raged at myself. Rasputin neared the gate. I bit with all my force the end of my left hand to force myself to concentrate and I fired a third time. The bullet hit him in the shoulders. He stopped. I fired a fourth time and hit him probably in the head. I ran up and kicked him as hard as I could with my boot in the temple. He fell into the snow, tried to rise, but could only grind his teeth."

By this time Yussoupov had reappeared and began viciously clubbing the fallen *staretz* as blood splattered the snow. The killers then rolled up the body in a curtain, tied it securely, proceeded to the frozen Neva River, and shoved the corpse through a hole in the ice. Now the Holy Devil really was dead. Or was he? According to some accounts, the autopsy performed on Rasputin after his body was eventually recovered from the river indicated there was water in his lungs. If true, it meant that after being poisoned, shot, and beaten, the *staretz* ultimately died by drowning.

News of his demise was greeted with jubilation in the capital, as if a dragon had at last been slain. The assassins were hailed as heroes, the national anthem was played and sung in churches, and people crowded into the Cathedral of Our Lady of Kazan to give thanks. "The very cabmen in the street are rejoicing over the removal of Rasputin," reported one British officer in the capital at the time, "and they and many others think that by this the German influence has received a check."*

Even the empress's saintly sister Ella—the grand duchess turned nun—was exultant. "Prayed for you all darlings," she telegraphed Grand Duke Dmitri, who was soon banished to the Persian front for his role in the murder. And to Yussoupov's mother, Ella wired: "All my deepest and most tender prayers surround you all because of the patriotic act of your dear son. May God protect you all."

Of course not all the royals were quite so ecstatic. "There is nothing heroic about Rasputin's murder," wrote the tsar's sister Olga, still bristling fifty years after the fact. "It was . . . premeditated most vilely. Just think of the two names most

---

* It should be noted that the murder was not universally celebrated. "For the peasants Rasputin has become a martyr," one noble, recently returned from the countryside, related to Paléologue. "He was from the people, he made the voice of the people known to the tsar; he defended the people against the court, and so courtiers killed him! That's what is being said in all the *izbas* [traditional countryside dwellings, usually constructed of logs]."

closely associated with it even to this day—a Grand Duke [Dmitri], one of the grandsons of the Tsar-Liberator [Alexander II], and then a scion of one of our great houses [Yussoupov] whose wife was a Grand Duke's [Sandro's] daughter. That proved how low we had fallen."

And though he was conveniently rid of a pesky interloper whom he indulged mostly for his wife (and son's) sake, Nicholas II was nevertheless "filled with shame that the hands of my kinsmen are stained with the blood of a simple peasant." The emperor was merciless toward his cousin Dmitri, declaring, "Murder is murder," and even a joint letter from a number of members of his extended family pleading for leniency left him unmoved. In fact, he was furious. "I allow no one to give me advice," he wrote on the margin. "In any case, I know that the consciences of several who signed that letter are not clean."

Through the swirl of family drama that resulted from the tsar's harsh response, one essential truth remained: Nicholas was not wrong about some of his relatives' clouded consciences. Indeed, quite a few of them had long been plotting against him and, especially, his wife. This was particularly true of the tsar's domineering uncle Vladimir, once described by a visiting American as having a "fat and rather meaningless face," which was accompanied by dangerous ambition. The grand duke was entirely contemptuous of his softhearted nephew and never quite accepted that it was Nicholas, not he, who sat on Russia's throne. There were even genuine fears upon Alexander III's death that Vladimir would try to seize the throne—just as there were six years later when Nicholas II nearly succumbed to typhoid fever in the fall of 1900.

After the grand duke's death in 1909, his widow, Miechen, pursued her late husband's grandiose schemes and barely hidden grudges with equal vigor. She had long despised the Empress Alexandra, who occupied a position Miechen deemed rightly hers (see Chapter 13), but by the time of Rasputin's murder, simmering resentment had turned to rage as the grand duchess and other Romanovs felt the world upon which they rested so comfortably begin to crumble beneath them. They blamed this all on the empress and the disastrous policies she dictated to her husband. "She must be annihilated!" Miechen declared.

Amid all the jubilation and recriminations that surrounded Rasputin's murder, Empress Alexandra quietly grieved for the holy man she once addressed as her "beloved, unforgettable teacher, redeemer and mentor." Pierre Gilliard, the loyal tutor who would remain with the Romanovs almost to the very end, later wrote "how terribly she was suffering. Her idol had been shattered. He who alone could save her son had been slain. Now that he had gone, any misfortune, any catastrophe was possible."

Before he was buried on the grounds of the palace at Tsarskoe Selo, Alexandra placed in Rasputin's coffin an icon signed by her whole family, as well as a written plea for his protection from above. As it turned out, the Holy Devil would not rest in peace for long. And given what was in store for the Romanovs, the efficacy of his heavenly intercessions on their behalf would have to be deemed negligible.

Emerging from the grave site, the empress dusted the dirt off her hands, raised her head high, and with defiance flashing through her gray-blue eyes, went forward with the work that still had to be done. God had given the Russian crown to her husband, and with faith in Gregori's holy intercession from above, she would do everything she could to preserve it for her son. "From that point," wrote biographer Robert K. Massie, "through the months left to her to live, Alexandra never wavered."

Such fortitude in the face of personal tragedy might have been admirable, had it not been accompanied by the empress's fatal determination to proceed along the same perilous path as before, the one that would eventually lead her and the rest of her family down the shaft of an abandoned mine pit. It was she who still ruled Russia while her husband passively stood by—a dynamic perfectly illustrated when Alexandra carved out a secret nook adjacent to Nicholas's office, from where she could conveniently monitor all his conversations. She eventually installed a couch in the hidden space to lounge more comfortably as she eavesdropped.

The ministerial shuffle continued. Prime Minister Alexander Trepov was out, replaced by the aged and extremely reluctant Prince Nicholas Golitsyn, who ineffectively begged the tsar to reconsider the appointment. "If someone else had used the language I used to describe myself," Golitsyn wrote, "I should have been obliged to challenge him to a duel." The only minister to consistently maintain his position was the half-mad Protopopov, who now believed he could channel the spirit of Rasputin. Yet still he was unable to get food supplies to the starving populace. Russia was hurtling toward revolution.

"It seems as certain as anything can be that the Emperor and Empress are riding for a fall," reported General Sir Henry Wilson, an old acquaintance of Alexandra, visiting Russia with an Allied mission. "Everyone—officers, merchants, ladies—talks openly of the absolute necessity of doing away with them."

The Dowager Empress Marie also noted the increasingly sinister mood and openly worried about her son and daughter-in-law's apparent blindness to it. "All the bad passions seem to have taken possession of the capital," she wrote to her daughter Xenia. "The hatred augments daily for her [Alexandra] that is disastrous, but doesn't open eyes yet. One continues quietly to play with fire. . . . What my poor Nicky must suffer makes me mad to think! Just everything might have been so excellent after the *man's* [Rasputin's] disappearance and now it is all spoiled by her rage and fury, hatred and feeling of revenge! . . . so sad!" Then Marie's letter took on a more ominous tone, one that seemed to echo her sister-in-law Miechen's call for the empress's annihilation: "Alexandra Feodorovna must be banished. I don't know how but it must be done. Otherwise she might go completely mad. Let her enter a convent or just disappear."

Michael Rodzianko, president of the Duma, had long shared the imperial family's concerns about the empress. "Alexandra Feodorovna is fiercely and universally hated, and all circles are clamoring for her removal," he told the tsar's younger brother Michael. "While she remains in power, we shall continue on the road to ruin."

On January 20, 1917, at Michael's urging, Rodzianko brought these worries to the emperor in a private meeting at Tsarskoe Selo. "Your Majesty," he said, "I consider the state of the country to have become more critical and menacing than ever. The spirit of all the people is such that the greatest upheavals may be expected. . . . All Russia is unanimous in claiming a change of government and the appointment of a responsible premier invested with the confidence of the nation. . . . Sire, there is not a single honest or reliable man left in your entourage; all the best have either been eliminated or have resigned. . . . It is an open secret that the Empress issues orders without your knowledge, that Ministers report to her on matters of state. . . . Indignation against and hatred of the Empress are growing throughout the country. She is looked upon as Germany's champion. Even the common people are speaking of it."

At this point the tsar interrupted. "Give me facts," he insisted. "There are no facts to confirm your statements."

"There are no facts," Rodzianko acknowledged, "but the whole trend of policy directed by Her Majesty gives ground for such ideas. To save your family, Your Majesty ought to find some way of preventing the Empress from exercising any influence on politics. . . . Your Majesty, do not compel the people to choose between you and the good of the country."

In a sign of burgeoning despair and resignation, Nicholas pressed his head between his hands. "Is it possible," he said, "that for twenty-two years I tried to act for the best and that for twenty-two years it was all a mistake?"

With little more to say than the absolute truth, Rodzianko responded: "Yes, Your Majesty, for twenty-two years you have followed the wrong course."

The March Revolution of 1917 was sparked not by Lenin, Trotsky, or any other radical party—they had simply not made plans for one. It started in the streets, with a basic lack of bread. Day after day, people formed long lines in subzero temperatures to buy essentials at wildly inflated prices, only to be turned away when the meager supplies ran out. Confronted with this daily privation, they began to take on what the French ambassador described as a "sinister expression" on their faces, until hunger and frustration finally exploded into rage. "They [the radical left] were not ready [for revolution]," wrote Basil Shulgin, a monarchist deputy in the Duma, "but the rest were."

On March 8, people began smashing into bakeries, chanting, "Give us bread!" Their numbers grew the following day, as Cossack patrols began to share with the mob gestures of solidarity. "Don't worry," they declared, "we won't shoot." By Saturday, March 10, the protesters were joined by hordes of workers who went on strike that day, effectively shutting down the capital. Together they marched through the streets, waving red flags for the first time and shouting, "Down with the German woman! Down with Protopopov! Down with the war!"

With the capital seething with rising turbulence, the tsar's ministers desperately sought a solution to the food shortages. Failing that, they offered to resign as a group—all except Protopopov, the minister most responsible for the desperate supply situation, who still believed the spirit of Rasputin would guide him to a resolution of the problem. The emperor refused their offer, as well as their suggestion that a ministry acceptable to the Duma be appointed to replace them.

Several days before the crisis started, Nicholas had left Petrograd (as St. Petersburg had been renamed)* to return to military headquarters—and he was clearly on the verge of a nervous breakdown. Maurice Paléologue, the French ambassador, reported a most disconcerting meeting he had with the tsar in the weeks before his departure: "The Emperor's words,

---

* In reaction to the ferocious anti-German agitation among the Russians during the war, Nicholas II changed the name of the capital from St. Petersburg to the more Slavic Petrograd. For similar reasons in Britain, King George V replaced the royal family surname of Saxe-Coburg-Gotha with the thoroughly English "Windsor."

his silences and reticences, his grave, drawn features and furtive, distant thoughts and the thoroughly vague and enigmatic quality of his personality, confirm in me . . . the notion
that Nicholas II feels himself overwhelmed and dominated
by events, that he has lost faith in his mission . . . that he
has . . . abdicated inwardly and is now resigned to disaster."

Former prime minister Vladimir Kokovtsov had a similar
impression after meeting the emperor on February 1. "During the year that I had not seen him, he became almost unrecognizable," Kokovtsov recalled. "His face had become very
thin and hollow and covered with small wrinkles. His eyes . . .
had become quite faded and wandered aimlessly from object
to object. . . . The whites were of a decidedly yellow tinge, and
the dark retinas had become colorless, grey, lifeless. . . . The
face of the Tsar bore an expression of helplessness. A forced,
mirthless smile was fixed upon his lips."

As the budding revolution continued to intensify that Sat-
urday in the capital, the emperor issued the following com-
mand to General Sergei Khabalov, the military governor of
Petrograd, from headquarters five hundred miles away: I
ORDER THAT THE DISORDERS IN THE CAPITAL, INTOLERABLE
DURING THESE DIFFICULT TIMES OF WAR WITH GERMANY
AND AUSTRIA, BE ENDED TOMORROW. NICHOLAS. He may as
well have ordered cats to bark, for as Khabalov later testified,
"this telegram was like being struck with the head of an axe.
How was I to bring the disorders to a halt tomorrow?"

Falsely assured by Protopopov that the situation in Petrograd was manageable, the emperor sought a simple solution
to what he believed was a simple problem—just send in the
troops. But the military presence in the capital was a desic-
cated vestige of what it had once been. "The regular soldiers
of the pre-war army—the proud infantry and cavalry of the

Imperial Guard, the veteran Cossacks and regiments of the line—had long since perished in the icy wastes of Poland and Galacia," wrote Massie. "The best men who remained were still in the trenches facing the Germans." What was left was a motley assortment of raw recruits—older men from the suburbs and backward country boys, unfit for the front and commanded by untested officers fresh out of military school. Confronted with the prospect of shooting at their own people, most of the soldiers simply refused.

Although two hundred people throughout the city were killed on Sunday, March 11, thousands more were spared. A company from the Volinsky regiment, ordered to shoot into a crowd, fired into the air instead, while another company of the Pavlovsky Life Guards opted to shoot their commander instead. Soon a mass mutiny would erupt among the entire Petrograd garrison.

That night Duma president Rodzianko sent the emperor an urgent telegram. "The position is serious," he wired. "There is anarchy in the capital. The government is paralyzed. Transportation of food and fuel is completely disorganized. . . . There is disorderly firing in the streets. A person trusted by the country must be charged immediately to form a ministry." Rodzianko then concluded, "May the blame not fall on the wearer of the crown."

Upon reading the telegram, Nicholas—still kept blissfully in the dark by Protopopov—turned to his chief of staff, General Michael Alexeiev, and announced derisively, "That fat Rodzianko has sent me some nonsense which I shall not even bother to answer."

The next morning, Monday, the tsar's government still held the last vestiges of its power it would lose that evening. Meriel Buchanan, daughter of the British ambassador, looked out her window over the capital and, as she later wrote, saw "the same wide streets, the same great palaces, the same gold spires and domes rising out of the pearl-colored mists, and yet . . . everywhere emptiness, no lines of toiling carts, no crowded scarlet trams, no little sledges. . . . [Only] the waste of deserted streets and ice-bound river . . . [and] on the opposite shore the low grim walls of the [Peter and Paul] Fortress and the Imperial flag of Russia that for the last time fluttered against the winter sky."

Paléologue also recorded his impressions of that pivotal day in Russian history: "At half past eight this morning, just as I finished dressing, I heard a strange and prolonged din which seemed to come from the Alexander Bridge. I looked out; there was no one on the bridge, which usually presents a busy scene. But almost immediately, a disorderly mob carrying red flags appeared at the end . . . on the right bank of the Neva and a regiment came toward them from the opposite side. It looked as if there would be a violent collision, but on the contrary, the two bodies coalesced. The army was fraternizing with the revolution."

In what amounted to a grand denouement to that momentous Monday morning, the mighty Fortress of Peter and Paul, along with all its artillery, fell to the rebels at noon. Meanwhile, as government buildings burned and rebellious soldiers, their bayonets decorated with red ribbons, marched side by side with surging mobs, the tsar's cabinet met for the last time. Protopopov, the unwitting architect of the unfolding disaster, was urged to resign. Upon doing so, he declared dramatically, "Now there is nothing left to do but shoot myself." (It so happened that the Bolsheviks would take care of that the following year.)

During that final assembly—before the ministers adjourned and gradually gave themselves up to be arrested (and protected) by the Duma—Grand Duke Michael left to send a final appeal to his brother at headquarters to form an acceptable government. He was left waiting for nearly an hour before Alexeiev called back and responded for Nicholas: "The Emperor wishes to express his thanks. He is leaving for Tsarskoe Selo and will decide there."

That afternoon a triumphant crowd marched into the Duma, housed at the Tauride Palace, built by Catherine the Great's favorite, Potemkin. "I must know what I can tell them," the leftist Duma leader Alexander Kerensky shouted to Rodzianko. "Can I say the Imperial Duma is with them, that it takes the responsibility on itself, that it stands at the head of government?"

Rodzianko had little choice but to agree. Still, he expressed deep reservations to Basil Shulgin for what was tantamount to a revolt by the Duma (which Nicholas had ordered suspended) against the emperor. "Take the power," Shulgin counseled. "If you don't, others will." And indeed they did, for that very evening a second, rival assembly took their seats across from the Duma in an opposite wing of the palace: the Soviet of Soldiers' and Workers' Deputies.

"Thereafter," wrote Kerensky, who emerged as the bridge between the Duma and the Soviet, "two different Russias settled side by side: the Russia of the ruling classes who had lost (though they did not realize it yet) . . . and the Russia of Labor, marching towards power, without suspecting it."

Nicholas and Alexandra—he at headquarters; she at Tsarskoe Selo—only gradually learned what was happening in the capital that Monday. Over the next three days, however, the full impact of what had occurred slammed into them with devastating force. On Tuesday, March 13, the Winter Palace—that magnificent edifice of imperial power and splendor—fell under the threat of the heavy guns aimed at it from the rebel-controlled Fortress of Peter and Paul across the river. The palace, Massie wrote, had been "the last outpost of tsarism" in the capital. Just outside the city, mutinous sailors at the Kronshtadt naval base slaughtered their officers, one of whom was still very much alive when he was tossed into a grave and buried. But perhaps most threatening, to the empress at least, a band of unruly soldiers set out for Tsarskoe Selo with the stated intent to seize "the German woman," along with her son, and drag them back to Petrograd.

Alexandra had been warned of the danger, but with half her children sick with the measles, she refused to leave. Her brave stance became irrelevant when the railroads were commandeered by the rebels, after which she couldn't escape even if she wanted. Instead, fifteen hundred loyal soldiers took up positions around the Alexander Palace to protect the frightened family inside. "Oh, Lili," the empress exclaimed to her friend, "what a blessing that we have the most devoted troops. There is the *Garde Equipage;* they are our personal friends." It was a mantra she kept repeating—so little did she know.

That night, as the tension grew, the empress ventured outside to meet and encourage the men charged to protect her family. "The scene was unforgettable," Baroness Buxhoeveden recalled. "It was dark, except for a faint light thrown up from the snow and reflected on the polished barrels of the rifles. The troops were lined up in battle order . . . the first line kneeling in the snow, the others standing behind, their rifles in readiness for a sudden attack. The figures of the Empress and her daughter [Marie] passed from line to line, the white palace looming a ghostly mass in the background."

The marauding soldiers, who had spent the day drinking themselves into a frenzy, arrived that night. One sentry was shot less than five hundred yards from the palace. Yet they were ultimately discouraged by the sight of machine guns manned on the roof of the palace and the masses of soldiers protecting the royal residence. By the next day, however, Alexandra's devoted "friends" had white ribbons tied to their rifles—an indication of a truce with the rebels, who were left free to loot and pillage the surrounding village.

Throughout the rest of that tumultuous night, barely sleeping as the sounds of rifle shot burst through the stillness, the empress clung to one hope: "Tomorrow the Emperor is due to come. I know that when he does, all will be well." Nicholas, however, had been detained elsewhere.

The emperor was traveling home from headquarters on Tuesday when his train stopped in the town of Malaya Vishera—just one hundred miles south of the capital. There had been reports that rebels controlled the railroad ahead and so it was decided to divert the imperial train west to Pskov, headquarters of the Northern Group of Armies. Nicholas arrived on Wednesday night, only to receive the shattering news that his own personal guard had defected.

Paléologue witnessed that fateful event earlier in the day, as the Imperial Guard strode toward the Tauride Palace to declare allegiance to the Duma. "They marched in perfect order, with their band at the head," the ambassador wrote of the first three regiments to pass. "A few officers came first, wearing a large red cockade in their caps, a knot of red ribbon on their shoulders and red stripes on their sleeves. The old regiment

standard, covered with icons, was surrounded by red flags. . . .
Then came His Majesty's Regiment, the sacred legion which
is recruited from all the units of the Guard and whose special
function is to secure the personal safety of the sovereigns."

Also marching was the *Garde Equipage,* the "personal
friends" the empress was so pleased to see protecting her at
the palace. And leading them was their commanding officer,
Grand Duke Cyril, the tsar's first cousin and the son Miechen
earnestly hoped would replace him on the throne. Having
bowed before the Duma, Cyril returned to his palace and
hoisted a red flag over his roof. But the grand duke's treachery
did little to endear him to the new order. "Only rats leave a
sinking ship!" sniffed one radical newspaper.

As events rapidly began to crush in around him, the emperor determined at last to make some concessions, including
the appointment of a ministry acceptable to the Duma and a
prime minister who would maintain total control over internal affairs. The opportunity to implement reforms had long
since slipped away, however, and now Nicholas II was no longer in control.

"His Majesty . . . [is] apparently unable to realize what is
happening in the capital," Rodzianko telegraphed upon receiving Nicholas's proposals. "A terrible revolution has broken
out. Hatred of the Empress has reached fever pitch. To prevent bloodshed, I have been forced to arrest all the ministers. . . . Don't send any more troops. I am hanging by a thread
myself. Power is slipping from my hands [as it ultimately did].
The measures you propose are too late. The time for them is
gone. There is no return."

The tsar's fate had already essentially been decided for him.
As the Provisional Government's new war minister, Alexan-

der Guchkov, declared, "The only thing which can secure the permanent establishment of a new order, without too great a shock, is his voluntary abdication." Either that, or Nicholas risked plunging his country into civil war—a prospect entirely repellent to the sovereign, who, if nothing else, was a true patriot. Confronted with this stark choice, the emperor consulted with his generals—all of whom were unanimous in urging him to renounce the throne. The tsar's cousin Grand Duke Nicholas, "Nikolasha," the imposing former commander in chief whose position the emperor had assumed, begged him "on my knees" to abdicate.

The decision was made. Nicholas, who had been silently staring out of a window, suddenly turned around and in a resolute voice declared, "I have decided that I shall give up the throne in favor of my son, Alexis." Then, after crossing himself, he personally addressed the men surrounding him: "I thank you . . . for your distinguished and faithful service. I hope it will continue under my son."

Thus the young boy of twelve, cursed with an incurable and frightening disease, reigned for six hours as Russia's uncrowned sovereign, Emperor Alexis II. But in the time it took to prepare the proper documents, Nicholas had a change of heart. He recognized what trauma would accompany the accession of his precious son—torn away from his family, set to rule as a mere figurehead over a strife-ridden nation, controlled by unscrupulous men who cared neither about him nor the hideous affliction that might kill the child at any unguarded moment.

With these fears in mind, Nicholas made a new declaration: "I have decided to renounce my throne. Until three o'clock today I thought I would abdicate in favor of my son,

Alexis. But now I have changed my decision in favor of my brother Michael.* I trust you will understand the feelings of a father." Then, with the scratch of his signature, Nicholas II swept both himself and his son off the Russian throne. Now only humiliation and death awaited them.

The emperor relinquished his crown with such calm and thoroughness of purpose as to be unsettling to some. "He was such a fatalist that I couldn't believe it," recalled General Dmitri Dubensky. "He renounced the Russian throne just as simply as one turns over a cavalry squadron to its new commanding officer." Yet Nicholas's apparent stoicism in the face of his profound and irrevocable decision masked something far deeper, touching his very soul. Abdication "was for him an immense sacrifice," wrote historian Richard Pipes, "not because he craved either the substance of power or its trappings— the one he thought a heavy burden, the other a tedious imposition—but because he felt by this action he was betraying his oath to God and country." The emperor stepped aside for one reason: to facilitate Russia's ultimate triumph over Germany. "He chose . . . to give up the crown to save the front," wrote Pipes.

The impact of Nicholas's renunciation of his throne was seismic. To a nation that for centuries believed deeply that the sovereign was semidivine—an essential part of the equilibrium between heaven and earth†—his absence was for many

---

* In the midst of rising antimonarchical sentiment, Michael almost immediately renounced the throne as well. "He was frail and gentle," Shulgin wrote of the grand duke, "not born for such difficult times, but he was sincere and humane. He wore no masks. It occurred to me: 'What a good constitutional monarch he would have been.'" Michael was murdered by the Bolsheviks just a few weeks before his brother.

† "As God is in heaven," generations of Russians had been taught, "so great is our Tsar on earth."

simply inconceivable. In the aftermath of the abdication, Paléologue visited several churches. "The same scene met me everywhere," he wrote: "a grave and silent congregation exchanging grave and melancholy glances. Some of the *moujiks* looked bewildered and horrified and several had tears in their eyes. Yet even among those who seemed the most moved I could not find one who did not sport a red cockade or armband. They had all been working for the Revolution; all of them were for it, body and soul. But that did not prevent them from shedding tears for their Father, the Tsar."

Among members of the royal family, the emperor's decision had more personal repercussions. "The news of Nicky's abdication came like a thunderbolt," recalled his sister Olga. "We were stunned. My mother was in a terrible state. She kept telling me it was the greatest humiliation of her life. . . . She blamed poor Alicky for . . . everything."

Alexandra was at Tsarskoe Selo, all but trapped, when she received the news from Nicholas's uncle, Grand Duke Paul. Her friend Lili Dehn remembered the two spoke privately, after which "the door opened and the Empress appeared. Her face was distorted with agony, her eyes were full of tears. She tottered rather than walked, and I rushed forward and supported her until she reached the writing table between the windows. She leaned heavily against it and taking my hands in hers, she said brokenly 'Abdicated!' I could not believe my ears. I waited for her next words. They were barely audible. 'The poor dear . . . all alone down there . . . what he has gone through, oh my God, what he has gone through. . . . And I was not there to console him.'" Then she sat down and sobbed.

While Alexandra wept, others were appalled by what the emperor had done. "Nicky must have lost his mind," wrote his brother-in-law and cousin, Grand Duke Alexander, "Sandro," who was married to Nicholas's sister Xenia and happened to be the father-in-law of Yussoupov, one of Rasputin's killers. "Since when does a sovereign abdicate because of a shortage of bread and partial disorders in his capital? . . . He had an army of fifteen million men at his disposal. The whole thing . . . seemed ludicrous."

What was particularly galling to some was Nicholas's decision to renounce the crown for Alexis as well. "I needn't tell you of my love for the Emperor and with what devotion I served him," the ex-foreign minister Sazonov said tearfully to Paléologue. "But as long as I live, I shall never forgive him for abdicating for his son. He had no shadow of a right to do so. . . . Fancy destroying a three-hundred-year-old dynasty, and the stupendous work of Peter the Great, Catherine II and Alexander I. What a tragedy! What a disaster!"

The former emperor was permitted one last public act after his abdication—to travel back to field headquarters at Mogliev and bid farewell his beloved armies. On the way, Nicholas gave vent to feelings in the diary he had kept since he was a young man. "For the sake of Russia, and to keep the armies in the field, I decided to take this step. . . . All around me I see treason, cowardice, deceit." Upon arrival at Mogliev, he would also see some of the callous indifference and loss of respect that would plague him for the rest of his brief life.

Across from his room, two large red banners adorned city hall, while the town itself still celebrated the abdication with street parties. Outside Nicholas's window, the staff and troops of his escort loudly swore allegiance to the Provisional Government and removed the insignia and adornments that distinguished them as members of the emperor's suite. During the church service that followed, prayers for the tsar and the rest of the imperial family were omitted for the first time in centuries. Even Nicholas's written message to the troops, in which he encouraged them to keep fighting bravely and to support the new government, was rejected by that very government and never delivered.

"My heart is full of grief and despair," wrote the Dowager Empress Marie, who joined her fallen son for five days in Mogliev. "I don't even know how I am still alive after seeing how my poor dear son was treated. I thank God I spent those terrible . . . days with him . . . when he was so lonely and abandoned by everyone. These were the most terrifying days of my life. . . . I can't even begin to describe . . . the kind of humiliation and indifference that my poor Nicky went through. I would not believe it if I did not see it with my own eyes. He was like a true martyr."

With his mother in such a state of anguish, the role of comforter fell upon the former tsar. As the American ambassador David R. Francis noted, "it was Nicholas, the son she had always lectured on behavior, who carefully steered his mother back to courage and self-control." After five days, it was time for mother and son to part—forever, as it turned out. Nicholas "went quietly and calmly," Ambassador Francis wrote, while Marie "was overcome with emotion." Her Cossack companion, Timofei Yaschik, reported that the dowager empress "hugged, gently kissed and blessed him. She really cried—more than I have ever seen the strong Danish Princess cry at any time before or after this." Then, as Nicholas's train pulled away, his mother blessed him with the sign of the cross for the very last time.*

---

* Dowager Empress Marie, once so beloved by the Russian people, would endure a degrading captivity by the Bolsheviks in the Crimea, along with her daughters and other members of the extended family. "Here, we are looked at as if we were real criminals and very dangerous people," she wrote. "It is difficult to believe in this."

The ex-sovereign returned to his beloved Tsarskoe Selo—
"that charming, dear, precious place"—a prisoner in his own
palace.* His degradation began immediately. Arriving by car,
Nicholas was stopped at the locked gates by a sentry who in-
quired mockingly who was inside. The guard then proceeded
to telephone an officer, who emerged from the palace.

"Who is there?" the officer hollered.

"Nicholas Romanov," the sentry shouted back.

"Let him pass."

After what Count Paul Benckendorff, Grand Marshal of
the Court, called "this offensive comedy," Nicholas and Alexandra were at last reunited. They grasped one another tenderly, as the once all-controlling empress gently reassured her
husband that the throne meant nothing to her—just the love
the two of them shared together. With that, the deposed tsar
who had so steadfastly restrained his emotions over the past
trying weeks "sobbed like a child on the breast of his wife."

A fresh recruitment of unruly, disrespectful guards—like
the ones at the gate—had arrived at the palace earlier and
basically taken it over. They roamed the halls, bursting into
bedrooms unannounced, and harassed the remaining staff for
serving "the bloodsuckers." Having already picked off all the
tame deer that once roamed the palace park, the soldiers next
turned their aggression toward Rasputin, whose putrefying
corpse they dragged out of its tomb, tossed onto a pile of logs,
and burned to ashes—just as the *staretz* had once predicted
would happen.

---

* On March 20, the Provisional Government resolved "to deprive the
deposed emperor and his consort of their liberty." The following day,
both Nicholas and Alexandra were under arrest.

The guards' behavior toward Nicholas was only marginally better. On his first day home, the deposed emperor received permission to take his customary walk in the park—only now under strict watch. No sooner did he begin his stroll than he was confronted by six armed soldiers determined to bring him low. When the first stepped into his path, Nicholas tried to turn and walk in another direction. But a second soldier ordered him back.

"With their fists and with the butts of their guns they pushed the Emperor this way and that as though he were some kind of wretched vagrant they were baiting on a country road," wrote Alexandra's friend Anna Vyrubova. "'You can't go there, Mr. Colonel.' 'We don't permit you to walk in that direction, Mr. Colonel.' 'Stand back when you are commanded, Mr. Colonel.' The emperor, apparently unmoved, looked from one of these coarse brutes to another and with great dignity turned and walked back to the palace."

Watching the degrading scene from a window above, Alexandra remained silent but gripped the hand of her friend Lili Dehn. "I do not think that until this moment we had realized the crushing grip of the revolution," Dehn wrote. "But it was brought home to us most forcibly when we saw the passage of the Lord of all the Russias, the Emperor whose domains extended over millions of miles, now restricted to a few yards in his own park."

Such ugly episodes would recur often during the family's five-month captivity at Tsarskoe Selo, and Nicholas accepted them all "with extraordinary serenity and moral grandeur," as Gilliard wrote. "No word of reproach ever passed his lips." Such fortitude was no doubt grievously tested, as on one occasion when a soldier thrust his bayonet into the spokes of a bicycle Nicholas was riding, causing him to come crashing to the ground. Young Alexis, his face burning with shame, witnessed his father's humiliation. But the boy also endured some equally discomfiting situations himself.

Derevenko, one of the sailors who had been assigned to protect the tsarevitch from injury—and did so for ten years with all the apparent love and tenderness of a father*—now viciously turned on his young charge. Anna Vyrubova witnessed a most distressing scene: "I passed the open door of Alexis's room and . . . saw lying sprawled in a chair . . . the sailor Derevenko. Insolently, he bawled at the boy whom he had formerly loved and cherished, to bring him this or that, to perform any menial service. . . . Dazed and apparently only half conscious of what he was being forced to do, the child moved about trying to obey."

Yet despite the monstrosities unfolding all around him, Alexis remained essentially the same good-natured boy he had always been, a child who managed to revive his family's flagging spirits with his own inherent exuberance. "He is very intelligent, has a great deal of character and an excellent heart," Count Benckendorff noted. "If his disease could be mastered, and should God grant his life, he should one day play a part in the restoration of our poor country. He is the representative of the legitimate principle; his character has been formed by the misfortunes of his parents and of his childhood. May God protect him and save him and all his family from the claws of fanatics in which they are at present." Alas, there would be no such bright future for Alexis Romanov.

Alexandra suffered with the rest of her family, both their traumas and her own. The empress who had once filled the palace with fresh flowers imported from the Crimea was now

---

* See previous chapter, page 264.

reduced to tears of gratitude when handed a measly sprig of lilac. When she ventured outside, she was often greeted with the gawks and jeers of crowds gathered at the park fence to observe her like a zoo animal. And the press remained merciless, depicting her in cartoons as a promiscuous ogress who bathed in the blood of her own people.

Yet Alexandra's true humanity gradually began to reveal itself to some of those who reviled her most. One day, as she sat quietly in the park, a soldier rudely plopped down next to her and began to harangue her as a hater of the Russian people. The former empress answered him calmly, relating her story and the deep feelings she had for the nation she once ruled. The soldier continued to bombard her with accusations, but after some time, the angry man began to see another side to the woman he had learned to despise. When the conversation was over, the soldier stood up, took her hands in his, and said to her, "Do you know, Alexandra Feodorovna, I had quite a different idea of you. I was mistaken about you."

Even the ardent antimonarchist Kerensky, who once shouted for the violent removal of the tsar and his wife, adopted a different view of Alexandra when he came to the palace to interrogate her about what he believed were her treasonous activities throughout the war. The former empress's assured and persuasive responses soon convinced Kerensky that she had been unfairly demonized. "She does not lie," he remarked to Nicholas. Later he wrote: "I had imagined her differently. She is very sympathetic. She is an admirable mother. What courage, what dignity, what intelligence and how beautiful she is!"*

---

* Kerensky also formed a favorable impression of Nicholas, whose violent overthrow he had once advocated. The socialist leader of the Provisional Government later acknowledged that he had been affected by his

Yet as impressed as he may have been with Alexandra, it was nevertheless Kerensky who ordered the arrest of her dear friends and faithful companions, Lili Dehn and Anna Vyrubova*—a loss that left her utterly forlorn. "With a tremendous effort of will, she forced herself to smile," Lili Dehn wrote of the farewell before she and Anna were taken away; "then, in a voice whose every accent bespoke intense love and deep religious conviction, she said: 'Lili, by suffering, we are purified for Heaven. This goodbye matters little. We shall meet in another world.'"

Perhaps what was most agonizing to Nicholas and Alexandra throughout their imprisonment at Tsarskoe Selo was the uncertainty of what would happen to them and their children next. "At best, they might be permitted to live abroad in exile," wrote historian W. Bruce Lincoln; "at worst, they faced the frightening prospect of a humiliating public trial and execution in the tradition of England's Charles I and France's Louis XVI and Marie Antoinette. In large measure, their fate depended upon which course the revolution might follow. In mid-March [1917], no one even dared predict what that might be."

"unassuming manner and complete absence of pose. Perhaps it was this natural, quite artless simplicity that gave the Emperor that peculiar fascination, that charm, which was further increased by his wonderful eyes, deep and sorrowful. . . . It cannot be said that my talks with the Tsar were due to a special desire on his part; he was obliged to see me . . . yet the former Emperor never once lost his equilibrium, never failed to act as a courteous man of the world."

* Lili Dehn was quickly released after her arrest, but Anna Vyrubova remained imprisoned for five months at the Fortress of Peter and Paul, where, due to widespread speculation about a sexual relationship with Rasputin, she underwent a mortifying gynecological exam that finally proved she was actually a virgin.

As it turned out, exile to Britain—the most practical and desired place—was no longer an option after the English king, Nicholas's maternal first cousin and friend, George V, turned his back on the man he once referred to as "my dear Nicky."* Then came the event that would ultimately answer the question of the now-helpless family's fate. Germany, aiming to sow further discord and rebellion within its enemy's borders, secretly arranged for the return from exile of the man Churchill called "the most grisly of all weapons": Vladimir Lenin. It was the reemergence of this most vicious of Bolsheviks, who once declared it "necessary to behead at least one hundred Romanovs," that would ensure the family's slaughter just over a year later.

Desperate to avert such a massacre, Kerensky quietly arranged to have the family moved to the Siberian town of Tobolsk—"an out-and-out backwater," as he described it, with "a very small garrison, no industrial proletariat, and a population which was prosperous and contented, not to say old-fashioned." It was in this remote place, Kerensky believed, that the Romanovs would be safe and "could live with some measure of comfort." Nicholas readily acceded to the plan. "I have no fear," he told Kerensky. "We trust you. If you say we must move, it must be. We trust you."

On August 12, 1917, Nicholas and Alexandra, along with their five children, spent their last day at the place they had

---

* The British government had actually arranged sanctuary for the Russian royal family, until the king, cousin "Georgie," stepped in to revoke it. With his own throne imperiled by a rising tide of republicanism in wartime Britain, George V feared the impression it might make if he were to give shelter to a fallen autocrat. Still, he was saddened by his cousin's fate the following year. "It was a foul murder," the king wrote in his diary. "I was devoted to Nicky, who was the kindest of men and a thorough gentleman: loved his country and people."

called home over two decades—most of their married life. It was Alexis's thirteenth birthday, and to celebrate a special service was arranged at the palace with a blessed icon from a nearby church. "The ceremony was poignant, all were in tears," recalled Count Benckendorff. "The soldiers themselves seemed touched and approached the holy icon to kiss it. [Afterward, the family] followed the procession as far as the balcony, and saw it disappear through the park. It was as if the past were taking leave, never to come back."

Setting aside the irony of a Russian emperor consigned to Siberia—that forbidding wasteland to which so many of Nicholas's ancestors had banished their enemies (and from which Rasputin had emerged)—conditions at Tobolsk were tolerable—at least during the early period of the family's eight-month imprisonment there. The Romanovs were housed in the recently refurbished governor's mansion, amid a populace fairly well disposed toward them. Gilliard, who still remained with the exiles, recalled that "on the whole, the inhabitants of Tobolsk were still very attached to the Imperial family, and our guards had repeatedly to intervene to prevent them standing under the windows or removing their hats and crossing themselves as they passed the house."

But that November, terrible news reached Tobolsk. After an abortive second revolution that accompanied Lenin's return the previous April, the Bolsheviks had now roared back and seized power. And to effect this socialist resurrection, Lenin promised peace with Germany. It came at a staggering price, essentially gutting the empire. Nearly every foot of territory acquired since the days of Peter the Great had to be ceded under the terms of the treaty, including Poland, Finland, the Baltic States, the Ukraine, the Crimea, and most of the Caucuses. Nicholas was enraged by Lenin's concessions, which he called "a disgrace" and "suicide for Russia."

"I then for the first time heard the Tsar regret his abdication," Gilliard wrote. "It now gave him pain to see that his renunciation had been in vain and that by his departure in the interests of his country, he had in reality done her an ill turn. The idea was to haunt him more and more."

Though Lenin's reemergence assured the destruction of the Romanovs, for now they were still safe in Siberia. That December provided snapshots of the doomed family in their final period of relative calm. There was Anastasia, bored and peering through a window, watching the passersby; Nicholas, huddled with his family around a small fire, reading aloud while his wife and daughters did their needlework, passing the time together on a long winter night. And then there was Alexis—once set to rule over a vast empire—rummaging around the fenced-in yard collecting old nails and pieces of string. "You never know when they will be useful," he wrote to Anna Vyrubova with a perspective that could only come from a boy eagerly exploring his environment—no matter how limited it was.

"One by one all earthly things slip away," Alexandra wrote in one of her last letters, "houses and possessions ruined, friends vanished. One lives from day to day. But God is in all, and nature never changes. I can see all around me churches . . . and hills, the lovely world. . . . I feel old, oh, so old, but I am still the mother of this country, and I suffer its pains as my own child's pains and I love it in spite of all its sins and horrors."

The family's circumstances began to rapidly disintegrate as the effects of the Bolshevik triumph in Petrograd began to seep into Tobolsk. "All the old soldiers (the most friendly) are to leave us," Gilliard wrote at the beginning of February. "The Tsar seems very depressed at this prospect; the change may have disastrous results for us." And indeed it did.

Reduced rations often left the family without the most basic staples, although sympathetic townspeople did sometimes make up for the deficit with what Alexandra called "little gifts from Heaven." And the new guard arrived with a deep reservoir of cruelty. The soldiers took to carving obscenities on the swing set used by the children, and painted pornographic images on the fence. An ice mountain the prisoners had spent weeks constructing together as a joint project was hacked down, simply to deprive the children of the pleasure they found in sliding down it. They are "disconsolate," Gilliard wrote.

The destruction of the mountain had another, more frightening consequence as well. Without this diversion, Alexis began to seek out other, more risky activities to amuse himself. Sliding down a stairway on a tray one day, he fell and was injured, after which the horrid effects of his ever-lurking disease manifested with monstrous fury. "He is frightfully thin and yellow, reminding me of Spala [five years earlier]," Alexandra wrote to Anna. This time, however, there was no Rasputin to alleviate the agony. Alexis would never walk again.

Though time was quickly evaporating, there was still hope in Tobolsk that a means of escape might be found for the desperate family imprisoned there. "All that is required is the organized and resolute efforts of a few bold spirits outside," Gilliard wrote on March 17. One such "bold spirit" was none other than Rasputin's own son-in-law, Boris Soloviev, who managed to centralize all monarchist rescue efforts with himself. The funds poured in but were never used. Instead Soloviev ran off with the money. Now there was nothing left for Nicholas, Alexandra, and their children but death.

While the family's fate was being debated in what would become Leningrad, leaders in the Siberian city of Ekaterinburg—capital of a region known as the "Red Urals" because of its long history of socialist rebellion—were braying for blood. And after a complicated series of maneuvers and political posturing, they would get just what they wanted.

"The atmosphere around us is electrified," Alexandra wrote in her final letter to Anna Vyrubova. "We feel that a storm is approaching, but we know that God is merciful and will care for us. . . . Though we know the storm is coming nearer and nearer, our souls are at peace. Whatever happens will be through God's will."

Nicholas and Alexandra arrived in Ekatcrinburg on April 30, 1918,[*] and were installed right away at Nicholas Ipatiev's commandeered residence—ominously renamed "the House of Special Purpose" and retrofitted as an impregnable fortress. More than one hundred guards were posted at strategic locations inside and outside the house, which was surrounded by an imposing stockade, and all the windows were whitewashed, barred, and sealed, rendering the interior a darkened, stifling tomb. The former sovereign and his wife, now more commonly referred to as "Nicholas the Blood-Drinker" and "the German Bitch," would endure monstrous abuse for most of the month and a half they had remaining.

---

[*] They would be joined three weeks later by their five children, and the remnants of their retinue—most of whom were then either shot or dismissed. It was at this time that the loyal Gilliard was separated from the family forever.

There was no running water in the house for weeks, and any small request was dismissed by the hard-drinking commandant, Alexander Avadeyev. "Let them go to hell!" he would belch. The commandant liked to invite his Bolshevik comrades to watch the family eat, as he showcased his cruelty. He reached past Nicholas to grab some bread from the table, purposely jabbing him in the face with his elbow, and snatched food out of the former emperor's hands. "You've had enough, you idle rich," Avadeyev gloated poisonously. "I will take some myself."

The guards frequently emulated their boss's behavior in their mistreatment of the prisoners. They taunted Nicholas and Alexandra's daughters with lewd asides and forced them to play revolutionary songs on the piano. When the young women had to use the lavatory—the filthy walls of which were covered with pornographic renderings of their mother having sex with Rasputin—they were always accompanied by a leering soldier who left them no privacy and reminded them to admire the "art."

On Alexis's bed, one guard noticed a thin gold chain upon which the boy had strung his collection of religious images. He went to snatch it, but was stopped by Nagorny—the loyal sailor who remained to protect Alexis after the heartless defection of Derevenko at Tsarskoe Selo, and who now carried the boy still immobilized after his fall at Tobolsk. "It was his last service to Alexis," Massie wrote. Nagorny was arrested for his efforts on the child's behalf and shot four days later.

The noose was tightening around the Romanovs. At the beginning of July, Avadeyev was replaced as commandant by Jacob Yurovsky. "This specimen we like least of all," Nicholas wrote in his diary of the man who would very shortly become his executioner. Two days before they were murdered, the family seemed to have some intimation of what was to come. A priest and deacon came to read them the service, and both noted their exhaustion. When the prayer, "At Rest with the Saints," was sung, the family fell to their knees in unison. Later, the deacon remarked to the priest, "They are all some other people, truly. Why, no one even sang."

The Romanovs went to bed on the night of July 16 at ten thirty. An hour and a half later they were roused from their sleep, ordered to get dressed, and told they were being evacuated because Ekaterinburg was in danger of assault by approaching White forces, then engaged in a ferocious civil war with the Bolshevik Red Army. After that, the family and four attendants* were led down to the basement of the house—Nicholas carrying a sleepy Alexis, his arms draped around his father's neck, and Anastasia clinging to their pet spaniel, Jemmy. There they were told to wait for the arrival of a car that was going to transport them to a more secure location.

None of the group seemed to sense what was to come. "There were no tears, no sobs, no questions," Yurovsky later reported. Two chairs were brought in for Alexandra and Nicholas, upon whose lap Alexis rested. The rest stood behind them, against a wall. Yurovsky then stepped before them and announced, "In view of the fact that your relatives are continuing the attack on Soviet Russia, the Ural Executive Committee has decided to execute you."

"What? What?" Nicholas exclaimed just before Yurovsky's bullet struck and killed him instantly. He fell forward to the floor on top of his son. Alexandra, too, died immediately, after the rest of the squad began to open fire. As the barrage of bul-

---

* The four loyal companions murdered along with the imperial family were Dr. Eugene Botkin; Alexandra's maid, Anna Demidova; the valet, Alexis Trupp; and their cook, Ivan Kharitonov.

lets continued over the next several minutes, the four grand duchesses huddled together in a corner, screaming and crying in terror. But they didn't die. Nor had their brother.

When the firing ceased, groans could be heard emanating from the thick, acrid smoke that filled the room. Then, as it cleared, Alexis could be seen crawling through his parents' blood, shielding his face in a futile effort to protect himself. Yurovsky shot him twice in the head, while the other soldiers began to attack his surviving sisters with their bayonets. Again and again they stabbed, until finally the screaming young women were silent. Now the only survivor of the massacre was Alexandra's maid, Anna Demidova, who was chased back and forth against the wall, tripping over corpses, before she, too, was brought down by the squad's lethal instruments.

The bodies were then wrapped in sheets and dragged outside to a waiting truck. As they were being loaded, however, a low moaning could be heard from beneath the sheets. Then one of the grand duchesses, believed to be dead, suddenly sat up and started to scream. Horrified, the men stabbed her repeatedly but were shocked to find how difficult it was to penetrate the body with their bayonets. Finally, all was still and the truck drove off to an abandoned mine in the forest outside the city. There the bodies were stripped naked and, according to some accounts, sexually violated. It was then revealed why both bullets and bayonets had been so ineffective on some of the victims. Sewn into corsets and other garments were rows upon rows of diamonds and other precious stones, all of which helped deflect the onslaught.

"No one is responsible for their death agonies but themselves," Yurovsky later stated. "There turned out to be eighteen pounds of such valuables. By the way, their greed turned out to be so great that on Alexandra Feodorovna there was a

simply huge piece of gold wire bent into the shape of a brace-
let of around a pound in weight. All these valuables were immediately ripped out so that we wouldn't have to drag the
bloody clothes with us."

After this plunder, the clothing was burned and the naked
bodies unceremoniously tossed into the mine pit. Then several hand grenades were thrown in to destroy any evidence of
the crime the Bolshevik government was determined to keep
secret. Yet it wasn't enough. The mine did not collapse and,
fearing the corpses would be discovered by the advancing
White Army, Yurovsky went back later and had them hauled
out with ropes. Once again the bodies were loaded onto a
truck for burial elsewhere. But when the vehicle got mired in
the mud several miles away, it was decided to dispose of the
Romanovs right there. While two of the corpses were burned
near the site, a hole was dug and the rest of the remains
dumped into it. Before the site was covered with dirt, however, the faces of the victims were smashed with rifle butts
and sulfuric acid poured into the grave. This ensured that no
one would ever recognize the Romanovs if their unmarked
resting place were ever discovered.

"My Lord, save my poor, unlucky Nicky," the Dowager
Empress Marie wrote in her journal on July 17. "Help him in
his hard ordeals." But by then the trials of Nicholas II were
over, and buried with him in that marshy Siberian forest was
all the splendor, infamy, and madness that was imperial Russia.

Concluding Chapter

Aftermath

As the Romanovs either lay moldering in unmarked graves or scattered into exile, relics of the imperial past remained. Crowns, orbs, and scepters were unceremoniously stashed away, but the Bolsheviks never saw fit to destroy all the grand monuments erected to the glory of long-dead monarchs. Thus the massive figure of Peter the Great could still be seen proudly mounted on his horse, while Catherine the Great stood imperiously overlooking what had become Leningrad— semideities, frozen in bronze, lingering in what now was an officially godless state. Their splendid palaces were preserved, but entirely devoid of the passion and intrigue that made them uniquely Romanov—merely elaborate shells, occupied only by ghosts.

Dowager Empress Marie, who had once enchanted Russia as the vivacious wife of Alexander III, barely managed to escape the Bolsheviks with her life. And, while she endured in exile, clashing with her cheap nephew King Christian X of Demark over such trivia as electricity bills, she stoutly refused to accept that her son and his family had been slaughtered. Indeed, upon arriving in England after leaving Russia, she tore off a black armband that the future King Edward VIII was wearing in honor of his fallen kinsmen. "It was clear," recalled Marie's loyal bodyguard Timofei Yaschik, "the Empress wanted to underline the fact that she did not believe and did not want to believe the news about the murder of the Imperial family."

Marie was far from alone in this, for almost as soon as the bodies of Nicholas II and his family had been dumped in their makeshift grave did reports emerge of the miraculous escape of at least some of them. Romantic legends were born, particularly about the impish Anastasia, youngest of the four grand duchesses. One of the most enduring revolved around a woman, known to the world as Anna Anderson, who in 1920 emerged dazed and confused from a Berlin canal she had fallen into and gradually began to reveal herself as Russia's lost tsarevna. Hers was a riveting tale of escape, and her resemblance to Anastasia was uncanny enough to convince some Romanov associates that she was indeed Nicholas and Alexandra's daughter.

The woman's amazing story of survival captured the imagination of millions; Ingrid Bergman played her in the Hollywood movie. Even after many decades, when Anna Anderson was just an eccentric cat lady living a decidedly unregal existence in Charlottesville, Virginia, the legend persisted. It was only DNA that ultimately destroyed it: After her death in 1984, a preserved tissue sample from the claimant was compared to a blood sample taken from one of the real Anastasia's royal relatives, Queen Elizabeth II's husband, Prince Philip. Anna Anderson was a fraud.

"I think it's a shame," her biographer Peter Kurth told author Robert K. Massie, "that a great legend, a wonderful adventure, an astonishing story that inspired so many people, including myself, should suddenly be reduced to a little glass dish."

Yet almost as soon as the myth of Anastasia's astonishing escape imploded, a Romanov revival of sorts began with the fall of the Soviet Union. In 1991, a collection of skeletal remains—discovered and reburied outside Ekaterinburg in 1978—were once again unearthed and forensically examined by several sets of scientists. All came to the conclusion that the bones were indeed the remains of Nicholas II, his family, and four servants. The murderers' attempt to destroy the identities of their victims had failed in the face of science. But the evidence of their brutal efforts still remained apparent more than eight decades later. Dr. Ludmilla Koryakova, a professor of archeology at the Ural State University, had examined many skeletons over the course of her career. "But never," she told the Sunday *Times*, "so many that were so badly damaged—so violated. I was ill."

On July 17, 1998, the remains of Nicholas and Alexandra, along with three of their five children, were at last ceremoniously laid to rest at St. Petersburg's Cathedral of St. Peter and St. Paul, the imperial mausoleum since the interment there of Peter the Great in 1725. Boris Yeltsin, the first president of the Russian Federation, paid tribute to the massacred family with a stirring apology:

"All these years, we were silent about this horrible crime. Those who perpetuated this crime and those who for decades have been finding excuses for it are guilty. All of us are guilty. One cannot lie to oneself and explain away wanton cruelty as political necessity. . . . We are all responsible to the historic memory of the nation. That's why I should come here as a person and as president. I bow my head before the victims of a senseless murder."

Eight years after the formal burial of Russia's last imperial family, Dowager Empress Marie joined them in perpetuity.

She had been laid to rest in her native Denmark after her death in 1928, but her wish had been to remain beside her husband, Alexander III. "Having fallen deeply in love with the Russian people, the empress devoted a great deal of effort for the benefit of the Russian fatherland," Orthodox Patriarch Alexis II said at the reinterment ceremony. "Her soul ached for Russia."

The family circle at the cathedral was still not quite complete, though. Only the remains of three of Nicholas and Alexandra's children had been found in the forest grave, once again giving rise to the hope that perhaps the others had survived. But the executioner's record was clear on this: two of the corpses were burned near the burial place of the rest. DNA analysis of charred bone and tooth fragments found at the site proved conclusively in 2011 that they belonged to Tsarevitch Alexis and his sister Marie. The siblings still await burial with the rest of their family.

Meanwhile, history took one of its strange turns in 2000 when Russia's last emperor and empress—once reviled as "Bloody Nicholas" and "the German Bitch"—were canonized, along with their five children, as saints.

ACKNOWLEDGMENTS

I am deeply indebted to my editorial team at Random House, Ryan Doherty and Anne Speyer, for their thoughtful guidance and encouragement, and to Ann Marie and Robert Lynch, as well as Bill Millard, for their generous research assistance.

I am also most grateful for the love and encouragement of my family and friends. I feel truly blessed.

SELECT BIBLIOGRAPHY

Alexander, John T. *Catherine the Great: Life and Legend.* New York: Oxford University Press, 1989.

Anisimov, Evgenii V. *Five Empresses: Court Life in Eighteenth-Century Russia.* Translated by Kathleen Carroll. Westport, CT: Praeger, 2004.

Buchanan, George. *My Mission to Russia.* London: Cassell, 1923.

Buchanan, Meriel. *Dissolution of an Empire.* London: Murray, 1932.

Buxhoeveden, Sophie. *The Life and Tragedy of Alexandra Feodorovna, Empress of Russia.* New York: Longmans, Green, 1928.

Bergamini, John D. *The Tragic Dynasty: A History of the Romanovs.* New York: G. P. Putnam's Sons, 1969.

Catherine II. *Memoirs.* Translated by Alexander Herzen. New York: D. Appleton, 1859.

———. *Memoirs of Catherine the Great.* Translated and with notes by Katherine Anthony. New York: Alfred A. Knopf, 1927.

———. *The Memoirs of Catherine the Great.* Edited by Dominique Maroger and translated by Moura Budberg. New York: Macmillan, 1955.

———. *The Memoirs of Catherine the Great.* Edited and translated by Mark Cruse and Hilde Hoogenboom. New York: Modern Library, 2005.

Charques, Richard. *The Twilight of Imperial Russia.* Fair Lawn, NJ: Essential Books, 1959.

Coughlan, Robert. *Elizabeth and Catherine: Empresses of All the Russias.* New York: G. P. Putnam's Sons, 1974.

Crankshaw, Edward. *The Shadow of the Winter Palace: Russia's Drift to Revolution, 1825–1917.* New York: Viking, 1976.

Dehn, Lili. *The Real Tsaritsa.* London: Thornton Butterworth, 1922.

de Jong, Alex. *The Life and Times of Grigori Rasputin.* New York: Dorset Press, 1982.

Dunning, Chester S. L. *A Short History of Russia's First Civil War: The Time of Troubles and the Founding of the Romanov Dynasty*. University Park: Pennsylvania State University Press, 2004.

Florinsky, Michael T. *The End of the Russian Empire*. New York: Collier-Macmillan, 1961.

Fülöp-Miller, René. *Rasputin: The Holy Devil*. Garden City, NY: Viking, 1928.

Gelardi, Julia P. *From Splendor to Revolution: The Romanov Women, 1847–1928*. New York: St. Martin's, 2011.

Gilliard, Pierre. *Thirteen Years at the Russian Imperial Court*. New York: Doran, 1921.

Hughes, Lindsey. *Peter the Great: A Biography*. New Haven: Yale University Press, 2002.

———. *The Romanovs: Ruling Russia, 1613–1917*. London: Hambledon Continuum, 2008.

———. *Russia in the Age of Peter the Great*. New Haven: Yale University Press, 1998.

———. *Sophia: Regent of Russia, 1657–1704*. New Haven: Yale University Press, 1990.

King, Greg. *The Last Empress: The Life and Times of Alexandra Feodorovna, Tsarina of Russia*. New York: Citadel Press, 1994.

Kleinmichel, Marie. *Memories of a Shipwrecked World*. London: Brentano's, 1923.

Knox, Alfred. *With the Russian Army*. New York: Dutton, 1921.

Kurth, Peter. *Anastasia: The Riddle of Anna Anderson*. Boston: Little, Brown, 1983.

Lincoln, W. Bruce. *In War's Dark Shadow: The Russians Before the Great War*. New York: Dial Press, 1983.

———. *Nicholas I: Emperor and Autocrat of All the Russias*. Bloomington: Indiana University Press, 1978.

———. *The Romanovs: Autocrats of All the Russias*. New York: Dial Press, 1981.

Lockhart, Robert Bruce. *British Agent*. New York: Putnam, 1933.

Longworth, Philip. *Russia: The Once and Future Empire: From Pre-History to Putin*. New York: St. Martin's Press, 2006.

Lowe, Charles. *Alexander III of Russia*. Charleston, SC: BiblioLife, 2009.

Massie, Robert K. *Nicholas and Alexandra: An Intimate Account of the Last of the Romanovs and the Fall of Imperial Russia*. New York: Atheneum, 1967.

———. *Peter the Great: His Life and World*. New York: Knopf, 1980.

————. *The Romanovs: The Final Chapter*. New York: Random House, 1995.

Mossolov, Alexander. *At the Court of the Last Tsar*. London: Methuen, 1935.

Paléologue, Maurice. *An Ambassador's Memoirs*. New York: Doran, 1925.

Pipes, Richard. *The Russian Revolution*. New York: Knopf, 1990.

Platonov, S. F. *The Time of Troubles: A Historical Study of the Internal Crisis and Social Struggle in Sixteenth- and Seventeenth-Century Muscovy*. Translated by John T. Alexander. Lawrence: University Press of Kansas, 1970.

Purishkevich, Vladimir. *The End of Rasputin*. Ann Arbor, MI: Ardis Press, 1985.

Radzinsky, Edvard. *Alexander II: The Last Great Tsar*. Translated by Antonia W. Bouis. New York: Free Press, 2005.

Riasanovsky, Nicholas V. *Nicholas I and Official Nationality in Russia, 1825–1855*. Berkeley: University of California Press, 1969.

Ragsdale, Hugh. *Tsar Paul and the Question of Madness: An Essay in History and Psychology*. Westport, CT: Greenwood Press, 1988.

Rice, Tamara Talbot. *Elizabeth, Empress of Russia*. London: Weidenfeld & Nicolson, 1970.

Schom, Alan. *Napoleon Bonaparte*. New York: HarperCollins, 1997.

Troyat, Henri. *Alexander of Russia: Napoleon's Conqueror*. Translated by Joan Pinkham. New York: E. P. Dutton, 1982.

————. *Catherine the Great*. Translated by Joan Pinkham. New York: E. P. Dutton, 1980.

————. *Terrible Tsarinas: Five Russian Women in Power*. Translated by Andrea Lyn Secara. New York: Algora, 2001.

Vorres, Ian. *The Last Grand Duchess: Her Imperial Highness Grand Duchess Olga Alexandrovna 1 June 1882–24 November 1960*. New York: Scribner's, 1964.

Zamoyski, Adam. *Moscow 1812: Napoleon's Fatal March*. New York: HarperCollins, 2004.

Zguta, Russell. "Peter I's Drunken Synod of Fools and Jesters," *Jahrbucher fur Geschichte Osteuropas* 21, no. 1 (1973): 18–28.

ABOUT THE AUTHOR

Michael Farquhar is the bestselling author of *A Treasury of Royal Scandals, A Treasury of Great American Scandals, A Treasury of Deception, A Treasury of Foolishly Forgotten Americans,* and *Behind the Palace Doors.* He is co-author of *The Century: History as It Happened on the Front Page of the Capital's Newspaper.* His work has been featured in a number of publications, including *The Washington Post,* where he was a writer and editor for ten years, specializing in history. He has appeared as a commentator on such programs as the History Channel's *Russia: Land of the Tsars* and *The French Revolution.* He lives in Washington, D.C.